Twin Cities Picture Show

NOW SHOWING..

TWIN CITIES PICTURE SHOW

A CENTURY of MOVIEGOING

Dave Kenney

MINNESOTA HISTORICAL SOCIETY PRESS

www.mhspress.org

The Minnesota Historical Society Press is a member of the Association of American University Presses.

Manufactured in the United States of America

10 9 8 7 6 5 4 3 2 1

∞ The paper used in this publication meets the minimum requirements of the American National Standard for Information Sciences—Permanence for Printed Library Materials, ANSI Z39.48–1984.

International Standard Book Number
ISBN 13: 978-0-87351-595-5 (cloth)
ISBN 10: 0-87351-595-1 (cloth)

LIBRARY OF CONGRESS CATALOGING-IN-PUBLICATION DATA

Kenney, Dave, 1961–
Twin Cities picture show : a century of moviegoing / Dave Kenney.
    p. cm.
Includes bibliographical references and index.
ISBN-13: 978-0-87351-595-5 (cloth : alk. paper)
ISBN-10: 0-87351-595-1 (cloth : alk. paper)
 1. Motion pictures—Minnesota—Minneapolis—History.
 2. Motion pictures—Minnesota—Saint Paul—History.
 3. Motion picture theaters—Minnesota—Minneapolis—History.
 4. Motion picture theaters—Minnesota—Saint Paul—History.
 I. Title.

PN1993.5.U753K46 2007
791.4309776′579—dc22

2007022585

For Helen and Grace
Remember the Cottage View

Publication of this book is supported, in part, by a gift from Blythe Brenden in honor of her grandfather Ted Mann.

Contents

Feature Presentations

Preface

*I*t was early December 2006, and the old movie theater that had served as one of the primary settings of my adolescence was dead. The Har Mar Theater in Roseville was not all that ancient, actually. It had opened in 1970, so it was just thirty-six years old—middle-aged by cinema standards. But a new fourteen-screen megaplex with stadium seating, attentive staff, and good coffee was opening that afternoon at Rosedale Center, less than a mile away. The Har Mar was no longer needed. I had meant to be on hand for its final show the night before, but I forgot to show up. Now I was standing outside the old cinema, running my fingers along its pebble-encrusted walls, looking up at the jumble of nonsensical letters splayed across its marquee. The Har Mar was where, during a junior high school field trip showing of Franco Zeffirelli's *Romeo and Juliet,* I had almost—*almost*—summoned the courage to slip my arm around a girl's shoulder for the first time. It was where a group of my friends and I, hopelessly uncool, had sung along with John Travolta and Olivia Newton-John during the musical finale of *Grease.* ("You're the one that I want. O, o, oo, honey.") I tried to calculate how many movies I had seen there over the years, but the number eluded me. Twenty? Fifty? One hundred? More? It had never occurred to me to keep track.

One of the theater's glass entrance doors was propped open, so I let myself in. The scene inside was unsettling. The weird, curvilinear fiberglass box office was stripped down and abandoned. Large cardboard packing boxes were scattered about the lobby. The concession stand's display cases were bare, candyless. A young woman stepped out from behind one of the lobby's gold lamé walls and eyed me warily. I introduced myself and explained that I was writing a book about moviegoing and movie theaters in the Twin Cities. She smiled and nodded, evidently relieved that I was not a scavenger come to pick the Har Mar's corpse. She told me that workers already were removing the seats from the auditoriums, that no one had shown any interest in taking over the theater from her employer, AMC, that she had turned down an offer to work at the new Rosedale megaplex and was transferring instead to a theater in Texas. I thanked her for indulging my curiosity and left.

As I walked back to my car, my mind shuffled through some of my most vivid moviegoing memories. The earliest one was of my mother

x TWIN CITIES PICTURE SHOW

taking me to see *Mary Poppins*. I couldn't place the theater, but I figured it must have been the Southtown in Bloomington—or maybe the Parkway in South Minneapolis. I remembered watching *Yours, Mine, and Ours* at the Maple Leaf Drive-in while simultaneously battling my sisters for the most comfortable spot in my parents' station wagon (the one with the mosquito-repelling window screens). There was my first James Bond movie, *Live and Let Die*, at the Orpheum in downtown St. Paul and the tedious afternoon I spent watching *The Emigrants* under the faux stars of the Uptown on Grand Avenue. I recalled sneaking into my first R-rated film, *Chinatown*, at the Roseville 4, with its clueless ushers; settling into the claustrophobic screening room of the recently twinned Grandview for a twisted double-bill of *King of Hearts* and *Bambi Meets Godzilla;* and taking my girlfriend, Lisa, to see *Alien* at the Plaza in Maplewood after being assured by a cocksure coworker that it would scare her into my awaiting arms. (He forgot to mention that it might frighten me more than it would Lisa.) And then there was my last trip to the Rose Drive-in, with a gaggle of high school friends. We absentmindedly watched what I declared the worst movie I had ever seen, a disaster flick called *City on Fire*. As it turned out, *City on Fire* was the last feature presentation ever to play at the Rose.

There is something about watching a motion picture in a movie theater that lodges in the brain. How else can you explain the ability to recall when, where, and with whom you watched a supremely forgettable film called *Hawmps?* (It had something to do with camels.) Often when I mention to someone that I'm writing a book about moviegoing, that person responds by regaling me with recollections of a certain film or a certain theater or both. Before you know it, we're filling in each other's moth-eaten memories and laughing at each other's favorite movie lines. It's then that I realize what a shared experience moviegoing really is.

We Twin Citians are not unique in our attachment to motion pictures, of course. Moviegoing is a diversion that we hold in common with millions of people around the world. But few communities between New York and Los Angeles can match our hometowns' rich history with the movies. We count among our number several nationally known showmen, including Moses Finkelstein, Isaac Ruben, and Ted Mann. We've spent countless hours in the darkened auditoriums of our favorite theaters—some of which rank as world-class architectural gems. Some of us have railed against films that offended our sensibilities, while others of us have defended the people who sought to show them. We've even served as a test market for some of the biggest motion pictures of all time.

We may not be Hollywood, but our lives are rich in movies.

The Har Mar may be closed now, but who knows, maybe someone will resurrect it. Stranger things have happened. Other old movie theaters like the State, Orpheum, and Pantages in Minneapolis and the World (now the Fitzgerald) in St. Paul have found new life recently. The Grandview, Highland, Riverview, Uptown, and Heights still show movies. The Terrace, Hollywood, and Palace have managed to avoid the wrecking ball and, if we're lucky, will experience a kinder fate than did the Radio City, Paramount, and Cooper. All of them—the ones still with us and the ones relegated to memory—are places worth remembering. They're where we've shared a common interest called the movies.

Acknowledgments

Although I didn't start working on this book until early 2006, its genesis dates back to the late 1960s. That's when a Minnesota Historical Society staff member named John Dougherty began collecting old newspaper clippings and other ephemera related to motion picture exhibition in the Twin Cities. As the years went by, Dougherty's collection of movie-related "stuff" continued to expand. Folders bulged. Boxes seemed to reproduce by themselves. In 1985 another longtime MHS staffer, Lucile Kane, joined the project. Together, she and Dougherty assembled a massive compilation of historical material unlike any other I'm aware of—twenty-five boxes of well-organized documents and photographs tracing the history of movies, movie theaters, and movie exhibitors in Minneapolis and St. Paul. Kane and Dougherty planned to turn their research into a book, but they never got around to finishing it. They wrote a fascinating article for *Minnesota History* about the earliest years of the Twin Cities' movie business, but that was it. The two researchers moved on to other projects. Their boxes of movie material migrated into the bowels of the Minnesota History Center. Only a handful of people at MHS even knew the collection existed.

One of the people who had heard rumors of Kane and Dougherty's work was Greg Britton, the director of the Minnesota Historical Society Press. For some reason, he thought I might be interested in tracking down the boxes and taking a look at their contents. He was right. With the help of several MHS staffers, including Jim Fogerty, Debbie Miller, and Nick Duncan, I gained access to what turned out to be a treasure trove of material that would have taken me years to assemble on my own. Almost from the moment I started thumbing through Kane and Dougherty's handiwork, I could tell I was looking at the makings of a book—or at least the makings of the first chapter or two of a book.

So, to John Dougherty and Lucile Kane: Many thanks for setting the stage for me.

Many thanks also to the people who shared their movie memories with me and helped me understand how the motion picture business in the Twin Cities really developed. Deserving special mention are Zelda Baker, Esther Bergman, Blythe Brenden, Nancy Chakrin, Harold Engler, Marvin Engler, Hal Field, Barbara Flanagan, Gerry Herringer,

Bill Irvine, David Lebedoff, Tom Letness, Steve Mann, Mike Muller, Dorothy Saltzman, and Jack Smith.

Some of the most intriguing items I unearthed during my research are stored in libraries and archives beyond the walls of the Minnesota History Center. I owe a great debt of gratitude to the following patient souls who fielded my questions and responded to my requests: Barbara Bezat and Al Lathrop at the University of Minnesota's Northwest Architectural Archives; Linda Schloff at the Jewish Historical Society of the Upper Midwest; Maureen McGinn at the Ramsey County Historical Society; Vonda Kelly at the Bloomington Historical Society; Heather Lawton in the Special Collections Department of the Minneapolis Library; and Sara Markoe Hanson of the White Bear Lake Area Historical Society.

Others contributed to this book by making available documents and photographs that I probably never could have obtained anywhere else. I send out my deepest thanks to Jeff Bartlett of the Southern Theater; Tom Campbell of the Fitzgerald Theater; Stacy Housman of the Hennepin Theatre Trust; Steve Siers of Landmark Theatres; former Mall of America 14 manager Mike Skradski; John Wadell of the *Highland Villager;* and the Riverview Theater's Loren Williams.

This is the fourth book I've written for the Minnesota Historical Society Press, and once again, I feel incredibly fortunate to have been given the opportunity to work with such a talented and likeable team of publishing professionals. Many thanks to Greg Britton, Alison Vandenberg, Will Powers, designer Cathy Spengler, photographer Bill Jolitz, and especially to my editor, Mike Hanson. (Sorry about all the extraneous commas.)

And, finally, to Nancy: Let's catch a movie—my treat.

Twin Cities Picture Show

ADMIT
ONE

466897
466897
466897

HUMBLE BEGINNINGS

*T*he Bijou Opera House on Washington Avenue, just north of Hennepin, was about the last place anyone would have wanted to spend the evening of August 3, 1896. The daytime temperature in downtown Minneapolis had spiked at around one hundred degrees. The mercury in the thermometer had retreated a bit since midafternoon, but the air remained oppressively still. Severe storms would soon rumble in and squeeze out some of the atmosphere's excess moisture, but for the time being, the city sweltered. It would take something extraordinary on an evening as uncomfortable as this to coax anyone into a poorly ventilated building like the Bijou. After all, many theaters closed during the summer months for good reason: they tended to bake their occupants.

Previous page:
Theo Hays's Bijou Opera House, about 1897.

The Bijou's young manager, Theodore Hays, hoped the attraction he had scheduled would make his audience forget its discomfort. A select company of well-dressed ladies and gentlemen had accepted his invitation to witness something that few people had ever seen. He was gratified to find that the heat had not kept them away. The ladies had arranged themselves in their seats and were now fanning themselves furiously. The men dabbed their temples and necks with sodden handkerchiefs.

The lights in the auditorium dimmed. The mechanical sounds of whirling gears and sprockets filled the air. Suddenly, images from nowhere flickered into focus on a white canvas screen hanging over the stage. And the images moved.

A cluster of horses, riders astride, hurtled silently around a track. The field began to thin. Soon it was a two-horse race. By this time most of the members of the Bijou audience knew what they were watching. Two months earlier, two of the world's greatest racehorses, Persimmon and St. Frusquin, had faced off at Epson Downs in England. Now, remarkably, Theo Hays's guests were watching the great race unfold, just as it had happened. It didn't matter that the outcome was already known. The two hundred or so people seated in the Bijou were mesmerized. The stifling air was an afterthought. When Persimmon crossed the finish, edging St. Frusquin by a neck, the people in the Bijou cheered as though they were in the grandstand at Epson Downs. The effect of the moving pictures was electrifying. As the *Minneapolis Tribune* reported the next day, "Nature could not be counterfeited more cleverly."

> *If the reader can picture in his mind Epson Downs . . . with all the accessories of that exciting finish—the horses dashing under the wire and running like the wind, the crowds of people in the amphitheater, the rush of thousands across the track at the moment the horses have*

passed—he will have an idea of the wonderfully life-like scenes which were presented at the Bijou last night.[1]

As the audience murmured its approval, Theo Hays's projectionist, George "Dad" Strong, removed *Persimmon Winning the Derby* from the hand-cranked Animatograph motion picture machine and replaced it with another film, depicting the arrival of a passenger train in Calais. During the course of the evening, Strong repeated the process several times with a succession of European motion pictures. As he turned the crank on the unwieldy machine, images of jump-roping girls, London foundry workers, and the steamship *Queen Victoria* appeared on the screen. The audience didn't seem to mind the headache-inducing flicker or the projector's mechanical foibles. "That [Animatograph] was a regular jack-o-lantern," Strong recalled years later. "Sometimes it worked and sometimes it didn't."[2]

Theo Hays, about 1901.

In the months that followed, Theo Hays introduced his patrons to other motion pictures, claiming each one superior to the previous one. By the fall of 1896, the Animatograph was yesterday's news. Local newspapers were lauding the arrival of the Biograph, which had recently debuted in New York and was now featured in an exclusive engagement at Hays's Bijou. "Motion photography has never been more cleverly demonstrated than by this [Biograph] machine," the *Tribune* gushed. "The views it projects upon the canvas are life-like in the extreme, and need only speech to make them real."[3] As another Minneapolis showman, Charles Van Duzee, later recalled, Hays was making a name for himself.

The first [moving picture] show I ever witnessed was in the old Bijou. . . . It was nothing more than a train traveling along at good speed, but we all thought it was wonderful. The train looked as though it were coming right into the audience and the people gasped with amazement. Some women fainted and children wept. . . . The effects turned out to be the funniest thing in the show. They consisted of Dad Strong, one of the pioneers in the film game, who was attached to the handles of a barrel truck. When the train would appear way down the track on the screen, Dad would race back and forth on the stage with his truck, trying to imitate a locomotive whistle, and the pounding of the engine on the rails. Poor old Dad must have covered a thousand miles that first day, for the film was short and the train was exhibited continuously.[4]

Theo Hays was not the first showman to bring projected motion pictures to the Twin Cities (an early projection system called the Eidoloscope made its first appearance at Minneapolis's Palace Museum a year earlier),[5] but he was now the region's undisputed champion of motion picture promotion. He was in an enviable position. He seemed to possess the very skills needed to bring the future of American entertainment to the people of Minneapolis and St. Paul.

The Palace Museum introduced projected motion pictures to the Twin Cities in 1895.

The Twin Cities' entertainment business, in which Theo Hays had immersed himself, was a something-for-everybody smorgasbord. Those who enjoyed refined stage plays (and who could afford to pay one dollar and up for a ticket) attended New York touring shows at the first-class Metropolitan theaters in both cities. "The great ladies and gentlemen of the stage [including Sarah Bernhardt, Edwin Booth, Helena Modjeska, and Tommaso Salvini] visited this community regularly," a

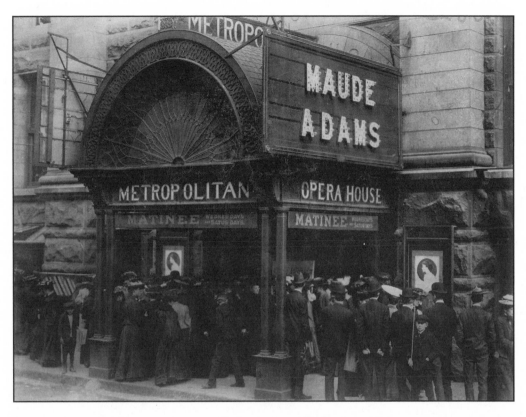

critic for the *St. Paul Pioneer Press* recalled years later. "[They brought] us the works of the better dramatists from New York and from all the foreign countries including, rather notably, the Scandinavian."⁶ Those who couldn't afford or appreciate the sophisticated offerings at the two Metropolitans turned to other venues. Devotees of the strange and exotic streamed into dime museums in both cities to gawk at human and animal oddities. Rowdy crowds of men hooted and hollered at the underdressed chorus girls of the Dewey burlesque theater in Minneapolis and the Star Theater in St. Paul. And those who disdained the highbrow pretensions of the New York touring shows flocked to the Bijou in Minneapolis and the Grand Opera House in St. Paul for comedies and crowd-pleasing melodramas featuring dashing heroes, mustachioed villains, and lovely damsels in distress. It was no coincidence that the Bijou and the St. Paul Grand both were managed by Theo Hays.

Hays understood the tastes of his working-class and middle-class patrons because he was, in many ways, much like them. His parents were German immigrants who had come to Minnesota during the 1850s with little money and few possessions. His father, Lambert Hays, had caromed from job to job—baker, sawmill laborer, lunchroom operator,

Theatergoers line up for a matinee performance at the Metropolitan Opera House, St. Paul's home of first-class theater, 1904.

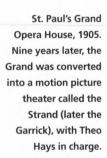

St. Paul's Grand Opera House, 1905. Nine years later, the Grand was converted into a motion picture theater called the Strand (later the Garrick), with Theo Hays in charge.

bartender—trying to make ends meet.[7] In the late 1870s the family moved into an apartment above Lambert's drinking establishment, the First and Last Chance Saloon, on the grimy three hundred block of Washington Avenue North.[8] Theo was heading into his teens by this time, and his prospects seemed limited at best. But then his father made a series of shrewd real estate investments, and the family's financial status improved considerably. In 1887 Theo's father embarked on his most ambitious project yet: a new theater two blocks south of his saloon. He called it the People's Theatre, and he put Theo—who had recently studied at Minneapolis's Curtiss Business College—in charge of bookkeeping.

Theo Hays proved himself a competent bookkeeper and soon took on even greater responsibilities. His chief patron during this period was Jacob Litt, a New York theatrical agent who specialized in producing inexpensive, or "popularly priced," entertainment for those who couldn't afford, or who weren't interested in, high-class theater. Litt and Hays first met in 1889 when Litt—looking to break into the Twin Cities' entertainment market—leased the People's Theatre from Hays's father. Hays convinced the New York impresario to retain him as treasurer and in the months that followed cemented his reputation as an up-and-coming theater man. When a fire destroyed the People's in the fall of 1890, Hays oversaw the construction of a replacement theater. His work on the new Bijou Opera House was so impressive that, when it opened in the spring of 1891, Litt promoted him to resident manager. A few years later, Hays took over management of Litt's St. Paul theater, the Grand, as well.[9]

Feature Presentation

●●●

**Miles Theater
46 South 7th Street,
Minneapolis
Opened 1908**

With more than six thousand lights illuminating its exterior and interior, the 1,400-seat Miles was billed as the "most heavily lit theater in the world." The crowds that packed the Miles during its first few years basked in sumptuousness. The auditorium was clad in marble and draped in red silk. The carpeting was a deep green. The seats were upholstered in gold plush.[1] But the lavish new vaudeville house soon fell on hard times. It closed in 1914 and underwent a major overhaul. The following April, it reopened as a "photoplay house" called the Garrick.[2] Like the Miles, the Garrick struggled to turn a profit, and in 1928 it too closed. The theater's new owners gutted the interior and built a new show house inside. The newly christened Century opened in the fall of 1929. For many years after that, the Century relied heavily on the patronage of women who interrupted their shopping excursions to enjoy a movie matinee. In 1954 the Century was converted into the Twin Cities' exclusive home of the wide-screen motion picture format called Cinerama. It closed for good and was demolished in 1965.

The Miles was easily the most brightly illuminated theater the people of Minneapolis had ever seen.

As the manager of Litt's two Twin Cities theaters, Theo Hays gave his audiences what he believed they wanted: professionally produced, unpretentious amusement. The romantic comedy *In Old Kentucky,* for example, was a perennial favorite at the Bijou and the Grand. Local newspapers praised Hays for having the good sense to set standards "in keeping with the taste of his patrons."[10] On those few occasions when he booked more sophisticated fare, he later wondered why he had bothered. "The moment any effort is made involving proper acting, higher intellectual work, and dramatic effort," a sympathetic reporter observed, "the management of the Bijou feel the [disappointing] results at the box office."[11] Hays further enhanced his reputation as a theater man with a common touch by keeping ticket prices low. No seat in the Bijou or the Grand cost more than seventy-five cents.

With his reputation as the Twin Cities' preeminent purveyor of inexpensive stage entertainment and his experience as an early exhibitor of motion pictures, Theo Hays seemed well positioned to exploit the commercial possibilities of film. But Hays was not a visionary. He was cautious with money, whether it was his or Jacob Litt's. He had built his success on a foundation of comedy and melodrama, and he was comfortable with them. Motion pictures were altogether different. They were exciting and full of potential, but they remained novelties. Even after the positive reviews that followed his showing of *Persimmon Winning the Derby,* Hays refused to fully embrace such an untested entertainment form. Others, however, were less reluctant.

The October 22, 1904, opening of the new Orpheum Theater on Seventh Street between Nicollet and Hennepin was, in the opinion of the *Minneapolis Journal,* "an epoch-making event" because it marked the city's formal introduction to "modern vaudeville."[12] Vaudeville was, in effect, a cleaned-up and repackaged version of the variety shows that had long been a common feature at saloon-theaters like the Theatre Comique in Minneapolis. Many Twin Citians regarded variety entertainment as low-class fare for unrefined tastes, but vaudeville was different. It had class. As a reviewer for the *Minneapolis Free Press* pointed out, vaudeville appealed to just about everyone, including "staid spinsters, matrons with their daughters, broad-minded clergymen, business men and women of all degrees."

> *A Vaudeville performance is made up today to afford the greatest pleasure to the greatest number. There is no attempt at plot. There is no strain on the mental faculties. You come there to be entertained, and*

Minneapolis's first Orpheum Theater, which opened in 1904, introduced Twin Citians to vaudeville.

you are, without any effort on your part. There is nothing taxed but the eye, the ear and the risibles. You hear good singing, see beautiful costumes properly worn, feats of strength and agility, agile dancing, and a goodly proportion of laughter compelling jokes, stories and situations, all of which make you feel better toward yourself and your neighbor.[13]

The opening night lineup at the Minneapolis Orpheum was typical of the vaudeville shows that were drawing huge crowds in many other parts of the country. Tom the mind-reading pony showed off his amazing psychic powers. J. A. Probst's birdcalls prompted one reporter to theorize that Probst must be a bird. Actress Valerie Bergere and two assistants condensed a five-act play into a fifteen-minute playlet. Jugglers juggled. Singers sang. A ventriloquist engaged in witty repartee with his dummy. The audience thundered its approval.[14] In the weeks that followed, crowds continued to pack the theater as word-of-mouth spread. The Orpheum was a smash hit. So, too, was another vaudeville house that opened in Minneapolis that year, the Unique on Hennepin Avenue. Not surprisingly, vaudeville's success came at the expense of older theaters like Theo Hays's Bijou. In 1905, the year after the Orpheum and the Unique opened, receipts at the Bijou declined 40 percent. When another Minneapolis vaudeville house, the Miles, opened in 1908, Hays once again watched business at the Bijou drop precipitously.[15]

Lost in hoopla over the openings of the Orpheum, Unique, and Miles (and, in 1905, a second Orpheum theater in St. Paul) was the fact that vaudeville managers in the Twin Cities and elsewhere were adding more and more motion pictures to their shows.[16] The opening night bill at the Minneapolis Orpheum, for example, included a motion picture finale depicting "the horrible plight of a newly arrived Frenchman who advertises for an American wife and then tries to escape from the embarrassingly large bevy of applicants for the position."[17] As

Feature Presentation

**Shubert Theater
22 North 7th Street,
Minneapolis
Opened 1910**

The Minneapolis Shubert opened the same night, August 28, 1910, as its sister theater in St. Paul. Modeled after the Maxine Elliott Theater in New York, the Minneapolis Shubert seated about 1,600 people and cost around $250,000.[1] It was one of several theaters that the brothers Lee and J. J. Shubert opened around the country in their effort to break the New York–based theatrical booking monopoly that dominated the nation's show business. For many years the Shubert was the home of the Bainbridge Players, a stock theater company managed by A. G. "Buzz" Bainbridge. In 1935 local movie exhibitor Al Steffes acquired the Shubert, gave it an extensive makeover, and reopened it as the Alvin (Steffes's middle

The stately Shubert dominated the Seventh Street block between Hennepin and First Avenue North.

name). Originally a motion picture house, the Alvin later switched to live burlesque. Another local showman, Ted Mann, acquired the Alvin in 1947. In the decade that followed, the theater served as both a burlesque house and as an evangelical church. In 1957 Mann transformed the Alvin into a sparkling new movie the-

ater called the Academy. For more than twenty-five years the Academy ranked as one of Minneapolis's top first-run motion picture houses. The old theater escaped demolition in 1999, when it was moved a block down Hennepin Avenue to make way for the new Block E development.

vaudeville strengthened its grip on the Twin Cities' entertainment market, motion pictures became even more prominent. The Miles opened with an eclectic bill featuring a juggler, several singers, a troupe of Arab acrobats, and two motion pictures that the management dubbed "Cameographs."[18] In St. Paul, the Star Theater, which was primarily a burlesque house, began booking vaudeville bills with multiple films, including *The Fireman's Dream,* a "thrilling" spectacle that "called forth deafening applause."[19]

Motion pictures were captivating Twin Cities vaudeville audiences, and local entrepreneurs were taking notice. Charles Van Duzee capitalized on the trend by converting the first floor of his Washington Avenue penny arcade, the Wonderland, into a small auditorium where "the grinding of the moving picture machine begins 10 o'clock each morning and continues without let-up until midnight."[20] Soon others followed his lead. In the words of film historian Merritt Crawford, "the 'gold-rush' was on."

> *Everyone was hastening to "stake a claim." The butcher, the baker, the candlestick-maker, all swarmed into this newest [source of wealth], eager to gather a share of the riches, which seemingly awaited anyone who could rent a vacant store, hire three or four dozen chairs from the nearest undertaker and arrange for a projection machine and supply of film.*[21]

In 1907 the *Minneapolis Tribune* noted that the city now accommodated a "mosquito fleet" of "moving picture theaters" where, for the price of a nickel, audiences could "witness a humble, but interesting form of entertainment at most any hour of the day after the hour of noon."[22] These new theaters, known widely (but rarely in the Twin Cities) as nickelodeons, were often converted shops or restaurants that had been gussied up to look—from the outside, at least—like fancy vaudeville houses. Inside, the auditoriums often were cramped and uncomfortable, with small cloth screens and rows of tightly packed removable chairs. Charles Van Duzee's Isis Theater on South Sixth Street was among the first of this new class of motion picture houses. It was an oddly long and narrow space—about 20 feet wide and 165 feet deep—that could seat about four hundred people. It played to about twelve thousand customers each week.[23] The Unique Theater, near the corner of Seventh and Jackson streets in St. Paul, was another typical storefront operation. Among other things, it was known for its sound effects. One of the Unique's early patrons remembered watching a scene in which the characters on the screen were throwing bricks at each other. "At the right time, some bricks were thrown in back of the curtain," he wrote. "As I recollect, the effect was very realistic."[24] Between 1906 and 1909, twenty similarly simple storefront motion picture houses opened in Minneapolis and St. Paul. By the end of the decade, they accounted for nearly half of all the Twin Cities' theaters.[25]

For years motion pictures had been forced to share time with other forms of entertainment at legitimate stage theaters, vaudeville houses, and penny arcades. Now they were popular enough to demand their own venues. And no one was more aware of the trend than Theo Hays. In a 1908 letter to Jacob Litt's partner, A. W. Dingwall, Hays noted that some theaters were successfully "giving motion pictures exclusively" and proposed that the Bijou try booking a week's worth of films to determine "whether there is any chance of getting enough business to make it pay."[26] Nothing ever came of his suggestion.

The proliferation of storefront theaters in the Twin Cities reflected the chaotic and largely unregulated nature of the early film business. But theaters and the exhibition of film constituted just one part of a much larger and complex motion picture equation. Before a film could be projected onscreen, someone had to produce it and someone had to distribute it. And to many theater owners' dismay, the film industry's production and distribution system already was as organized as the

St. Paul's Lyric, an early storefront theater, about 1909.

exhibition system was disorganized. It was, by most definitions of the word, a monopoly. The Motion Picture Patents Company, led by Thomas Edison, controlled the patents on raw film and on most of the equipment used in the making and screening of motion pictures. The Edison Trust, as it was widely known, vigorously enforced its patents by threatening to take legal action against any independent producer who failed to obtain the proper licenses. Its stranglehold on production and distribution limited the number of films available to theaters around the country, and it wasn't long before some independent producers and exhibitors began to rebel. In 1909 one particularly exasperated rebel came to the Twin Cities.

Carl Laemmle was a small-time theater operator from Chicago who recently had begun branching out into film distribution (one of his first branch offices was in Minneapolis).[27] Laemmle, like many independent film men, chafed under the iron grip of the Edison Trust, and he was determined to fight back. He formed a new film production firm, the Independent Moving Picture Company, and set out to make his own motion pictures. His first production was a one-reel adaptation of Henry Wadsworth Longfellow's poem *The Song of Hiawatha*. It was shot in August of 1909, not in Chicago or New York or California—but in Minneapolis.

In the years that followed, accounts of the making of *Hiawatha* varied widely. Some people said Laemmle chose to make the motion picture in Minneapolis only after his plans to film a reenactment of the battle of Gettysburg at the Minnesota State Fair fell through. Others insisted he just wanted to take advantage of the beautiful scenery at Minnehaha Falls. Information about the actors who appeared in the film was often contradictory as well. Some accounts said the role of Minnehaha was played by Mary Pickford, who soon went on to become one of the film industry's first major stars. Others credited either Gladys Hulette or Leah Baird, both of whom were established stage actors at the time. Whatever was the case, Laemmle's production crew shot most of the twenty-minute film at Minnehaha Falls and Lake Minnetonka.[28] Critics lauded Laemmle's decision to shoot the film on location. "We have nothing but praise for the way in which the scenes have been chosen, with the historic Minneahaha Falls as a background," wrote the reviewer for *Motion Picture World*. "It is stamped all over with the signs of success."[29]

The making and release of *Hiawatha* reinforced Laemmle's influence in the Twin Cities' rapidly developing motion picture market. Over the next several years, Laemmle fortified his distribution operations in Minneapolis. His presence in the market helped establish the city as the major distribution point for motion pictures throughout the Upper Midwest.[30] By the fall of 1911, he was running advertisements in Twin Cities newspapers, exhorting local entrepreneurs to get in on the motion picture action while they still could.

> *Do you know a single business on earth today that you can enter with only a few hundreds of dollars in capital and be your own "boss" manager and dictator, and become the happy earner of hundreds of dollars clear profit monthly? THAT'S what's being done by those in the moving picture business today everywhere—not only in larger cities than Minneapolis and St. Paul but in this city as well. Study it yourself. Don't watch one particular manager or theater, but just ask the manager nearest you if he wants to sell out? The moving picture business is growing rapidly—the people everywhere are awakening up—it's no fancy or fad—this time next year the business will be tripled what it is now. Don't wait for someone else to show you how foolish you have been in looking on. My plan is simple—you secure the location and building and I'll do the rest—I'll furnish you from entrance to exit— also the finest motion pictures in the world. Call and see me.[31]*

During its early years the motion picture business in the Twin Cities was strictly a downtown proposition. In Minneapolis nearly all the theaters that showed films were clustered near the corners of Hennepin and Washington or Hennepin and Sixth. And in St. Paul, Seventh and Wabasha served as the city's motion picture hub. But as film grew in popularity, its tendrils began reaching out from the downtown loops. By 1910 new theaters—most of them showing motion pictures exclusively— were springing up "as spontaneously as mushrooms."[32] Many popped up in neighborhoods bounded by busy arteries like Plymouth Avenue and West Broadway in North Minneapolis, Lake Street in South Minneapolis, and St. Paul's University Avenue. "The theater has become a neighborhood institution and a part of the routine of life rather than a luxury," one reporter observed. "The fifty theaters already in operation [in Minneapolis] are so well distributed that practically every streetcar intersection and every trading center has its show house."[33]

As the number of theaters grew, attendance skyrocketed. By 1911 the fifty or so theaters that dotted Minneapolis were showing films to nearly a quarter of a million customers each week.[34] With the price of admission topping out at ten cents, motion pictures were an affordable form of entertainment—especially among the working classes. But as one

reader of the *St. Paul Pioneer Press* noted, films had a wider appeal than many people were willing to acknowledge.

> I admit that a large portion of the better class of people in this city are not patrons of these theaters, but that is a condition showing that we are behind the times. In the larger cities, the picture shows are patronized by the best people, I mean by this, not only rich people but people of education and refinement. . . . So I claim that the moving picture show, like the automobile, is here to stay; it has come not as a menace, but as a blessing, not only to the illiterate poor but to the educated and refined.[35]

Still, not everyone shared such rosy assessments of the cinema and its potential to uplift the masses. Many Twin Citians worried that motion pictures posed a threat to public morality. Although public officials rarely took actions that might actually hurt business at motion picture theaters, they occasionally considered proposals designed to mollify morally scandalized constituents. In one such case, the Minneapolis city council considered an ordinance that would have banned theater operators from hiring girls as ushers. Some council members believed that girls should not hold jobs that might keep them out late at night. Such concerns struck many girl ushers as silly. "It will mean that deserv-

By 1915, Hennepin Avenue in Minneapolis was home to at least thirteen movie theaters, including the Mazda.

ing girls who have found employment as ushers will have to give up their positions," Gratia Hanson, an usher at a downtown theater, complained. "There is nothing at all that I know of, that the aldermen should object to. A neatly dressed girl who is quick and prompt can do the work well."[36] The council apparently abandoned the proposal without taking action on it.

Nonetheless, concerns about motion pictures and motion picture theaters remained. In a few cases residents fought to keep theaters out of their neighborhoods, arguing that children were being put at risk. One of the earliest such battlegrounds was in Minneapolis along the stretch of Hennepin Avenue between downtown and the Uptown area. This section of the city, adjacent to the upscale Lowry Hill neighborhood, was home to hundreds of people who considered motion picture theaters a threat to morality. When a pair of local businessmen sought licenses to open two theaters near the corner of Hennepin and Dupont, residents, educators, and clergy mobilized to block the proposals. In the fall of 1911, about two hundred people packed the city council chambers to express their disapproval. "I represent the people who wish to conserve the morals of the young people of this city," declared Andrew Gillies, the pastor of nearby Hennepin Methodist Episcopal Church. "We have enough difficulty in keeping young girls off the streets without adding the temptation of motion picture theaters." The council denied both license requests.[37] In the months that followed, other would-be theater operators encountered similar resistance. "Personally," argued one attorney on behalf of his theater owner client, "I would rather have my children attend picture shows near home than be compelled to go downtown, where they are exposed to real influences for evil."[38] Such arguments made little difference. The disputed section of Hennepin Avenue remained theaterless.

Rev. Andrew Gillies of Hennepin Methodist Episcopal Church was among the community leaders who believed that motion pictures were corrupting "the morals of the young people" of Minneapolis.

In those neighborhoods that already had theaters, critics focused their attention on another perceived danger: fire. The threat of fire had been ingrained into the public's consciousness since 1903, when at least six hundred people died in a conflagration at the Iroquois Theater in Chicago. The Iroquois disaster prompted plenty of hand-wringing in Minneapolis and St. Paul, and for several weeks officials in both cities fended off calls to close down all theaters.[39] But the public outcry quickly settled down. Audiences seemed to forget their worries about the theaters' safety as soon as the lights dimmed in the auditorium.

Fears of another Iroquois-like disaster resurfaced in 1911 with the rapid expansion of the motion picture business in the Twin Cities. Film presented a unique public safety problem: it caught fire easily. If the projectionist wasn't careful and stopped reeling the film for too long, the machine's arc lamp would eventually ignite the highly flammable nitrate stock. Theater owners could greatly reduce this danger by taking proper precautions, but some were reluctant to spend money on preventive measures when their financial status already was precarious. "The history of the erection of these theaters has been, in many instances, the story of money-getting enterprise on the part of persons of small capital," the *Minneapolis Tribune* reported. "[These people] have been willing to open moving picture shows in old, flimsy buildings with almost total disregard of the protection from fire or panic risk that is due to audiences that will attend these shows."[40]

An investigation by the *Tribune* found that the aisles in most theaters were too narrow to accommodate quick evacuations, that few theaters had firefighting equipment, and that most theater employees were too young to assume "the responsibility of the safety of audiences of children." The Iola, a new neighborhood theater on Franklin Avenue, was a good example. It had "no standpipes, fire hose, fire hooks, ladders, fire extinguishers or other apparatus for putting out a fire." It was, the *Tribune* implied, a firetrap.

> *The auditorium has a center aisle, with six-seat rows on each side running flush against side walls containing no windows, doors or other means of exit or egress. The entire building is a flimsy structure of wood, with an ornamental iron front and considerable electric wiring. It would be difficult for a hurrying crowd to get out of the single exit door at the rear, down the three steps, past the turn, and down two more steps at the outside of this door—especially for those who had been seated on the inside of the rows next to the side walls. The center aisle is four feet wide.*[41]

Theater owners suddenly had another public relations problem on their hands. Not only were they, as some critics contended, corrupters of youth, but their buildings were potential death traps. A week after the

Tribune published its findings, news of a fire at a theater in nearby Anoka only made matters worse (the audience had stampeded toward the exits when a flustered projectionist tossed flaming film into the theater's main entrance).[42] Even though no one was hurt in the Anoka fire, Twin Citians now wondered whether they were putting their lives in danger when they attended motion picture shows. Elected officials in both cities proposed new, stricter fire regulations for theaters. Theater owners—most of them from the smaller neighborhood venues—banded together to fight back. In the end, inspectors in Minneapolis and St. Paul found that most theaters were, in fact, quite safe. Even the Iola, which the *Tribune* had identified as one of the worst, passed the inspectors' muster. "No fire traps were found on the [inspectors'] tour," the *Minneapolis Journal* reported. "There were places for betterment in several theaters, but no menacing conditions."[43]

The criticism of the theaters as threats to public safety and public morals failed to dent the public's enthusiasm for the cinema. In 1913 a survey of ten thousand Minneapolis families found that about two-thirds of them attended motion picture shows and that the average family spent $7.50 a year on the movies, at a time when tickets rarely cost more than ten cents.[44] The city had sixty-nine motion picture houses, giving it a theater-to-resident ratio double that of New York City.[45] In St. Paul the numbers were similar. Reporters marveled that the film business there had "grown to an extent almost incredible."[46]

Motion pictures were becoming remarkably popular and, perhaps just as significantly, respectable. Several prominent Twin Citians now counted themselves among the cinema's biggest fans. Financier Thomas B. Walker, for example, rarely missed an opportunity to take in a picture show—especially when it featured "an amusing young fellow" named Charlie Chaplin. "The great thing of moving pictures is their democracy," Walker said. "There, the banker, the carpenter, the mechanic and laborer for a small admission price come with their families and enjoy a few hours in a common and wholesome amusement. The general association is good for the men, their families and for the community."[47]

The crowds that showed up for the grand reopening of Minneapolis's Lyric Theater on September 18, 1911, were stunned. They had come to see a moving picture show. What they instead experienced was a spectacle. A footman, gracious in the extreme, greeted them on their arrival. Inside, exquisitely mannered pages attended to their needs. Young African American women in carefully pressed uniforms ushered them to their seats. The show itself was a revelation. The Lyric, unlike every other theater in the Twin Cities, kept the lights on in its auditorium. Its powerful projector and new screen—of a secret "textile fabric and a composition of animal matter"[48]—made darkness obsolete (and impressed those who fretted over the safety of audiences in darkened auditoriums). The pictures on the screen were accompanied not by a tinny piano but by an eighteen-piece orchestra, a pipe organ, five

Feature Presentation

Shubert Theater
494 Wabasha Street,
St. Paul
Opened 1910

Although the St. Paul Shubert opened the same night as its Minneapolis namesake, it did not enjoy quite the same cachet. The St. Paul Shubert cost $165,000, as compared with the Minneapolis Shubert's $250,000, and it seated about only three-quarters as many people. Still, the Sam S. Shubert Theater, as it was initially known, ranked for several years as the capital city's most impressive show house. It was, like the Minneapolis Shubert, patterned after New York's Maxine Elliott Theater. "There has been no waste in filling the interior of this theater with 'tinselly' and cheap decorative devices," the *St. Paul Pioneer Press* noted. The Shubert was "a model of sanitary perfection."[1] In 1933 Al Steffes acquired the Shubert and turned it into a motion picture house called the World. The World continued to show movies until 1977, when its screen finally went dark. But the old show house quickly found new life as the home of

The Shubert Theater in St. Paul, while similar to its Minneapolis counterpart, was smaller and less ornate.

the public radio variety show *A Prairie Home Companion*. After an extensive renovation in 1986, the World was reborn as the Fitzgerald Theater.

vocalists, and a sound effects man armed with a dizzying array of noise makers.[49] This was no fly-by-night storefront theater or ramshackle neighborhood cinema. The refurbished Lyric was the Twin Cities' first premium motion picture house.

The Lyric was an unlikely venue for such a spectacle. It had opened twenty-six years earlier as the Hennepin Theater and had since gone through a succession of name changes: first the Harris, then the Lyceum, and finally the Lyric. Its recent history had been especially tumultuous. After reopening as the Lyric in 1908, it enjoyed modest success by offering a full calendar of stock theater productions. The following year, the brothers Lee and J. J. Shubert of New York leased the Lyric and turned it into the Minneapolis home of their rapidly expanding stage show empire. But the Shuberts never intended to hold on to the Lyric. They planned to build two new theaters—one each in Minneapolis and St. Paul—and they considered the Lyric a mere stopgap. When the new Shubert theaters opened in 1910, the Lyric went dark. The Shuberts didn't want it anymore. It took a prodigal Minnesotan to bring out the Lyric's potential as a motion picture house.

Samuel Rothapfel (he later dropped the *p* from his name) had grown up in Stillwater. He was the son of Jewish immigrants and was remembered by neighbors as a rebellious youngster with the instincts of a showman. (He supposedly organized a makeshift theater and charged a penny for admission, but it was never clear what kind of entertainment he offered.) At the age of twelve, he moved with his family to New York. Four years later, he set off to make a life of his own. After a succession of odd jobs, a long stint in the military, and a short career in semipro baseball, he landed a bartending job at a saloon in the coal mining town of Forest City, Pennsylvania. It was there, in 1908, that Rothapfel—or Roxy, as he was now known—opened his Family Theater in the saloon's back room.

From the beginning Roxy gave his patrons more than they ever could have expected for their five-cent admission price. For him the film was just part of the show. He hired the best musicians he could find to accompany the pictures he put onscreen. He developed a system for projecting films in a fully lighted auditorium to help his customers avoid eye fatigue. He even placed rose petals in front of electric fans and filled his theater with evocative aromas during the screening of a film depicting the Pasadena Tournament of Roses.[50]

It wasn't long before word spread about the upstart showman in Pennsylvania's coal country. The editors of the trade publication *Mov-*

ing Picture World commissioned Roxy to write a series of columns about motion picture exhibition. With each issue his reputation as an innovator in the film world grew. "Motion pictures are no longer a fad—they are here to stay, and are sure to become the greatest source of amusement in this country," he wrote. "The day of the ignorant exhibitor with his side-show methods is a thing of the past."[51]

The notoriety Roxy received from his column in *Moving Picture World* led to new jobs at theaters around the country. Benjamin Keith hired him to revive his struggling circuit of vaudeville houses. United Booking Offices asked him to improve the quality of projection at its theaters. And in early 1911, Herman Fehr contracted him to turn around one of the country's biggest—and least successful—legitimate theaters, the Alhambra in Milwaukee. Roxy introduced motion pictures to the Alhambra and infused the theater with an air of elegance. Audiences responded. Within weeks the Alhambra was drawing bigger crowds than it ever had before.[52]

When Roxy arrived back in Minnesota in the summer of 1911, he was on the verge of becoming a national celebrity. He kicked off his Twin Cities run in early September with the opening of the Colonial Theater in St. Paul. As anyone familiar with his history could have anticipated, he introduced a series of innovations at the Colonial, including daylight motion pictures (with the auditorium lights on), an orchestra, vocalists, girl ushers, and a matron to "look after the wants of women and children."[53] Two weeks later, he presided over an even grander opening at the Lyric in Minneapolis. And there Samuel Rothapfel cemented his standing as a film exhibition wunderkind. His colleagues at *Moving Picture World* were happy to heap on breathless praise.

> *The Lyric on Hennepin Avenue, between 7th and 8th Streets, with a capacity of 1,700 seats, is the largest exclusive picture theater in Minneapolis. There are larger theaters in the country devoted solely to pictures, but there is none, and I can say it without the slightest fear of eating my words, that can lay claim to such model management as controls the destinies of the Lyric. By model management is meant the most intelligent, up-to-date, progressive presentation of moving pictures, the sure instinctive grasp of their full values and the talent—indeed the aspirations—that seizes the most effective means to reveal successfully these full values to an audience.[54]*

In the months that followed his Minneapolis debut, Roxy continued to make improvements at the Lyric. He added, among other things, a lighted canopy, an electric fountain, and a children's playground with slides and sandboxes.[55] But his tenure at the Lyric was short lived. In the summer of 1912, the brothers John and Tom Saxe of Milwaukee acquired the Lyric. A year later, Roxy was gone. (John Saxe claimed that "Mr. Rothapfel's management had not been satisfactory.")[56] Roxy went on to much bigger and better things in New York, but his legacy in the Twin Cities was lasting. He had proved that motion picture audiences in Minneapolis and St. Paul appreciated showmanship. No longer could theater owners—especially those in the two downtowns—afford to

Feature Presentation

**Southern Theater
1420 Washington Avenue
South, Minneapolis
Opened 1910**

The Southern was among the first of the new neighborhood theaters that began sprouting up in the Twin Cities during the early years of motion picture exhibition. The Southern was, unlike many of its counterparts, an ethnic theater catering primarily to the largely Scandinavian community congregated near Cedar Avenue (widely known as "Snoose Boulevard"). On Saturday afternoons neighborhood kids crammed the Southern's compact auditorium to watch matinee movies, but the theater was best known as a legitimate playhouse specializing in Swedish-language dramas by the likes of August Strindberg and Bjørnstjerne Bjørnson. As the years went by, the Southern gradually abandoned live theater in favor of the movies. In the mid-1940s the theater shut down and was converted into a garage and warehouse. In the three decades that followed, it went through vari-

The Southern, around the time of its opening.

ous incarnations, including a stint as a popular restaurant called the Gaslight. In 1975 the building underwent an extensive renovation that turned it back into a live performance space called Guthrie 2 (an adjunct of the much larger Guthrie Theater). A few years later, ownership of the theater transferred to a nonprofit corpora-

tion called the Southern Theater Foundation. The theater reopened under its original name, the Southern, in 1981 and established itself as the stage home for a variety of independent performing artists.[1]

ignore the finer points of film presentation. "It is now accepted," Roxy wrote a few years later, "[that] our picture theatres in the large cities are catering to an audience as fine as any legitimate attraction."[57]

*F*or a while, during the summer of 1912, it looked as though the cautious Theo Hays would finally get his chance to show regularly scheduled motion pictures at the Bijou. The Saxe brothers, who had acquired the Roxy-managed Lyric a couple months earlier, now controlled the Bijou, too. They planned to convert the Lyric back into a legitimate theater and move its motion picture business over to the Bijou, where Hays would continue as manager. But that plan didn't last long. On second thought, the Saxes decided, it made no sense to remove films from the Lyric. Business there, under Roxy's guidance, remained brisk. Instead, they refurbished the Bijou and instructed Hays to continue running stage plays there.[58]

The decision to maintain the Bijou as a legitimate theater failed miserably. Trends in the entertainment industry—especially the rise in the popularity of motion pictures—were working against traditional venues like the Bijou. Before long Hays was resorting to promotional tactics he had never previously considered, including the mailing of complimentary tickets to a "selected list of Minneapolitans."[59] But nothing he tried worked. One year after acquiring the Bijou, the Saxes sublet the old theater to a pair of Twin Cities showmen, Harry Blaising and Clyde Hitchcock. Blaising and Hitchcock immediately instituted a new show policy that, for the first time at the Bijou, included regular motion pictures. "Heroes will fight, beautiful maidens will be rescued and stories of love and adventure [will be] told on canvas at the Bijou," the *Minneapolis Journal* reported. "The theater that for nearly twenty-six years has been the home of the melodrama will become a picture and vaudeville house."[60] Seventeen years after premiering *Persimmon Winning the Derby* at the old opera house on Washington Avenue, and five years after trying unsuccessfully to convince A. W. Dingwall to jump on the film bandwagon, Theo Hays was on the verge of becoming the manager of a true motion picture house.

But Blaising and Hitchcock had other ideas. They brought in their own manager and told Hays to move on. Hays's long association with the Bijou was over, and with it, his best chance yet to move into the film exhibition business. Still, there was always the Grand in St. Paul.

Herman Fehr, the man who owned the Roxy-revived Alhambra Theater in Milwaukee, had leased the St. Paul Grand from the Jacob

Litt estate in 1912 and turned it into a burlesque house. As the longtime manager of the Grand, Hays had done everything he could to make Fehr's new adults-only policy work, but he found it impossible to beat St. Paul's most successful burlesque theater, the Star, at its own game. Hays's days at the Grand might have ended there had Fehr not signed over his lease to a pair of novice theater operators, the brothers Charles and Joseph Friedman of St. Paul.

The Friedmans were not interested in continuing burlesque at the Grand. They had something else in mind: motion pictures. They renamed the venerable theater the Strand, in honor of the new and phenomenally successful Strand Theater in New York City (which just happened to be managed by the recently departed Samuel Rothapfel), and instituted a new policy of "high-class photoplays."

While some St. Paulites lamented the "cruelties of passing time" represented by the Grand-to-Strand switch, others took comfort in the fact that the day-to-day management of the theater remained in good and experienced hands. Theo Hays was still on the job. "We believe that there is a place in St. Paul for a photoplay house of unusual quality," Hays declared at the Strand's grand opening on November 1, 1914. "We shall cater to ladies and children and it shall be our aim to provide in the fullest measure for their safety, comfort and amusement."[61] Hays soon relinquished his managing duties at the Strand, but he continued to oversee the local financial affairs of the theater's owner, the Jacob Litt estate. Although he didn't realize it yet, he was now in position to make a permanent jump into the motion picture business.

*M*ost motion picture houses in the Twin Cities shut down during the summer. With no effective system for cooling the air, the windowless auditoriums in which the movies played became oppressive sweatboxes. Even the most rabid film enthusiasts were happy to forgo motion pictures during the sultry months of June, July, and August. Movies were not worth the risk of heatstroke. But that didn't mean summer films couldn't succeed under the right conditions.

For several years exhibitors in other cities—especially in warmer climates—had experimented with open-air theaters called "airdomes." The typical airdome was a vacant lot surrounded by a tall fence, with a screen at one end, an entrance at the other, and rows of wooden benches in between. What the airdomes lacked in amenities, they made up for in fresh air. Film-hungry audiences flocked to outdoor screenings in numbers that forced the managers of traditional indoor theaters to take notice.

Exhibitors in Minneapolis and St. Paul were slow to pick up on the airdome trend. Open-air theaters performed best in places where they could stay open most of the year, and the Twin Cities, with their inhospitable winters, did not fall into that category. But in the summer of 1914, Samuel Neuman, the manager of the Metropolitan Opera House in St. Paul, decided to take a chance on the concept. He opened the Twin Cities' first airdome, called the Airdome, at the corner of Wabasha and College Avenue, about four blocks northwest of the city's main theater district. The grounds, occupying about 1,500 square feet, were "commodiously laid out." The Metropolitan's orchestra, under the direction of W. W. Nelson, furnished the music. And in a move that set the Airdome apart from most other theaters, Neuman played up the fact that "refreshments can also be had on the grounds." Programs at the Airdome began promptly at 8:00 PM and lasted three and a half hours. Advertisements encouraged patrons to "Enjoy a Smoke and Show with the Blue Sky Above You."[62] Later that summer, a second airdome opened in Minneapolis, at the corner of Tenth and Hennepin. The *St. Paul Pioneer Press* predicted that Neuman's "novel place of amusement" would "no doubt become popular."[63] The following summer, the St. Paul airdome was gone.

*M*otion pictures were becoming immensely popular, but few, if any, qualified as artistic masterpieces. When the cinema boom hit around 1910, most films were still one-reel shorts—simple comedies, dramas, or scenics. In most theaters a single show consisted of four to six one-reelers run back to back. But it wasn't long before filmmakers began experimenting with longer, multiple-reel movies. Storylines became increasingly complex. Previously anonymous actors became stars. Audiences were entranced. Theater owners soon discovered they could charge higher admission prices for these new, longer films, and soon they were screening features, as they became known, seven days a week.[64]

In early 1915 word began spreading that a new feature, unlike any previously made, would soon arrive in the Twin Cities. *The Birth of a Nation* was at the time the longest movie ever produced—three hours plus—and it was arousing passions in every city it played. The film, produced and directed by D. W. Griffith, told the story of two families caught in the turmoil of the Civil War and Reconstruction. It was an enthralling

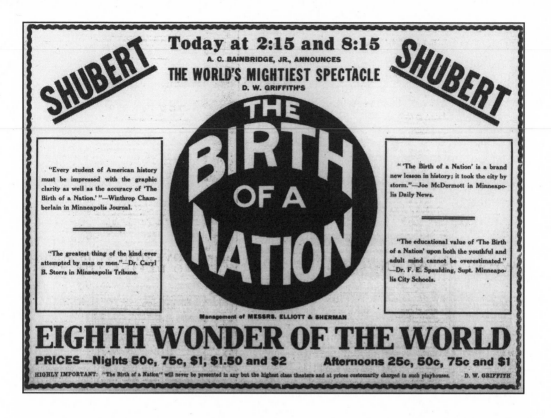

Today at 2:15 and 8:15

A. C. BAINBRIDGE, JR., ANNOUNCES

THE WORLD'S MIGHTIEST SPECTACLE

D. W. GRIFFITH'S

SHUBERT   SHUBERT

THE BIRTH OF A NATION

"Every student of American history must be impressed with the graphic clarity as well as the accuracy of 'The Birth of a Nation.'"—Winthrop Chamberlain in Minneapolis Journal.

"The greatest thing of the kind ever attempted by man or men."—Dr. Caryl B. Storrs in Minneapolis Tribune.

"'The Birth of a Nation' is a brand new lesson in history; it took the city by storm."—Joe McDermott in Minneapolis Daily News.

"The educational value of 'The Birth of a Nation' upon both the youthful and adult mind cannot be overestimated."—Dr. F. E. Spaulding, Supt. Minneapolis City Schools.

Management of MESSRS. ELLIOTT & SHERMAN

EIGHTH WONDER OF THE WORLD

PRICES---Nights 50c, 75c, $1, $1.50 and $2   Afternoons 25c, 50c, 75c and $1

HIGHLY IMPORTANT: "The Birth of a Nation" will never be presented in any but the highest class theatres and at prices customarily charged in such playhouses.   D. W. GRIFFITH

The *Minneapolis Journal* ran this advertisement for *The Birth of a Nation* on November 7, 1915.

epic featuring many cinematic innovations, like close-ups, flashbacks, and fades. But it also was blatantly racist. It depicted African Americans as either infantile or depraved and the Ku Klux Klan as heroic. Black activists already had attempted to keep the film from showing in several large cities. The premiere in Boston, for example, had triggered an outbreak of egg throwing, stink bombings, and angry protests. But no matter how loud the objections, the film continued to run. *The Birth of a Nation* broke box office records wherever it appeared.[65]

New films usually debuted in cities on the East and West Coasts, so it was no surprise that *The Birth of a Nation* had not yet arrived in Minneapolis and St. Paul. But African American leaders in the Twin Cities knew it was just a matter of time. They began to prepare.

In May of 1915, an African American newspaper called the *Twin City Star* reported that *The Birth of a Nation* had "been warned not to book [in Minneapolis]."[66] But that warning—whatever it might have been—went unheeded. A few months later, the editor of the *Star* acknowledged that "the infamous photo-play" undoubtedly would show up in the Twin Cities.[67] The only question was when—and where. The simmering controversy came to a boil in mid-October when theater owners announced plans to screen the film at two Twin Cities show houses: the Auditorium in St. Paul and the Shubert in Minneapolis.

St. Paul was the first of the two cities to tackle the issue. The brouhaha broke into the open when three St. Paul theater men—the brothers Charles and Joseph Friedman, of the Strand, and their partner, George Granstrom—rented an old theater called the Auditorium and applied for a license to show *The Birth of a Nation*. Aware of their formidable opposition, the Friedmans and Granstrom invited about one thousand people, including Mayor Winn Powers and the entire city council, to a private showing on October 20. The crowd at the Auditorium that evening reflected the full range of opinion regarding the film. When the movie was over, members of the audience shared their impressions with a reporter from the *St. Paul Daily News*. Physician Arthur Sweeney, like most of the white people in attendance, thought the film was "a magnificent spectacle that should be seen by everyone for its historical and artistic value." But most black guests, including Rev. Stephen L. Theobald of St. Peter Claver's Catholic Church, left the theater dismayed.

> *I do not think there is any question that such an exhibition is capable of creating sentiments of prejudice if not hatred for colored people. I do not say the picture would cause riots. We haven't the class of people here who would express their antipathies with violence. The feeling against the colored people is growing and the picture, therefore, is harmful in this community. As far as the historical value is concerned, if the producers are trying to educate the public in the history of the nation, they are doing so by emphasizing incidents which would be a discredit to civilization.*[68]

When the city council met a few days later to formally consider the license request, passions erupted. About five hundred people—most of them African American—packed the council chambers to express their feelings about the film. Speeches for and against the production were interrupted by hisses and applause. At least one fight broke out when a black man spoke in support of the film. Most of those expressing opposition to the motion picture were African Americans, but a few white people spoke out as well. "This picture is one of the most immoral things that could possibly be shown," declared Marguerite Bend, a prominent society matron. "I left the theater with a feeling of shame and nausea after seeing it."[69]

Black activists had worked behind the scenes at city hall for several weeks, hoping to build a resilient opposition to the motion picture, but in the end they could not overcome the efforts of the film's supporters. The Friedmans and Granstrom got their license. In a concession to the film's opponents, the three partners agreed to cut two scenes from the movie, including a famous sequence in which a young white woman leaps to her death when a black man threatens to rape her.[70] But as soon as the film began its run, the Friedmans and Granstrom reneged on their agreement with the city and restored parts of the edited scenes.[71] The city council could have revoked the license, but it chose to look the other way.

As the struggle over *The Birth of a Nation* reached its climax in St. Paul, a similar fight was brewing in Minneapolis. At the center of the controversy was the city's mayor, Wallace Nye. Earlier in the year, Nye had told black leaders in Minneapolis that he would block any attempts to show the film in the city. For a while it appeared as though he would stick to his promise. When the manager of the Shubert, A. G. "Buzz" Bainbridge, announced that he had scheduled *The Birth of a Nation* for an eight-week run beginning October 31, Nye reaffirmed his pledge to keep the film off the city's motion picture screens. "My decision is final," he proclaimed. But Buzz Bainbridge, who already had made elaborate plans to move his stock acting company, the Bainbridge Players, to another theater during the film's run, was not one to surrender without a fight. "I see no reason to stop the [photo] play here when it is permitted in every other city in the country," he said. "I think there are more people who want to see the play in this town than there are who want it stopped."[72]

Alexander "Buzz" Bainbridge, manager of the Minneapolis Shubert and the man most responsible for bringing *The Birth of a Nation* to the city.

The confrontation moved to the courts. On October 30 a district court judge in Minneapolis issued a temporary injunction preventing Nye from interfering with the showing of the movie. *The Birth of a Nation* opened at the Shubert as scheduled the following day. A week later, however, the same judge ruled that Nye did, in fact, have the authority to revoke the Shubert's license, assuming he had legitimate reasons for doing so. Faced with the possibility of imminent closure, Bainbridge reluctantly halted all screenings of the motion picture while he appealed the case to the Minnesota Supreme Court. At this point the facts in the case seemed to favor Bainbridge. *The Birth of a Nation* had shown at the Shubert for a full week without causing any public unrest, and courts in three other cities—Chicago, St. Louis, and Pittsburgh—had recently turned back attempts to suppress the photoplay.[73] Bainbridge expressed confidence that he would prevail, but the high court ruled against him. Nye's decision to block the movie stood.[74] Or so it seemed.

Shortly after the Supreme Court handed down its decision, Nye received a petition asking him to let a group of one hundred representative citizens pass judgment on the motion picture. Under the petitioners plan if a majority of the censors approved the film, the mayor could then lift the ban, confident that he was acting according to the public will.[75] Nye, who previously had insisted his decision on the matter was final, endorsed the proposal spelled out in the petition. When the committee of censors voted overwhelmingly in favor of the film, Nye jumped at the chance to remove an unwanted and politically uncomfortable burden from his shoulders. "I was highly pleased with the work of the committee," he said, "and as a result, 'The Birth of a Nation' will be allowed to run."[76]

The Birth of a Nation forced elected officials in the Twin Cities—and the people they represented—to confront inconvenient questions about a new form of entertainment that apparently was not going away. Should the government prevent the showing of motion pictures that some people found objectionable? If so, who should decide what was objectionable and what was not? In the case of *The Birth of a Nation*, officials in both cities ultimately proved unwilling to prevent the exhibition of a controversial film. But difficult questions stemming from the growing popularity of motion pictures were not simply going to vanish once *The Birth of a Nation* played itself out. Film was establishing itself as a powerful medium, and it would continue to stir passions among Twin Citians of every imaginable background. "We did not succeed in having the showing of [this] vicious film stopped," the editor of the black newspaper the *Appeal* wrote in the aftermath of the dispute over *The Birth of a Nation*, "but we have put up such a fight that we do not intend to have our rights utterly ignored or ruthlessly trod upon without protest."[77]

*I*t had been about three years since the Friedman brothers switched the name of the Grand Theater in St. Paul to the Strand and converted it into a motion picture house. Now, in the summer of 1917, word arrived that someone wanted to buy the Strand. As financial representative of the Jacob Litt estate, the theater's owner, it was Theo Hays's job to negotiate a fair deal.

The would-be buyers were Moses Finkelstein and Isaac Ruben. Over the previous few years Finkelstein and Ruben had assembled a stable of movie theaters—three in St. Paul and four in Minneapolis— that was second to none in the Twin Cities. Now they wanted to add the St. Paul Strand to their collection. Hays invited the two men to his office at the Bijou in Minneapolis (his family still owned the building) to work out the details.[78] The price they agreed to was the most lucrative in Twin Cities theatrical history: $100,000.[79]

On August 12, 1917, the new Garrick Theater—as the St. Paul Strand was now known—opened with *The Little American*. The theater sparkled with new furnishings. The sounds of a new ten-thousand-dollar pipe organ added depth to the already impressive orchestral accompaniment.[80] And overseeing the entire event was a familiar figure. "Messrs. Ruben & Finkelstein sprung a big surprise when they announced the manager for the new house," the trade publication *Moving Picture World* reported. "The executive is none other than Theodore L. Hays, perhaps the best known showman in the entire northwest."[81] Theo Hays had made his name as the manager of theaters specializing in live stage entertainment. He had detoured briefly into the motion picture field when the Friedmans took over the Strand but had since concentrated mostly on legitimate theater projects (including a short stint as business manager of the Minneapolis Shubert). Now he was poised to make a big splash in the film world. Not only was he the new manager of a newly refurbished cinema, he now worked for the two most powerful men in the Twin Cities' motion picture business.

ADMIT TWO

466898
466898
466898

AGE OF ELEGANCE

The exact details would blur with the passage of time, but the rough outlines of the fateful encounter were never seriously in dispute. One morning in St. Paul—it was probably 1908 or 1909, or maybe even 1910—a clothier and small-time theater owner from Des Moines named Isaac Ruben walked into Moses Finkelstein's jewelry store on East Seventh Street, across from the Golden Rule department store. According to an account published years later, the initial exchange between the two men began inauspiciously. After introducing himself, Ruben made a proposal that sounded more like a demand.

"I want you to build a theater for me," he said.

Finkelstein was taken aback. "I'm a jeweler," he said. "Why should I build a theater?"

The two men bickered for a while until Ruben left. About a week later, Ruben returned, only to be rebuffed. But he didn't give up. He came back again and again, until finally Finkelstein had a change of heart. "I like you," he said. "I'll build a theater and you can operate it. But it must be done under your name. If it is successful then we'll see."[1] Those initial encounters between Isaac Ruben and Moses Finkelstein constituted the genesis of an uncommonly lucrative partnership.

Finkelstein was an immigrant. Born in Lithuania in 1869, he left home at the age of fourteen and spent nearly all the money he had on passage to the United States. He arrived in New York with no knowledge of English, only a few cents to his name, and even fewer prospects for employment. Desperate for help, he wrote to his uncle, a St. Paul jewelry merchant named Lewis Finkelstein. Lewis arranged for his nephew to come to Minnesota and quickly put him to work as a traveling jewelry salesman.[2] Soon, young Moses had earned enough money to set up his own shop. His business grew throughout the 1890s. By the turn of century, his store on Seventh Street was known as "a favorite place for the newest things, the best things, and 'catchy' ideas where there is originality and not imitation."[3]

Ruben was born in 1868 in Syracuse, New York. His father had emigrated from Poland. His mother was from Germany. As a boy Isaac earned money by selling newspapers on the streets of Syracuse. (Among his fellow vendors were two other Syracuse natives who would go on to show business fame and fortune—Lee and Jake Shubert.) Eventually, he moved into retail. He clerked at clothing stores in Cleveland and Chicago and finally, around 1900, opened his own shop in Des Moines. But Ruben itched to try something new. About 1907 he opened a small theater called the Lyric, a block away from his clothing store. Not long after that, he opened a second theater, the Star, just down the street.[4] Ruben was bitten by the show business bug. But the opportunities to expand in Des Moines appeared limited. So he turned his attention to bigger markets—including the Twin Cities.

The Finkelstein and Ruben partnership made its public debut on July 18, 1910, with the opening of the Princess Theater, a block down from Finkelstein's jewelry shop on East Seventh. The Princess's streetside façade was "an elaborate affair of marble, onyx, stained glass and stucco work."[5] Inside, the unassuming auditorium could seat about eight hundred people. Finkelstein owned the building. Ruben managed the business.[6] The arrangement seemed to suit both men. Ruben, who by now qualified as something of a theater veteran, was in his element. He reveled in the crowds and the excitement. Finkelstein, worried that his association with show business might reflect poorly on him and his fam-

Finkelstein and
Ruben's first movie
theater, the Princess,
on East Seventh
Street in St. Paul.

ily, was happy to remain behind the scenes. He even went so far as to enter the building only through the rear door, where he wouldn't be spotted by the people he most wanted to impress.[7] The Princess was an immediate success. On Saturday evenings crowds spilled out of the auditorium, into the foyer, and out onto the sidewalk, forcing passersby into the street.[8]

With the Princess drawing large audiences and impressive profits, Finkelstein and Ruben began making plans for a second theater—this one in Minneapolis. On September 18, 1911, F&R opened the Grand, a 1,500-seat vaudeville house on Hennepin Avenue. Advertisements declared—with the usual hyperbole—that the new theater was "a total eclipse of any previous amusement [enterprise] anywhere."[9] It was, in fact, something that Twin Citians had never encountered before: a luxurious but affordable theater where all seats cost just ten cents. "Considering the price," the *Minneapolis Journal* reported, "the patron receives the same attention as though he or she had paid a dollar for a seat."[10]

Moses Finkelstein had always felt that the theater business was somehow beneath him. Now, with the Princess and the Grand performing better than he had hoped, his reservations about show business were fading. In the spring of 1913, he and Ruben took over management of the Majestic Theater in St. Paul. With three theaters in two cities, F&R now looked like a chain in the making. Finkelstein decided the time had come to stop hedging his bets and make a full commitment to his theaters. In December of 1913, he ran his last newspaper ad as a jeweler.

> *Say! Have you ever heard of a live merchant going out of business when he was making money? Well, I should say not. I am going out of the jewelry business because I am forced to. Forced on account of my other enterprises which need all my attention . . .*
>
> *Have been in the jewelry business in St. Paul for 26 years and every article can be depended upon to be just as represented.*
>
> *Watch our windows for bargains.*
> *Yours truly,*
> *M. L. Finkelstein*[11]

With Finkelstein now committed to the theater business, F&R embarked on an expansion campaign unlike anything the Twin Cities had ever seen. The two partners opened the Palace ("a building of Venetian red brick, massive, palatial"),[12] the Aster (named "after the flower which blooms so profusely in Minneapolis gardens in the late summer"),[13] and the Unique, all on Hennepin Avenue. They also purchased the nearby Miles Theater (which they soon renamed the Garrick) and

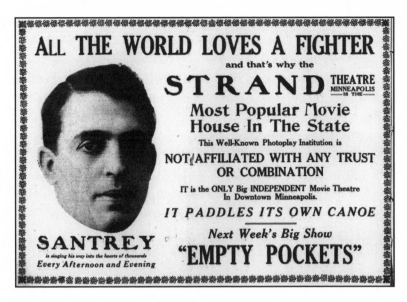

ALL THE WORLD LOVES A FIGHTER
and that's why the
STRAND THEATRE
MINNEAPOLIS
IS THE
Most Popular Movie
House In The State
This Well-Known Photoplay Institution is
NOT AFFILIATED WITH ANY TRUST
OR COMBINATION
IT is the ONLY Big INDEPENDENT Movie Theatre
In Downtown Minneapolis.
IT PADDLES ITS OWN CANOE
SANTREY
is singing his way into the hearts of thousands
Every Afternoon and Evening
Next Week's Big Show
"EMPTY POCKETS"

By early 1918, when this ad ran in the *Minneapolis Labor Review,* the Saxe brothers' Strand was the only major movie theater in downtown Minneapolis not owned by Finkelstein and Ruben.

Roxy's old haunt, the Lyric.[14] In St. Paul they opened their biggest theater yet, the 3,000-seat Palace, on the site of the old public library at Seventh and Wabasha.[15] And in the summer of 1917, they acquired the St. Paul Strand, hired Theo Hays to manage it, and—as they had with the Miles in Minneapolis—rechristened it the Garrick. Finkelstein and Ruben now operated nine theaters in the Twin Cities, including the five largest show houses on Hennepin Avenue. In fact, they controlled every major motion picture theater in downtown Minneapolis except one: the Strand on South Seventh Street.

The Saxe brothers of Milwaukee had opened the Minneapolis Strand (originally called the Saxe) four years earlier, after trying and failing to turn the Lyric into a moneymaking venture. The Strand was "designed and arranged exclusively for motion picture productions" and was "the only theater of its class in the middle northwest built expressly for [that] purpose."[16] The Saxes were proud of their $150,000 picture house, and as F&R tightened its grip on the Minneapolis market, they clung to their independence. They even trumpeted their autonomy in their advertisements. "All the world loves a fighter," one ad proclaimed, "and that's why the Strand Theatre Minneapolis is the most popular movie house in the state."[17]

The Saxes and F&R were engaged in what *Moving Picture World* called a "merry war," but there was little mystery as to who would ultimately prevail.[18] In the spring of 1918, the increasingly acquisitive Finkelstein and Ruben finally convinced the Saxes to sell. The Strand was now theirs, as was every other cinema of any consequence in downtown Minneapolis. In addition, their simultaneous acquisition of the Hippodrome in St. Paul made them just as dominant in that city. Industry insiders couldn't help but take notice. *Moving Picture World* reported that F&R was "getting into 'select' circles" that included, among others, New York–based theater magnate Marcus Loew.[19] And for the first time newspapers in the Twin Cities began using the word "monopoly" to describe F&R's growing regional empire.[20]

*W*hile Finkelstein and Ruben concentrated on the two downtowns, many of their competitors were looking elsewhere—to the outlying neighborhoods where city dwellers were settling in ever-greater numbers. Neighborhood theaters had begun sprouting in the Twin Cities around 1910, and before long it was hard to find any place in Minneapolis or St. Paul that didn't have a movie house within easy walking distance. One area that produced a particularly heavy concentration of theaters during the 1910s was North Minneapolis.

Minneapolis's north side had long been a haven for immigrants. During the late 1890s its residents were mostly Scandinavian. But around the turn of the century, a new group—Jewish immigrants from Eastern Europe—began to move in, and the north side assumed a distinctly Jewish, working-class character. Men eked out livings as peddlers, carpenters, tailors, and cobblers. Women took in boarders and washed laundry.[21] Many of them were strivers who had not yet attained the economic independence that earlier Jewish immigrants—like Moses Finkelstein—enjoyed. They worked hard to better their lot, but good-paying jobs were often in short supply. And Minneapolis had a reputation as one of the nation's most anti-Semitic cities, with many of its largest employers simply refusing to hire Jews.[22] The recently arrived Jewish immigrants of the north side bit their tongues and took their opportunities as they came. Among the more intriguing opportunities available to them was film exhibition.

During the early years of the motion picture business, owning a theater was a risky proposition. For one thing, film had an unsavory reputation. The refined and well-to-do attended stage plays and operas, not picture shows. Upper-class and middle-class Twin Citians often dismissed motion pictures as cheap entertainment for the masses. Even Moses Finkelstein was initially reluctant to enter the theater business because he knew many people held a low opinion of the cinema. In addition to its poor reputation, film had to overcome questions about its viability. Many industry insiders believed film was a fad that eventually would run its course. Charles Van Duzee, for example, disposed of six theaters in downtown Minneapolis because the future of motion picture theaters "didn't look so bright."[23] For many would-be entrepreneurs the movie theater business was simply not worth the risk. But this reluctance by members of the Twin Cities' establishment to embrace the cinema left the door wide open for dice-rolling outsiders who felt they had little to lose. Among them was a relative newcomer to North Minneapolis named Sol Lebedoff.

Lebedoff was a Russian immigrant who had fled to the United States in 1909 after deserting from the Russian army. Like most of his neighbors in North Minneapolis, he was Jewish. For several years after his arrival, Lebedoff bounced from job to job—clothes presser, tailor, peddler—but none was to his liking. Finally, in about 1912, he purchased a little theater on Sixth Avenue North called the Milo and embarked on a new career in the motion picture business. After five years at the Milo, he acquired another Sixth Avenue theater, the Liberty, which until then had offered "a distinctly Jewish vaudeville program three times a week."[24] Lebedoff knew that many, if not most, of his customers were Jewish, and he catered to them. "He used to have a large Chanukah party for all the kids from all the shuls," his son Martin Lebedoff recalled years later. "And they'd come and they'd fill up the six hundred seats, and they'd give them gifts and it was a wonderful occasion."[25] The Liberty functioned as a center of community life on the north side until 1924 when Lebedoff built a new theater, the Homewood, on Plymouth Avenue.

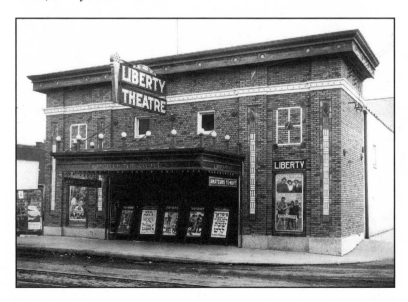

Sol Lebedoff's Liberty Theater in North Minneapolis catered to a predominantly Jewish clientele.

Feature Presentation

**Pantages Theater
708 Hennepin Avenue,
Minneapolis
Opened 1916**

The Minneapolis Pantages was the eighteenth theater in the chain of show houses owned or operated by West Coast vaudeville impresario Alexander Pantages.[1] Pantages's Minneapolis theater was groundbreaking in several respects. It was the first Twin Cities theater to include a mezzanine—a carpeted, balcony-level lobby where patrons could congregate before and after the show. It also was the first to feature automatic temperature control (forced air cooled by tons of ice) during the sweltering summer months. The Pantages was the height of comfort and elegance. Every seat in the house had an unobstructed view of the stage. The auditorium was carpeted, flanked by two tiers of proscenium boxes, and ensconced in molded stucco of ivory and gold.[2] But soon the Pantages was overshadowed by newer, even more ornate theaters like the nearby State. In 1922 it underwent a major refurbishing that included the addition of a glass dome above the auditorium, but it continued to struggle. In 1946 RKO acquired the Pantages and subjected it to a radical modernization that removed much of its vaudeville-era charm. The new RKO Pan was

Pantages Theater, Minneapolis, 1920.

the latest in stripped-down, postwar simplicity, and it operated for the next decade as one of the city's most successful second-tier motion picture houses. Ted Mann bought the Pan—along with the Orpheums in both cities—from RKO in 1960. He spent $350,000 to turn it into a top-notch movie house. The new Mann Theater screamed of the 1960s, with gobs of shiny metals, plastics, and abstract designs. After

more than twenty years as one of downtown Minneapolis's most recognizable movie theaters, the Mann finally closed in 1984. Sixteen years later, the city bought the theater from Mann and restored it to something approximating its former vaudeville self. The reborn Pantages began its new life as the city's newest live performance venue in 2002.

Lebedoff was just one of many local entrepreneurs who thought they could make a living by showing motion pictures in North Minneapolis. By 1915 the north side of Minneapolis was home to no fewer than thirteen motion picture theaters. Plymouth Avenue alone had four: the Dreamland, the Oak Park, the Plymouth, and the Third Ward. A few north side theater owners, including Lebedoff and William "Al" Steffes of the Northern on West Broadway, would go on to long and successful careers as motion picture exhibitors, but most discovered that the theater business was not as easy or lucrative as they thought it would be. North Minneapolis simply did not need thirteen movie theaters.

And it wasn't just North Minneapolis. The entire Twin Cities area was awash in motion picture theaters. By 1915 Minneapolis had nearly eighty. St. Paul had about thirty. Over the next several years the numbers continued to increase, albeit at a much slower pace. The theater glut was getting so pervasive that some owners began advocating restrictions. Charles Van Duzee, for one, believed that a limit on theater licenses would "elevate the business."[26] The editors at the *Minneapolis Journal* concurred. "Overcompetition in purveying motion pictures [is] decidedly against the public interest," they wrote. "From almost any point of view, except that of the man who wants to get into a new business that seems invitingly profitable, it is wise to limit the number of licensed theaters in the City."[27] What Twin Cities neighborhood theater owners didn't know—or didn't acknowledge—was that the overabundance of motion picture houses was the least of their problems.

*T*he crowd started forming outside the new Capitol Theater in St. Paul during the afternoon of September 8, 1920, several hours before the grand opening show was scheduled to begin. By 6:45 PM the line of people waiting to get into the new theater stretched down Seventh Street to Wabasha, turned the corner, and continued for nearly a block. When the doors were thrown open a half hour later, streams of people flooded into the lobby.[28] Jostling amid the throng was a critic for the *St. Paul Pioneer Press* named James Gray.

> *When you first step inside the Capitol theater you think "Wheeoo" and feel for the nearest support. Standing in the lobby, I experienced the same feeling of absolute incredulity which led the country farmer, making his first acquaintance with a giraffe, to exclaim, "There ain't no sich animal." In the midst of such complete luxury, the average man can merely rub his eyes and wonder whether they are serving him aright. . . .*
>
> *But it is not an illusion. It is all real.*

Nearly everyone who showed up for the grand opening was agog. The new theater on Seventh Street was, as James Gray suggested, something almost beyond comprehension. Girl ushers in black satin blouses, white satin pantalettes, and "black plush tams set at a rakish angle" escorted ticket holders to their seats. The auditorium, with its three levels, velvet wall hangings, and ubiquitous gold leaf, exuded luxury. It seated around 2,500 people (the exact number seemed to change daily, depending on who was asking), making it the largest movie theater in St. Paul and one of the largest west of Chicago.

The Capitol was the latest, biggest, and—at a price tag of about $1.5 million—most expensive theater in Finkelstein and Ruben's small empire of Twin Cities show houses. They already owned several fancy theaters, including the Minneapolis Strand and the St. Paul Garrick, but the Capitol outshined them all. It was the first example in the Twin Cities of a new trend in theater design: the picture palace. The most striking characteristic of the new palaces was their size. The largest ones, including the Capitol, had between 1,800 and 3,000 seats. But no matter how many people they accommodated, they never skimped on service or atmosphere. Ushers, doormen, and ticket takers were well trained and unfailingly polite. Blinding marquees illuminated the nighttime cityscape. Ornate interior decorations enveloped the audience in elegance.[29] The Capitol was modeled after two recently completed theaters that defined the modern picture palace—the new Roxy-managed Rivoli in New York and Grauman's Million Dollar Theatre in Los Angeles—although Moses Finkelstein insisted it exceeded both in "cost and beauty."[30]

The picture palaces, dripping as they were with opulence, may have looked like dolled-up refuges for society's pampered upper crust, but Finkelstein and Ruben—like their counterparts in other cities—were determined to avoid any charges of elitism. To that end their new general manager, Theo Hays (recently promoted from his position at the St. Paul Garrick), talked up the Capitol's democratic credentials.[31] The local press, including critic James Gray, was happy to oblige. The Capitol was a "castle," Gray wrote, a "palace" where "her ladyship, the manicurist, will have the same right to its use as her ladyship, the society woman." It was, he concluded, a grand "institution for the people."[32]

Finkelstein and Ruben probably could not have afforded to build the Capitol without the financial backing of their new partner, millionaire brewer William Hamm. Hamm had dabbled in the movie business for several years (he owned the Majestic, Gem, and Alhambra theaters in St. Paul),[33] but his association with Finkelstein and Ruben didn't begin until the spring of 1918, when he provided much of the capital for F&R's purchase of the Minneapolis Strand.[34] That experience led to the creation of a new partnership, the Twin City Amusement Trust Estate, which was controlled jointly by Finkelstein, Ruben, and Hamm. The estate financed the construction of the Capitol Theater (which actually was just part of a larger structure called the Hamm Building) and a second picture palace, the 2,800-seat State Theater on Hennepin Avenue in Minneapolis.

Millionaire brewer William Hamm used his considerable wealth to fuel Finkelstein and Ruben's expansion during the 1920s.

The opening of the State on February 5, 1921, rivaled the unveiling of the Capitol in almost every way. As in St. Paul, theatergoers in Minneapolis began gathering outside the new show house hours before the doors were scheduled to open. The crowd eventually swelled to such proportions that police were called in to clear people from the Hennepin Avenue streetcar tracks. Inside, ticket holders marveled at creative lighting schemes that washed the auditorium in "dazzling brilliance" and then blended into "subdued, softer tints." Theo Hays kicked off the evening's entertainment with a formal welcome to the audience and a bold declaration that the State was "the largest, best appointed and most perfectly ventilated motion picture theater in the West." Amid all the hoopla the opening night film, *Mama's Affair*, starring Constance Talmadge, was something of an anticlimax. One critic, unimpressed by the presentation on the screen, noted that the movie "proceeds to prove the proposition that continued display of feminine tears and hysterics will wash away the hardest stone."[35]

With the additions of the Capitol and the State, Finkelstein and Ruben permanently raised the expectations of many Twin Cities moviegoers. Audiences were no longer content to watch flickering motion pictures in shoddy surroundings. They expected to escape, however briefly, into a make-believe world. "Naturally patrons when they can be comfortably seated in a modern cinema theater which has been built expressly for the showing of pictures, will not pay as much for a seat in an old store building," a reporter with the *Pioneer Press* observed. "They are a bit discriminating nowadays, these movie patrons."[36]

*W*ho could object to a motion picture titled *Purity?* Perhaps the more appropriate question was, who wouldn't?

The ads for *Purity* that appeared in Twin Cities newspapers in the fall of 1916 slyly hinted at the film's plot. The story that unfolded on the screen was considerably less modest. As it turned out, *Purity,* played by actress Audrey Munson, was an innocent country girl who came to the big city and found work as an artist's model. Her beau, a young poet named Thornton Darcy, became distraught after learning that the woman he loved was posing nude. Among the characters threatening the undraped heroine were villains with such names as Evil, Luston Black, and Judith Lure. *Purity,* joked a reviewer with the *New York Times,* was a film to be relished by "specialists in furtive photographs."[37]

Entertainment critics in the Twin Cities were not so readily amused. "The motives of the men who produce such tainted films are often cloaked hypocritically, for the public eye, under high-sounding 'uplift' titles such as the grossly ironical 'Purity,'" the *Pioneer Press* complained. "The 'Purity' producers, forgetting their devotion to art, call attention [in their advertisements] simply to 'the Perfect Woman in Daring Nude Poses.'" Disrobed women on the movie screen? It was time, the newspaper suggested, to confront "the serious social danger confronted by children who, without restriction, see our motion picture plays."[38]

Women's groups in both cities took the lead in the campaign to clean up the movies. In Minneapolis the Women's Welfare League—a reform-minded organization focused on issues such as poverty, homelessness, and prostitution—tried to convince theater operators to submit their films to a voluntary censorship board. It scored its biggest success at the Gayety (which actually was a burlesque house, not a movie theater), where manager William Koenig pledged not to run "unclean or suggestive" acts.[39] In St. Paul a consortium of women's clubs urged theater owners to counteract the negative effects of salacious motion pictures by providing more movies made specifically for children. "If we are going to keep the children from the undesirable motion pictures we must offer a substitute," explained one club leader.[40] Several sympathetic exhibitors, including the Park Theater's George Granstrom, responded by scheduling special Saturday matinees of films like *Alice in Wonderland, Rumpelstiltskin,* and *Little Lord Fauntleroy.* Granstrom and his fellow theater owners claimed the matinees regularly drew crowds of five hundred or more, but the numbers were not sufficient to keep the programs going. The children's matinee became a rarity after 1916.[41]

Efforts to rid Twin Cities theaters of scandalous motion pictures languished until 1921, when the Minnesota Senate took up a bill providing for the creation of a new state censorship board. Supporters of the bill argued that censorship was necessary because the motion picture industry had failed to police itself. A group of Minneapolis school principals summed up the most common complaint: motion pictures were corrupting the city's youth.

> *In a fourth grade class . . . a little boy was talking with his principal about the terrible crime prevalent in the city. The principal tried to show the child that criminals always get the worst of it. He said, "Oh, I don't know. They get lots of money, and then go off and have a good time. And lots of 'em don't get caught. I've seen it in the movies, too."*

By the 1920s many children had become regular moviegoers. Critics of the motion picture industry lambasted Hollywood for producing violent and suggestive films that they considered inappropriate for children.

*Another boy in the same class at school is often in trouble. His mother
came, and inquired earnestly about the cause of the trouble. The teacher
told her that his head was full of the movies, and he entertained her day
after day with wild tales.*

*"Is that so?" innocently inquired the mother. "He doesn't tell them
at home."*

Of course he doesn't.[42]

Theater operators mobilized to defeat the legislation. The last thing
they wanted was the government's passing judgment on every film they
hoped to screen. Al Steffes, the owner of the Northern Theater in North
Minneapolis and the president of the United Theatrical Protective
League, promised "to bury the Capitol post-office under an avalanche of
[anticensorship] mail."[43] Theo Hays, now speaking as general manager
of the Finkelstein and Ruben chain, quoted statistics from Twin Cities
law enforcement officials suggesting there was no link between motion
pictures and juvenile delinquency.[44] But as hearings on the legislation
continued, exhibitors began to fear that momentum was working
against them. Five states already had censorship commissions (in Ohio,
for example, moviegoers were not allowed to see a woman smoke), and
thirty-six others were considering legislation similar to the bill in the
Minnesota Senate.[45] The outcome in Minnesota could have gone either
way. Opponents of the legislation needed someone without financial
links to the motion picture industry to step forward and explain why
state censorship of films was a bad idea.

On the evening of February 8, 1921, a relative newcomer to Minnesota politics, Catheryne Cooke Gilman, appeared before a senate committee to express her opposition to the censorship bill. Gilman was the
driving force behind the Better Movie Movement of the Women's Co-
operative Alliance of Minneapolis. In her testimony before the committee, she described how alliance volunteers had recently visited all sixty-
two movie theaters in Minneapolis. Their purpose, Gilman explained,
was to determine the quality of the shows being presented in each
house and to cultivate cooperative relationships with theater managers.
The results were encouraging. "True," Gilman said, "there are objectionable features in some of the houses, but these are being corrected
willingly by the managers when pointed out to them and I am sure that
should this bill pass it will hamper us in the work we are doing and this
work is really bringing about a better grade of motion pictures."[46]

Gilman argued that the best way to improve the quality of motion
pictures shown at Twin Cities theaters was to convince theater opera-

tors there was a market for superior films. She advocated cooperation with the exhibitors, not confrontation. Her arguments struck a chord. "The comments made by [Gilman] . . . were packed with common sense," one editorial writer observed. "Every experienced theatrical manager knows that in the long run obscenity and filth will never pay."[47] Gilman's testimony provided the weight that tilted the scales in the exhibitors' favor. The Senate committee rejected the censorship legislation by a single vote.[48]

Feature Presentation

●●

**Palace Theater
19–21 West 7th Street,
St. Paul
Opened 1916**

The St. Paul Palace opened on November 27, 1916, as Finkelstein and Ruben's sixth and most spacious theater. Advertisements for the new vaudeville house proclaimed that "its adorable charm and appeal" were "irresistible alike to juvenile and grown-up." The 3,000-seat theater offered every patron an unobstructed view of the stage. Its lavish décor featured ornate stuccowork finished in shades of ivory and putty.[1] In 1923 the Orpheum vaudeville circuit acquired the theater and changed its name to the Palace-Orpheum.[2] (The first St. Paul Orpheum, at Fifth and St. Peter, shut down and later reopened as the President.) The new Palace-Orpheum brought in some of the biggest vaudeville acts of the day, including the up-and-coming George Burns and Gracie Allen (Burns later described the theater as "large, beautiful—and with indoor toilets"), but it continued

By the late 1920s, the vaudeville theater originally known as the Palace had been converted into a motion picture house called the Orpheum. This 1933 photograph shows a crowd gathered outside the Orpheum for the regional premiere of Frank Capra's Lady for a Day.

to struggle.[3] In 1928 it switched to motion pictures and soon shortened its name to the (RKO) Orpheum. For four decades the Orpheum and its neighbor across the street, the Capitol (later the Paramount), reigned as the top first-run motion picture theaters in St. Paul. But by the mid-1970s downtown movie theaters like the Orpheum were hemorrhaging cash and customers in a losing battle with the increasingly popular suburban

houses. The old vaudeville theater showed its last movie in 1982. In the years that followed, entrepreneurs and politicians put forward a series of plans to revive the Orpheum, but none of them took. Nine decades after it opened, the Palace (it had regained its original name) stood empty, as if waiting for the chance to once again show off its finery.

Gilman's role in the bill's demise endeared her to movie men—both locally and nationally. In the Twin Cities her primary ally in the motion picture business was none other than F&R's Theo Hays. Hays encouraged Gilman in her efforts to forge cooperative relationships with Twin Cities theater managers and assured her that the movie industry was committed to reform. But Gilman soon began questioning Hays's sincerity. A few weeks after the defeat of the censorship bill, Gilman confronted Hays about a film titled *The Truth about Husbands*. The movie, which contained "nude figures," "suggestive dancing," and a banquet scene with obvious "sex appeal," had just completed a four-day run at F&R's Strand Theater in Minneapolis, and Gilman was incensed. She felt that Hays, F&R, and the manager of the Strand had, by booking such a "subtly vicious and destructive" motion picture, humiliated her in front of her colleagues at the Women's Co-operative Alliance. "It was very difficult for me, Mr. Hays, to have this [controversy] arise at the close of a thirty minute talk in which I had urged the sincerity of the distributors and exhibitors," she wrote. "As one woman expressed it, 'you have been very considerate of the exhibitors but we feel you have been betrayed by the manager of the Strand.'"[49]

Gilman was having second thoughts about her cooperative strategy, but she was not ready to abandon it—at least not yet. The following year, in a move that burnished her credentials as a leader in motion picture reform, Gilman forged an alliance with another Hays—Will Hays— the president of the Motion Picture Producers and Distributors of America. The Hays Office, as it was widely known, was the brainchild of some of the nation's most powerful movie producers—among them Carl Laemmle, D. W. Griffith, and Adolph Zukor. Its primary purpose was to fend off government regulation. As the motion picture industry's hand-picked self-regulator, Hays was intrigued by Gilman's commitment to reform through cooperation. He considered her approach the perfect antidote to the growing calls for state-sponsored censorship. He asked Gilman to fashion a nationwide program based on the Minneapolis Better Movie Movement. She accepted the assignment.[50]

Gilman spent the next two years trying to make her alliance with the Hays Office work. But it didn't take long for her to begin suspecting that Will Hays—like Theo Hays—was using her as a public relations prop. In a letter to Theo Hays, Gilman expressed dismay "that the motion picture situation had not improved materially," despite her efforts to work with the industry.[51] Hays responded that, to the contrary, he thought quality was rising.

I hold definitely and sincerely to the thought that there has been much improvement in every angle that enters into the consideration of the "motion pictures."

I believe as never before, the producers of motion pictures realize their responsibility to the public of this great commonwealth and that they are sincere in their effort to "sense" the sentiment and desire of the majority of motion picture patrons and are attempting in a constructive way to improve the standard of cinema entertainment.[52]

Gilman disengaged from the Hays Office and aligned herself with groups that advocated federal regulation of the film industry. She still opposed censorship (which she defined as changes made to films by a group of government-appointed censors), but she had come to believe that the federal government must step in because Hollywood was incapable of reforming itself. "When banks failed, we accepted government regulation for stabilizing banking," she said. "Now when motion pictures need regulating we should accept it."[53]

Catheryne Cooke Gilman, about 1916.

But as Gilman soon came to realize, few Americans were clamoring for government regulation of motion pictures. Hollywood was, for the most part, giving moviegoers what they wanted, and most politicians were loath to tell their constituents what they should and should not see. Gilman continued to agitate for reform, but she failed to make much headway. In the Twin Cities her former colleagues at the Women's Co-operative Alliance turned their attention to other movie-related issues that seemed more manageable. In 1928 the alliance lambasted Finkelstein and Ruben's Kiddie Revue, a popular semiannual attraction featuring dozens of young entertainers from around the Twin Cities. Alliance leaders called the revue "child labor of the worst sort."[54] But most Minnesotans failed to see the problem. A bill that would have prohibited young people from appearing in theatrical performances died a quiet death in the state legislature.[55]

Finkelstein and Ruben had always seemed content to limit their
holdings to downtown theaters. But the downtown loops in Minneapolis and St. Paul could accommodate only so many motion picture
houses. If F&R was to maintain its rapid growth, it would have to look
elsewhere for expansion opportunities. In 1918 Finkelstein and Ruben
turned their attention toward Minneapolis's Uptown neighborhood, a
few miles south of downtown.

The Uptown area had two neighborhood theaters—the Calhoun, at
the corner of Lake and Fremont, and the Lagoon, at the intersection of
Hennepin and Lagoon. The Calhoun was the older of the two. Opened
in 1914, it was a modest structure of mosaic brick with a seating capacity of 800.[56] The Lagoon, a 1,500-seat theater of gray terra-cotta and
textured brick, was two years younger than the Calhoun and was widely
considered "one of the finest houses" outside downtown Minneapolis.[57] The two picture houses competed directly with each other, but
both drew enough customers from the surrounding area to make a
decent profit.

The success of the Calhoun and the Lagoon helped convince Finkelstein and Ruben to make their first foray into the neighborhood theater

business. First they purchased the Calhoun in late 1918. Then they approached the owner of the Lagoon, Joseph Cohen.

According to Cohen, Finkelstein and Ruben forced him out of business. After informing him that they had purchased the Calhoun, they proposed that the two theaters combine operations and split the profits. But instead of waiting for his reply, they quickly hired away his manager and made job offers to his remaining employees. Soon Cohen received word from three film distributors that they would no longer supply him with motion pictures. (He denied that his failure to fulfill contract obligations with those distributors had anything to do with their decision to cut him off.) Unable to secure an adequate supply of films, Cohen surrendered, and F&R took over the Lagoon's lease.[58] Although Cohen's account of his dealings with Finkelstein and Ruben were impossible to confirm, one undisputable fact remained: F&R had assumed complete control of the Uptown district's motion picture business.

Finkelstein and Ruben's move into the Uptown area signaled a major shift in their business strategy. Over the next several years F&R developed a voracious appetite for neighborhood theaters. In Minneapolis it acquired the Lyndale, Loring, Rialto, and Nokomis. In St. Paul it added the Como, Dale, Mounds, Venus, St. Clair, Park, and Faust. In 1921 a committee of the Minnesota House of Representatives launched an investigation to determine whether F&R (or more specifically, the Twin City Amusement Trust Estate) constituted an illegal monopoly and whether it was guilty of unfair trade practices. On the eve of the opening of the committee's hearings, William Hamm issued a statement that made no apologies for F&R's aggressive expansion.

> *Far from being a monopoly, which is gouging the public, the interests which are represented in this statement by myself have endeavored to give the public of the cities the highest class of entertainment at the very lowest possible price.*
>
> *It is only because of the organization and the investment of capital that this has been possible.*
>
> *In a field which is as keenly competitive as the amusement field, at the present time, only those who are in a position to purchase in quantity and discriminately can obtain the best there is in the market and can, because of the organization, reduce operating expenses and increase efficiency, give to the public the class of entertainment we are at the cost which we are giving it.*[59]

Most of the testimony heard over the next two weeks concerned the extent to which F&R dominated the movie exhibition business in the

Feature Presentation

Capitol Theater
22 West 7th Street, St. Paul
Opened 1920

Located within the new Hamm Building, and accessible from Seventh Street, Finkelstein and Ruben's Capitol Theater was the Twin Cities' first true picture palace. Unlike the Palace Theater (later the Orpheum) across the street, the Capitol was built specifically to accommodate motion pictures. Its architects, George and Cornelius Rapp of Chicago, ranked among the nation's top theater designers. But while most of the Rapps' previous work echoed the French Renaissance, their designs for the Capitol oozed with Spanish-inspired flare. The exterior was a gaudy carnival of terra-cotta, iron, and bronze festooned with columns, cherubim, and gargoyles. The ornate décor continued inside, where the grand lobby, clad in grayish Italian travertine marble, led to a vast—and slightly less flashy—dome-ceiling auditorium.[1] The Capitol kept its original name through most of the 1920s, but in 1929 Finkelstein and Ruben sold it and the rest of their theaters to the powerful Hollywood studio Paramount. The new owners gave their new St. Paul show house a name more in keeping with their corporate sensibilities. The Paramount, as it was known from then on, remained at or near the

Top: Capitol Theater, St. Paul, 1923. Bottom: a 1920s view of the Capitol's cavernous auditorium.

top of St. Paul's movie theater pecking order for another three and a half decades. In 1965 demolition crews ripped out the Paramount's sumptuous interior so that a smaller movie theater called the Norstar could take its place. The Norstar lasted only thirteen years. It closed in 1978 and was eventually converted into an even smaller live performance theater.

Twin Cities. One witness insisted F&R controlled 85 percent of the area's seating capacity, but the state fire marshal refuted that claim. He presented statistics showing that Finkelstein and Ruben's theaters accounted for only one-third of the seats in Minneapolis and less than 39 percent of the seats in St. Paul.[60] As for the theaters themselves, William Hamm told the committee that F&R controlled fourteen houses in Minneapolis and fifteen in St. Paul—numbers that allowed the firm to benefit from economies of scale. "It must be apparent to this committee," Hamm testified, "that individual ownership of theaters is not financially successful [and] that there are advantages to all concerned from efficient centralized organization and the economy which goes with it."[61] The committee members apparently agreed. In their final report they concluded that "it did not appear that the business of Finkelstein and Ruben, as carried on by them, was unfair either to other exhibitors or to the film companies or to the public."[62] They were off the hook—at least as far as the legislature was concerned.

Still, some independent theater owners remained convinced that F&R was bent on complete domination of the Twin Cities' movie market. And one of them decided to do something about it. In the fall of 1921, about seven months after the house committee issued its report clearing F&R, Joseph Friedman opened a new theater, the Tower, on Wabasha Street in downtown St. Paul. Friedman had made a name for himself back in 1914 when he, his brother Charles, and George Granstrom brought *The Birth of a Nation* to St. Paul. Now he was trying something even more audacious. Friedman was loosely related by marriage to Moses Finkelstein (two of Friedman's brothers had married daughters of Lewis Finkelstein, the uncle who brought Moses to St. Paul during the 1880s), but he apparently didn't think much of his distant relative. Friedman had lost the St. Paul Strand to Finkelstein and Ruben in 1917. Now he was determined to show them that they were not invincible. The opening of Tower Theater constituted his shot across F&R's bow.

The Tower was a poor man's picture palace. Built at a cost of $250,000 (one-sixth the price of F&R's Capitol) and with a seating capacity of about 1,100, it was designed in a style that its architect called Northern Italian Renaissance. From the street it appeared vaguely Old World. Its tower, rising seventy-six feet above the sidewalk, recalled a similar feature at Madison Square Garden in New York. Inside, a paneled ceiling created the illusion that the auditorium was bigger than it actually was. "The Tower is not gaudy or overdeveloped from an artis-

Seventh Street East, just east of Wabasha, was the site of St. Paul's largest concentration of theaters during movie exhibition's first decade. In this photograph the Princess and Majestic are visible on the left; the Alhambra, Gem, and Blue Mouse are across the street.

tic standpoint," *Moving Picture World* reported. "It impresses one as being lastingly beautiful because of its artistic simplicity."[63]

Friedman advertised the Tower as "the people's playhouse," a theater where "all classes of screen followers" could see quality films at reasonable prices. And to make sure there was no confusion, each ad reminded readers that the Tower was "the only independent exclusive first-run photo-playhouse in the Twin Cities." In other words, it did not belong to Finkelstein and Ruben. "I have full confidence in the people of St. Paul," Friedman said, "and hope that my efforts at the Tower will merit [their] full confidence."[64]

For a while it appeared Friedman might succeed in his challenge to Finkelstein and Ruben. In its first year the Tower attracted large crowds and screened some of the season's most successful motion pictures, including D. W. Griffith's *Way Down East* and Douglas Fairbanks's *The Three Musketeers*. But Friedman soon discovered that the burdens of running a first-class motion picture theater were nearly impossible for an independent to bear. "Only a few houses in the Twin Cities are outside the Ruben-Finkelstein syndicate," one reporter noted, "and it is especially difficult for a high grade theater [like the Tower] to make it a success."[65] Friedman added a ballroom next door in an effort to increase revenues, but it made little difference. He couldn't make the theater profitable. Less than five years after opening the Tower, Friedman gave up. He leased the theater to Finkelstein and Ruben and announced he was getting out of the motion picture business. "As a result of this move," *Moving Picture World* observed, "competition, which has often been keen, comes to an end in St. Paul."[66]

With their acquisition of the Tower, Finkelstein and Ruben officially vanquished their most determined local competitor. Now all they had to worry about were the outsiders.

Summer had always been the seasonal bane of the exhibitor's existence. The heat and humidity that descended on the Twin Cities during the summer months made theaters nearly uninhabitable. Most motion picture houses, facing an inevitable drop in patronage, simply shut down after Memorial Day. A few theater owners tried to cool their auditoriums by blowing air across mounds of ice, but such systems were inefficient and unreliable.[67] Twin Citians continued to shun the movies in favor of other more refreshing summertime pursuits like a jump into the nearest lake.

But by the early 1920s theaters in Minneapolis and St. Paul were beginning to shed their reputations as warm-weather saunas. Some of the area's biggest show houses, including the State, Hennepin, and Pantages in Minneapolis and the Capitol in St. Paul, installed elaborate air conditioning systems designed to keep their patrons cool during the hottest months. The State's system was typical. Cold water, drawn from a specially drilled 300-foot well, was the primary source of refrigeration. Once the air was cooled, it was "whirled into the theater in a 20 mile gale." The State's managers claimed that the "artesian well" cooling system kept the temperature inside the theater fifteen degrees lower than the temperature outside.[68]

It didn't take long for exhibitors to begin touting their theaters' relatively frosty environs. Stylized icicles began appearing in newspaper advertisements and on marquees. The manager of F&R's Capitol in St. Paul instituted an ad campaign built around a fictional character that he called Miss Very Cool. The first ad in the series, for example, hyped the advantages of being inside the Capitol on a recent summer scorcher.

> *Miss Very Cool says—*
> *"On the hottest day of the year when 97 degrees was registered outside, it was 70 DEGREES in THE CAPITOL, and thousands found relief from the smothering heat in St. Paul's Million Dollar Theater."*
> *"Were you one of them?"*[69]

Movie theaters around the country began recording phenomenal summertime box office receipts. Exhibitors attributed the spike in business almost exclusively to the advent of air conditioning.[70] "Previous to our 'Miss Very Cool' campaign Capitol Theatre patrons had never stopped to think that we were pumping water and cooling the air artificially for their benefit," the manager of the Capitol wrote. "They realize it now and are talking about it on all sides."[71]

Feature Presentation

State Theater
809 Hennepin Avenue, Minneapolis
Opened 1921

The State was, in many respects, the fraternal twin of the Twin Cities' first authentic picture palace, the Capitol in St. Paul. Its architect, J. E. O. Pridmore of Chicago, described the State's style as free Italian Renaissance. Its original façade featured a marquee running the full length of the building and a vertical projecting "State" sign centered above a steel canopy. The 2,400-seat auditorium contained no boxes or loges that might obstruct views. Its elaborate proscenium arch and frontispiece framed the stage from under a curved, coffered ceiling. The glass stage floor was lit from underneath to create stunning visual effects. The State was the first theater in the Twin Cities to keep its patrons cool during the summer without depending on ice (as the Pantages did). Its rudimentary air conditioning system delivered cool air from an artesian well more than eight hundred feet below

Exterior view of the State from the intersection of Eighth and Hennepin, about 1930.

Hennepin Avenue. The State underwent several significant renovations over the years, including a 1929 art deco makeover designed by the Twin Cities' most successful theatrical architecture firm, Liebenberg and Kaplan.[1] Its run as a motion picture theater ended on New Year's Eve 1975 with a late showing of the rock opera *Tommy.* For six years, beginning in 1979, it served as the home of an evangelical Christian con-

gregation called the Jesus People Church. Private investors renovated the State as part of a larger, city-financed urban development project in 1990 and 1991. The city acquired the State under the financing deal and later added two other Hennepin Avenue show houses—the Orpheum and the Pantages—to its portfolio of live performance venues.

$\mathcal{T}$he following is from the February 6, 1923, minutes of the St. Paul Society for the Prevention of Cruelty—subject: "Animals used for advertising purposes in front of the Moving Picture Theatres."

This is another practice which should be stopped. In most cases these animals displayed have no connection with the show that is going on inside and they are placed there merely to attract the crowds, which frightens them. We receive many complaints against this means of advertising but we can do nothing as our hands are tied. Upon investigation we find the animals are being given the best care and they are usually in very good shape, but they have become so cowed from fright because of the noise and confusion that they act as if they are sick. Then, the complaints start pouring into the office. This is particularly true of the Theatres on Seventh Street where the traffic is so heavy. We have taken this matter up with the City Prosecutor but he says there is nothing in the City Laws which would prevent Theatre Owners from showing these animals in front of their show [houses] and suggested the only thing we could do was for the Society to have an ordinance established, prohibiting the showing of animals in cages outside of theatres.[72]

$\mathcal{O}$n the evening of November 18, 1926, three young women walked up to the ticket window at the Lyceum Theater, a former Finkelstein and Ruben house in downtown St. Paul. They wanted to see a show, which that night happened to be a stage farce called *Here Comes the Bride*. But when they asked for three seats on the main floor, the ticket vendor apologized and informed them there were no seats available. Seemingly disappointed, the three friends walked away. Moments later another patron—an older woman—walked up to the same window and asked for four seats on the main floor. This time the cashier obliged. She gave the woman her four tickets and told her to enjoy the show. That's when the trouble started.

The woman who succeeded in purchasing the tickets was Mrs. W. J. Murray. Her daughter Elizabeth was one of the three young women who had tried and failed to purchase tickets from the Lyceum's cashier. All four of the women—Mrs. Murray and the three friends—were African American, but Mrs. Murray had very light skin. The ticket vendor apparently assumed she was white.

The women had come to the Lyceum hoping to prove that the theater's reputation for racial discrimination was well deserved. And everything was going according to plan. The three friends returned to the Lyceum and joined Mrs. Murray. When they tried to enter the theater with the tickets Mrs. Murray had purchased, the doorkeeper refused to let them take their seats on the main floor and told them they should ask for their money back. Instead, they walked over to the county attorney's office.[73]

Within days the county attorney filed charges against the Lyceum's cashier and doorkeeper, accusing them of criminal discrimination. A few weeks later, a Ramsey County District Court jury found the doorman guilty. The judge in the case fined him three hundred dollars. It was the first time that a criminal discrimination case in Minnesota had resulted in a conviction. Black leaders in the Twin Cities, including editor Earl Wilkins of the *St. Paul Echo,* were elated.

> *The open discrimination which was being practiced at the [Lyceum] theater was the boldest aspect of similar treatment which Negro patrons had been given in other theaters and eating places the city over. In the case of the Lyceum, it had grown so odious that there was no longer any subtlety about it. Negroes simply were not allowed to sit in certain parts of the theater. . . .*
>
> *Viewed from all angles, the case was a milestone upon the march of Twin Cities Negroes up the path to unquestioned civil rights.*[74]

The case against the Lyceum's employees exposed an ugly truth: African Americans were not welcome in some Twin Cities theaters. The Lyceum may have been the most notorious, but most black Twin Citians knew that other movie houses discriminated as well. The practice had emerged from the shadows ten years earlier when two prominent African Americans filed a civil lawsuit against the Pantages Theater in Minneapolis claiming that black patrons were regularly barred from the theater's main floor.[75] The verdict in the Lyceum case provided welcome vindication for those who, over the years, had chafed at the unfair treatment they received from some Twin Cities movie houses. Perhaps now, the *Echo* surmised, theater owners would be "hesitant about adopting a 'policy' toward colored patronage."[76]

The Lyceum discrimination case roughly coincided with another racially charged controversy—this one involving Finkelstein and Ruben. A few months earlier, F&R had reopened the old Como Theater on University Avenue and hired an African American man to manage it. The *St. Paul Echo* lauded the event, claiming that the new Como was "a type of venture which has never before been successfully tried by Negroes in the city."[77] But the Como soon ran into trouble. Rumors began spreading that the firm had opened the Como only because it wanted to lure African American patrons from one of its other theaters, the Faust, just a block away on University. The implication was that Finkelstein and

St. Paul's Lyceum Theater was well known for discriminating against African American customers.

Ruben wanted the Como to be a black theater and the Faust to be a white theater. The *Echo*'s Earl Wilkins, noting that the Como's small audiences were made up almost entirely of white moviegoers, chided his readers for failing to support a black-managed business. "The New Como is *not* a segregation proposition," he wrote. "Any person or group of persons spreading such a version of the cause of its opening is willfully and maliciously lying."[78] Wilkins's protests went unheeded, and the Como closed just five weeks after its grand reopening.

"*C*an you imagine what conditions would be like if we had no ushers?" Moviegoers were asked to ponder that unthinkable proposition as they perused a 1924 edition of F&R's *Capitol Theatre Magazine*. "If at times you chafe under the restraint of waiting for a seat," the writer continued, "please remember that without ushers and their direction of patrons chaos would reign in our theatres."[79]

Chaos, indeed! No wonder good ushers were in such high demand.

In the first decade or so after motion pictures began catching on in the Twin Cities, ushering was almost exclusively a young woman's job. Moviegoers expected to be escorted to their seats by pretty usherettes decked out in stylish uniforms. Theater managers assumed that their patrons "would obey girl ushers, but not men ushers."[80] And the young women who assumed ushering duties in Minneapolis's and St. Paul's most popular show houses usually acquitted themselves well. Nellie Dodson, one of the early ushers at the Shubert Theater in Minneapolis, remembered that the girls on the theater's main floor had to be ready for anything, "regardless of unhooked uniforms, or twisted stockings."

There were always people who thought they could find their seats without the help of an usher. Nine times out of ten they would get into the wrong seats and we would have to move 'em to where they belonged. Did they get mad at themselves for being so smart-alec? No sir, they

Finkelstein and Ruben's Capitol Theater continued to employ female ushers into the mid-1920s.

took it out on us! There were always people who changed their seats
and threw everything into a grand muddle. There were always people
who were discontented with the seats they had been given, and threat-
ened to have Billy, who worked in the box office, discharged. It took a
world of patience to be sweet and nice to some of them. There were
always bald-headed men who grinned, and fresh young men who
would just have to make some wise retort as you handed them their
programs. All of us got bawled out by some blockhead for something
which was entirely the blockhead's fault and not ours. I never will for-
get the evening when an irate old lady came up to me and demanded I
do something about the gentleman in the row behind hers who was
eating peanuts so loudly and rustling the bag so viciously that she
couldn't hear half the lines which were being spoken on the stage![81]

But by the mid-1920s theater operators in the Twin Cities were having second thoughts about female ushers. For whatever reason—perhaps
it was the rise of World War I veterans through the cities' managerial
ranks—the managers of local show houses concluded that the seating of
theatergoers was a job that called for military efficiency. Men, it seemed,
were "better generals than women." The State Theater in Minneapolis
was the area's gender-bending trendsetter. It employed sixteen male
ushers—all of them college students. "Nobody but a college man can be
an usher," the *Minneapolis Journal* reported. "Any man who can work
as an usher is almost certain to be a success in business." According to
the new militaristic approach to ushering, men—unlike women—could
command respect by employing just a few choice words. "You salute,
bow, [and] lead the patron to his seat," the *Journal* explained. "You
speak only when you are spoken to, beyond three phrases, 'Please,'
'Thank you' and 'This way, please.' You must know exactly what tone of
voice to use. In your commands, you must let the patron know exactly
what you mean, but you must be completely courteous, always polite."

By 1928 female ushers were almost impossible to find in Twin Cities
theaters. Women and girls were relegated to box office duty. Men
patrolled the aisles. "They form a new kind of army," the *Journal* proclaimed. "They have taken over jobs traditionally reserved for girls, and
made good. They are the unknown soldiers who make up the army that
works to put you in your theater seat. And their job is an art."[82]

*I*f anyone had ever seriously held out hope that the Twin Cities
would become a filmmaking center, that hope had long since been
dashed. Hollywood was now the undisputed capital of motion picture
production. Filmmakers hardly gave Minneapolis and St. Paul a second

thought—or a first thought, for that matter. Carl Laemmle had made his first film, *Hiawatha*, in Minneapolis back in 1909, but *Hiawatha* was an anomaly. The only other film of any consequence to be shot in the Twin Cities was the 1922 feature *Free Air*. Minnesota author Sinclair Lewis had adapted the screenplay for *Free Air* from his novel of the same title.[83] The six-reel film played briefly in theaters around the country and then faded into motion picture oblivion. The Twin Cities remained a filmmaking nonentity.

But in the spring and summer of 1927, the people of Minneapolis and St. Paul got to indulge in the illusion that they lived in Hollywood

Feature Presentation

●●●

**Hennepin Theater
910 Hennepin Avenue,
Minneapolis
Opened 1921**

The Orpheum vaudeville circuit already had the old Orpheum Theater on Seventh Street when officials with the company announced in 1920 that they intended to build a new show house at Hennepin Avenue and Ninth Street. The new theater, called the Hennepin, was to be a "junior" Orpheum offering motion pictures and vaudeville at "popular prices."[1] But from the moment it opened on October 16, 1921, the new 3,500-seat theater easily outshone its older counterpart on Seventh Street. Big-time vaudevillians—including opening night up-and-comers the Marx Brothers—began making regular stops there. In 1922 company officials bowed to the inevitable and renamed the Hennepin the Orpheum. (From then on the old Orpheum was known as the Seventh Street.)[2] Vaudeville continued

Even before it officially changed its name in 1922, the Hennepin Theater was widely known as the Orpheum.

at the Orpheum into the late 1920s, but eventually motion pictures crowded out the live acts. For half a century the Orpheum ranked as one of the top first-run movie houses in Minneapolis. After a return to live theater in the early 1960s (its new owner, Ted Mann, brought in a string of high-profile Broadway touring productions) the Orpheum fell into a long and slow decline. It showed its last movie in 1979 and, after that, hosted occasional stage shows and rock concerts. In 1988 the city purchased the Orpheum from a group of investors that included Bob Dylan. After a major renovation the Orpheum reopened as a live theatrical venue in early 1994.

East. It was an illusion inspired by Joseph Friedman. Five years earlier, Friedman had drummed up publicity for his new Tower Theater by arranging to have a two-reel motion picture shot entirely in St. Paul, using amateur actors from the surrounding area. The stunt generated story after story in the St. Paul newspapers. (The *Pioneer Press* and the *Dispatch* cosponsored the film.) Hundreds of would-be actors jostled for the chance to star in a hometown feature. When the film, *A Romance of St. Paul,* opened at the Tower, hundreds more lined up to see it. Friedman's motion picture may have had little artistic merit, but it was a commercial success.[84]

Friedman's public relations triumph did not go unnoticed by his archrivals, Moses Finkelstein and Isaac Ruben. A few months after putting Friedman out of business, F&R appropriated his hometown movie idea and improved on it. In the spring of 1927, Finkelstein and Ruben announced that they had inked a deal to finance "amateur movies" in twenty-two cities—including Minneapolis and St. Paul—where they owned theaters. A Hollywood firm, Berkova Productions, would produce the movies. Local newspapers, in cooperation with F&R, would handle publicity. Residents in each city would be encouraged to submit scripts and to audition for roles. Each film would be a "quickie"—cast, shot, edited, and screened in a matter of days.[85]

St. Paul was the first city on F&R's movie list. Eighty-nine would-be screenwriters submitted script synopses for consideration. A committee of judges including St. Paul mayor Laurence Hodgson and F&R's Theo Hays chose a submission titled *Thief,* by local businessman Peter Bies. (The title was considered unsuitable, however, and was quickly changed to *Twin Mix.*) The casting call at the Capitol Theater attracted nearly four hundred people—most of them men. The raucous cattle call produced a leading man (a St. Paul resident with the unlikely name Gordon Awsumb) but no female ingénue. With time to find a suitable heroine running out, the *St. Paul Dispatch* advertised for one—preferably a young woman "five foot four inches in height, [with] small, even teeth, a trim figure, and a demure expression." Twenty-year-old El Nora Howard filled the bill and landed the part.[86]

Twin Mix told the convoluted story of a man whose twin brother was on trial for theft. But the plot was beside the point. The filmmaker's primary job was to put on the screen as many local faces and local businesses as possible. Peter Bies, the local screenwriter, was embarrassed with the outcome. "They disregarded the plot," he complained years later. "They made a shopping film. They took pictures inside this store and that. Just advertising, really." Even the *Pioneer Press* film critic found it hard to write anything nice about the picture. Only the stars, El Nora Howard and Gordon Awsumb, merited any praise. "Both are good looking," the critic wrote, "and both make creditable showings as motion picture actors."[87]

When the filmmakers were done in St. Paul, they moved across the river to Minneapolis to begin production of their next F&R extravaganza, *Pleasure Pirates*. About two thousand Minneapolis residents auditioned for fifty roles. Among the homegrown stars of the show were Louis Priem (as Jim Blake, a cub reporter with the *Minneapolis Journal*), Marguerite Mattern (as the vivacious heroine), five-year-old Leroy Hammond (as a dancing newsboy), a German Shepard named Chekko, and a flashy automobile with "six spare tires, washtub disc wheels, [and] chintz curtain top" owned by Minnesota Gophers all-American fullback Herb Joesting. The title, *Pleasure Pirates,* referred to the dozens of extras who rushed between various locations—Minnehaha Falls, Lake of the Isles, Glenwood Grotto—searching for clues in a treasure hunt. As with *Twin Mix,* the plot of *Pleasure Pirates* was secondary to its public relations value.[88]

Pleasure Pirates opened a one-week run at the State Theater just a few days after shooting wrapped up. Unlike the St. Paul critic who struggled to find anything nice to say about *Twin Mix,* the reviewer at the *Minneapolis Journal* was more than willing to heap praise on a film conceived primarily to generate publicity for F&R and the newspaper. "Thrills and laughs aplenty follow each other in rapid succession," the reviewer gushed. "All through the picture, members of the audience kept exclaiming . . . 'Oh, there she is, there's Betty!' or 'There's Jack,' or 'I saw that scene taken at the State,' or 'There's the new auditorium!'"[89] Finkelstein and Ruben couldn't have asked for better publicity. They might even have tried to make more movies the following summer if events had not intervened.

*T*he small crowd that gathered to watch the demolition of the old stone house and the filling station at the corner of Ninth and La Salle in downtown Minneapolis was oblivious to the forces of commerce that were colliding at that moment on that very spot. A group of prominent Minneapolis businessmen planned to build one of the largest theaters in the country there, and motion picture people in the Twin Cities and elsewhere were eager to see how the project played out. The developers had already leased the yet-to-be-built show house to Paramount-

Publix—the theater-operating arm of the company once known as Famous Players-Lasky. If Paramount-Publix retained the lease, it would become the first of the big Hollywood production companies to gain a foothold in the Twin Cities' motion picture exhibition market. But there was no guarantee that Paramount would hold on to the lease. Construction on the new theater hadn't even started yet, and everyone in the business assumed that the owners of a certain locally owned theater chain would do everything they could to maintain their virtual monopoly in Minneapolis and St. Paul.[90]

Finkelstein and Ruben had kept a wary eye on Paramount for more than a decade. Paramount had emerged as a motion picture powerhouse back in 1916, when Adolph Zukor's production company, Famous Players, merged with the Lasky Feature Play Company. Feature films starring well-known actors were becoming increasingly popular about that time, and Famous Players-Lasky moved quickly to lock up some of the industry's most popular stars—performers like Lillian Gish, Douglas Fairbanks, Fatty Arbuckle, and Mary Pickford. With its impressive assemblage of actors, Famous Players-Lasky forced exhibitors around the country to screen whatever films it was offering—the bad as well as the good—with a system called "block booking." Under this arrangement theater owners could obtain the most popular films only when they accepted package deals that included inferior motion pictures of dubious quality. Many exhibitors—including Finkelstein and Ruben—resented such high-handed tactics, and they began plotting ways to fight back.[91]

In 1917 Moses Finkelstein, Isaac Ruben, and twenty-five other regional theater chain executives formed a new company called First National Exhibitors Circuit to compete directly with Famous Players-Lasky. First National signed several big stars, including Charlie Chaplin, produced its own movies, and supplied them to its franchise holders. It seemed that F&R and the other First National founders had found a way to neutralize Famous Players-Lasky's production advantage. But Adolph Zukor was not one to be intimidated. He had to make sure there were always enough theaters to show his movies. So he started buying theaters.

Famous Players-Lasky's buying spree began in 1920. By the following year, it had acquired more than three hundred theaters nationwide.[92] It was now a vertically integrated entertainment company capable of producing, distributing, and exhibiting its own motion pictures. It had regained its advantage over First National. Other companies, including Loew's (the owner of MGM), Warner Bros., Fox, and Radio-Keith-Orpheum (RKO), would join the rush toward vertical integration, but Famous Players-Lasky was the front-runner. By 1925 Paramount—as it was now widely known—and its Publix theater chain had grown to about five hundred movie houses. It dominated the motion picture field in the South, New England, and a large swath of the Midwest. But not the Twin Cities.

Feature Presentation

Minnesota Theater
36 South 9th Street,
Minneapolis
Opened 1928

The Minnesota, the most palatial of the Twin Cities' picture palaces.

The Minnesota was easily the most spectacular theater the people of the Twin Cities had ever seen—or ever would see, for that matter. Designed by the Chicago architectural firm Graven and Mayger, the Minnesota was a temple of French Renaissance excess. From the street its domed corner tower, sprawling marquee, and imposing vertical sign dominated what was otherwise a fairly simple patterned brick facade. Inside, the effect was palatial. The lobby, flanked by two rows of Bunyanesque marble columns, was larger than many theaters. A grand marble staircase, dubbed the "stairway to happiness," led to the magnificent, yawning space that was the auditorium. The Minnesota was capable of seating more than four thousand people under its backlit ceiling dome. Its stage, stretching more than sixty feet across, featured a hydraulic orchestra lift and was framed by a soaring proscenium arch. But splendid as it was, the Minnesota was literally too much of a good thing—too big to keep filled with paying customers and too expensive to operate. Any chance that it would succeed vanished with the coming of the Great Depression. The monstrous theater went dark for much of the three-year period between 1932 and 1935, and in 1938 it shut down for six years. When it reopened in 1944, it was called the Radio City (KSTP radio had set up shop on the theater's old mezzanine). The early postwar years were good to the Radio City, but by the mid-1950s the overblown show house was once again losing money at an alarming rate. The owners of WCCO radio and television bought the Radio City in 1958 and demolished it the following year to make way for a parking deck.[1]

Carl Laemmle's Universal Pictures had attempted in 1925 to break Finkelstein and Ruben's stranglehold on the Twin Cities' market. Laemmle was convinced that Universal had to construct a theater in Minneapolis "as a matter of self preservation." But his efforts, including an attempt to buy Joseph Friedman's Tower Theater in St. Paul, fell short. Finkelstein and Ruben retained their near monopoly.[93]

But the news that Paramount Publix planned to lease the new, gargantuan theater under construction at the corner of Ninth and La Salle was a matter of deep concern for Finkelstein and Ruben. Paramount posed a much larger threat than Universal ever did. If it followed through with its plans to open the palace of all Twin Cities picture palaces, F&R's theaters in downtown Minneapolis would almost certainly see their audiences shrink. But what could Finkelstein and Ruben do about it?

About six months after construction began on the new theater at Ninth and La Salle, Moses Finkelstein announced that F&R had reached a deal with Publix. Under the agreement, Finkelstein and Ruben would take over management of the new picture house. In return Publix would assume partial control of F&R's theaters in downtown Minneapolis and St. Paul. The local press wasn't sure how to describe the deal. The *Minneapolis Journal* called it an "arrangement." The *St. Paul Pioneer Press* preferred "affiliation." Whatever the proper term, both newspapers agreed that the pact averted "a threatened invasion, by another circuit, of the Twin Cities and Northwest theatrical territory."[94]

The new theater that opened at Ninth and La Salle on March 23, 1928, was called the Minnesota, and it easily out-palaced every other Twin Cities picture palace, including the Capitol in St. Paul and the State in Minneapolis. With a seating capacity of more than four thousand, it ranked as the fifth-largest theater in the country. Only the Roxy and Paramount in New York, the Uptown in Chicago, and the Michigan in Detroit were bigger. The Minnesota's cavernous lobby was 150 feet long, 45 feet wide, and four stories high. Its saucer-shaped auditorium, with its splendid ceiling dome, was spacious beyond comprehension. Its staff of three hundred included fifty-five ushers (nearly all of them students at the University of Minnesota) and a specialist whose only job was to change lightbulbs.[95]

The opening night gala was an invitation-only affair that attracted a smattering of celebrities (the biggest name was composer Irving Berlin) and a multitude of theater executives, including the president of Publix, Sam Katz. Local newspapers published the names of about two

dozen theater people—all of them from other cities—who attended the opening, but nowhere in their coverage did they indicate that the roster of dignitaries included the two men who supposedly had taken over management of the Minnesota: Moses Finkelstein and Isaac Ruben.

The absence of the Twin Cities' two most successful theater owners signaled a power shift that would radically alter moviegoing in Minneapolis and St. Paul. Finkelstein and Ruben were preparing to get out of the motion picture business. Even as the Minnesota Theater was opening its doors to the public, rumors were rife that F&R was about to be sold. William Fox, the owner of the Fox theater chain, was looking to expand into the Upper Midwest and had set his sights on F&R. Trade publications reported that a deal was imminent.[96] At the same time the relationship between F&R and Publix was looking increasingly one-sided. Not only had Finkelstein and Ruben been shunted aside during the Minnesota opening, but now all advertisements for their downtown theaters in Minneapolis and St. Paul carried the Publix logo.[97] It was hard to guess what they planned to do next.

It all became clear in the summer of 1929. Fox had, by this time, dropped out of the running. Paramount was F&R's only remaining suitor. On July 15, William Hamm announced that Paramount had purchased all of F&R's holdings, including its 120 theaters in 27 Upper Midwest cities. The total value of the transaction was said to be about eleven million dollars. "My judgment is that as far as the public interest is concerned, the change will be highly beneficial," Hamm said. "Paramount is better able to give service and provide programs than any other organization."[98] Moses Finkelstein and Isaac Ruben did not comment publicly on the sale, but reports indicated that they were well compensated. While Hamm reportedly received cash for his holdings in the company, Finkelstein and Ruben exchanged their shares in F&R for a large chunk of Paramount stock.[99] With the stock market going gangbusters, it appeared that they had made a shrewd decision.

STREAMLINED

ADMIT THREE

466898
466899

*hen the movies talked. The silent motion picture era had officially ended in the Twin Cities on March 22, 1927, when Finkelstein and Ruben's Capitol Theater in St. Paul debuted Vitaphone talking pictures. (The State Theater in Minneapolis was supposed to get the honor, but a dispute over the number of projectionists needed to screen the new films prompted F&R to switch to the Capitol.)[1] The first talking movies actually were filmed versions of live stage acts much like those commonly seen in vaudeville shows. The big premiere at the Capitol, for example, included performances by vaudeville star George Jessel and the operatic tenor Giovanni Martinelli.[2] A reviewer with the *St. Paul Dispatch* declared that, thanks to the Vitaphone, audiences in the Twin Cities now could enjoy "the music of the greatest symphony orchestras as well as the vocal entertainment of the most popular star of the operatic, concert and musical comedy fields."[3] Talking features were still a few months away (Al Jolson's *The Jazz Singer* wouldn't debut at the Capitol until the following February), but nearly everyone—exhibitors and audiences alike—assumed that the talkies had come to stay. "Hollywood will still be beautiful but not, technically speaking, dumb," the skeptical editors of the *Minneapolis Tribune* observed. "The 'talkies,' bless their mechanical larynges, will care for that."

Every movie theater in the Twin Cities, including the Capitol and the State, had been constructed for silent motion pictures. Theater operators who wished to show talking pictures in existing houses had to install new equipment at considerable expense. And those who planned to open new theaters likewise had to figure the extra cost of Vitaphone or Movie-

Previous page: The former Grand Theater on Hennepin Avenue is reborn as the Gopher, an art deco showcase designed by the firm of Liebenberg and Kaplan, 1938.

Vitaphone sound system in St. Paul's Capitol Theater, the first Twin Cities cinema to show "talking pictures."

Neighborhood theaters, including the Nokomis in South Minneapolis (shown here in 1929), began converting to sound once it became clear that talkies were not a passing fad.

tone machines into their financial equations. If anyone was going to take a chance on building the Twin Cities' first sound-equipped movie theater, Finkelstein and Ruben—with their experience and the financial backing of William Hamm—seemed the logical candidates. But the timing wasn't quite right—F&R was focused elsewhere. Its newest theater, the palatial Minnesota, was under construction, and its relationship with Paramount-Publix was in flux. Finkelstein and Ruben seemed happy for the moment to let the Capitol and the State serve as talkie guinea pigs while the studios worked out the technical bugs. The door was open for someone else to build a made-for-talkies picture house.

Sometime in the late summer or early fall of 1927, a local contractor and builder named William Berg began making plans to construct a new movie theater in Minneapolis's Uptown district, about a block away from Finkelstein and Ruben's Lagoon (F&R had converted its other property in the area, the Calhoun Theater, into a ballroom). But Berg specialized in construction. He didn't know anything about designing or managing movie theaters. So he teamed up with people who did. He leased his still-to-be-constructed movie house to a pair of experienced neighborhood-theater operators, Louis Rubenstein and Abe Kaplan of the Arion Theater in Northeast Minneapolis. To design the theater, he hired a little-known local architect named Jack

Liebenberg. Berg eventually faded into the background of the Twin Cities' movie scene, while Liebenberg soon established himself as a theater designer extraordinaire.

Jack Liebenberg.

Liebenberg had happened into the theater business. A native of Milwaukee and the son of German Jewish parents, Liebenberg came to Minneapolis in 1912 to work on the construction of the Leamington Hotel. While there, he learned that a new architecture school was opening at the University of Minnesota. He applied and was accepted.[4] As a member of the School of Architecture's first graduating class, Liebenberg learned his chosen trade well. The university's 1916 yearbook included four lines of verse that suggested that Jake, as he was known, was leaving campus with high expectations.

> *Ambition is his keynote.*
> *Nothing will he shirk;*
> *Persevering ever.*
> *"Jake, he does the work."*[5]

Liebenberg left Minnesota to do graduate work at Harvard, though the war in Europe soon interrupted his studies. After a short stint in the U.S. Army Air Force, he returned to the University of Minnesota to teach architecture for a year. Among his students was Seeman Kaplan, a son of Russian Jewish immigrants and a draftsman by trade. Liebenberg and Kaplan forged a close relationship outside the classroom (Liebenberg married Kaplan's sister), and soon teacher and student went into business as partners.

Liebenberg and Kaplan struggled to find work during their first few years together as the Minneapolis business community's widespread anti-Semitism limited the opportunities available to a pair of Jewish architects.[6] But it was during this time that Liebenberg first dabbled in the kind of work that ultimately defined his career. As it happened, Seeman Kaplan's brother was Abe Kaplan, the co-owner—with Louis Rubenstein—of the Arion Theater on Northeast Minneapolis's Central Avenue. The Arion was one of the city's oldest neighborhood theaters, and it needed updating. In 1923 Rubenstein and Kaplan hired Liebenberg and Kaplan to do the design work. The remodeled Arion was undistinguished, especially when compared to many of the newer movie houses constructed during the 1920s, but the project whetted Liebenberg's appetite for theater design.[7]

After completing his work on the Arion, Liebenberg moved on to other projects that had nothing to do with motion pictures. In 1926 he began work on his most high-profile commission yet: the design of a new synagogue, Temple Israel, just north of the Uptown district. Among the synagogue's most outstanding architectural features was

Feature Presentation

**Granada Theater
3020 Hennepin Avenue,
Minneapolis
Opened 1928**

One of only two atmospheric theaters ever to open in the Twin Cities (the Uptown on St. Paul's Grand Avenue was the other), the $250,000 Granada was a whimsical fantasy worthy of the most audacious Hollywood dream factory. In the minutes before the start of the show, the Granada's patrons couldn't help but absorb their exotic surroundings—the statues, mock walls, and fake shrubbery of a stylized Spanish garden. When the lights went down, the ceiling transformed into a nighttime sky, complete with twinkling stars, rolling clouds, and a glowing moon. The 800-seat Granada was the first movie theater in the Twin Cities to incorporate stadium-type seats, with the rear rows installed on a steeper-than-normal incline. It was also the first theater in the Twin Cities built

The Spanish-flavored whimsy of Jack Liebenberg's atmospheric Granada Theater.

specifically for sound motion pictures.[1] The Granada weathered the Great Depression and World War II, but it finally shut down during the cinema slump of the early 1950s. In 1953 Ted Mann took over the Granada and turned it into a first-run art house called the Suburban World. In the years that followed, the Suburban World earned a reputation for showing quirky art films, foreign films, and—on occasion—highbrow adult fare. The old atmospheric theater finally closed in 1994 and remained mostly dark until 2000, when it was converted briefly into a cinema-grill combo. As it approached its eightieth birthday, the Suburban World—with most of its original atmospheric décor still intact—remained a prime candidate for a major restoration.

its main sanctuary, a 950-seat worship space known for its superior acoustics. The sound-enhancing tricks that Liebenberg learned on the Temple project served him well in the years to come.

By the fall of 1927, it seemed almost inevitable that Jack Liebenberg would be the man to design William Berg's new theater near the corner of Lake Street and Hennepin Avenue. Liebenberg already had designed one movie theater, the Arion. He had proven on the Temple Israel project that he knew how to work with acoustics (a talent that would come in handy in this new age of talking motion pictures). And then, of course, there was the family connection: Liebenberg's partner was the brother of the new theater's comanager.

For several years theaters built in what was known as the atmospheric style had been gaining in popularity around the country. Atmospheric theaters were designed to give moviegoers the illusion that they were sitting in an elegant outdoor garden. Liebenberg's plans for the new motion picture house near Lake and Hennepin reflected this latest trend. Stucco walls with faux balconies and wrought-iron railings would surround the audience. A curved ceiling of deep blue, pointilised by twinkling lights and a roving artificial moon, would approximate the night sky. The new cinema would be the first in the Twin Cities to introduce bleacher seating and the first to use a new echo-absorbing acoustical tile called Celotex. In a nod to its Spanish-inspired design, it would be called the Granada.[8]

The Granada opened on September 25, 1928. Nearly everything went as Liebenberg had hoped, except for one thing: Rubenstein and Kaplan were nowhere to be found. In the early months of construction, the old monopolists, Finkelstein and Ruben, had announced plans to convert the nearby Calhoun Theater into an atmospheric show house that would compete directly with the yet-to-be-completed Granada. Finkelstein and Ruben were probably bluffing, but it was a bluff that Rubenstein and Kaplan could not afford to call. In the spring of 1928, Rubenstein and Kaplan sold their lease on the Granada to Finkelstein and Ruben, and F&R immediately shelved its plans for the Calhoun. In the Granada's opening night program, Finkelstein and Ruben took full credit for bringing the "House of Features" to the Uptown neighborhood.

With the grand opening of the Granada theatre, you are presented with the first Atmospheric theatre in the Twin Cities. It marks the beginning of a new era of entertainment in your district, bringing the best obtainable motion picture programs presented amid an enchanted atmosphere.

The Granada, Minneapolis' most beautiful and picturesque theatre, is yours to enjoy. It is dedicated to your enjoyment. To contribute toward your happiness and contentment is its purpose and, with this end in mind, Finkelstein & Ruben and the Management bid you a most sincere welcome.[9]

The Granada turned out to be Finkelstein and Ruben's last new motion picture house. (They opened another Liebenberg-designed atmospheric theater, the Uptown in St. Paul, a few months after the Granada debuted, but the Uptown was actually a remodeled version of the old Oxford Theater.) After selling out to Paramount-Publix in the summer of 1929, F&R left behind the movie business for good. But the Granada represented something altogether different to Jack Liebenberg. It was the first hint that he had the makings of a top-flight theater architect.

$\mathcal{N}$ot everyone welcomed the arrival of talking motion pictures. "Real art has vanished and in its place has come the monster motion picture with its latest ungodly squawking," the editors of the *Minnesota Union Advocate* complained. "The entire effect of . . . sitting in a theater is to paralyze your faculties by transferring you to an unreal world with

Liebenberg's original plans for the atmospheric Granada were considerably more ornate than the designs his client eventually approved.

Eddie Dunstedter at the State Theater's organ console, about 1925.

its artificial scenes and noises; canned pictures, canned voices and canned music! What a nightmare!"[10] The *Union Advocate* and its readers had good reason to resent the talkies: jobs were at stake.

No one at the movie houses had more to fear than the musicians. Live music—whether by piano, organ, or orchestra—had always been an integral component of theaters' silent motion picture programs. But now talkies, with their synchronized dialogue and music, were threatening to make movie accompanists obsolete. Many musicians, including organist Eddie Dunstedter of the State and the Minnesota, felt compelled to jump to the defense of their chosen profession.

> *The advent of synchronized music was a novelty and still is, to a certain extent. . . . Synchronized music is too dead. As an accompaniment to a film, where it plays only a secondary role, it has its proper place. However, when people want music for the sake of music, they want something that is real, that is tangible. Only a musician or musicians on the stage or in the orchestra pit can satisfy that desire for the human touch.*[11]

But Dunstedter seriously misjudged the technological revolution that was taking place in the motion picture industry. By the summer of 1929, the Minnesota, where he worked, was the only movie theater in Minneapolis or St. Paul that still employed an orchestra. Musicians at the State and Uptown in Minneapolis had recently been given their notices. The orchestra pit at the Capitol in St. Paul had been converted into a glorified flowerpot.[12] The human touch that Dunstedter championed no longer seemed to apply. "It was bad enough when the living actor was supplanted by the screen," the *Union Advocate*'s editors lamented, "but now ghoulish noises imitating human voices and musical instruments have been added to the torture."[13]

*U*ntil the New York stock market had crashed in October 1929, nobody knew that the nation's economy was heading for a free fall. If the powers-that-were at Paramount had known, they probably would not have bought out Finkelstein and Ruben. If Finkelstein and Ruben had known, they probably would have asked to be paid in something other than Paramount stock. But nobody knew. And even those who suspected that a downturn was coming would have been hard pressed to accurately predict just how bad things would get. In the months that followed the crash, the nation descended into a broad-based economic depression. Conditions became increasingly desperate. Storefronts went dark. Soup lines and unemployment lines stretched for blocks. Calamity was at hand.

Theater owners suffered along with everyone else—at least at first. By the second half of 1930, attendance at many Twin Cities motion

Children of the Great Depression, outside the Minnesota Theater, 1931. Sagging box office revenues forced the Minnesota to close its doors the following year.

picture houses had dropped to business-busting levels. The laws of supply and demand seemed to call for a cut in ticket prices, but theater operators initially refused to budge. When Al Steffes, the fiery exhibitor from Minneapolis's north side, dropped matinee prices to ten cents at his Paradise Theater, many of his colleagues from around the cities were aghast. Didn't he understand that theaters couldn't afford to operate at dime-a-ticket prices?[14] Still, as T. E. Mortensen, the editor of the regional trade publication *Greater Amusements*, pointed out, the logic of lower admission prices was hard to deny.

> *The general public is not interested in theatre operation cost. It only knows that its earning power has decreased and that it must therefore get more for its money. . . . People have less money in dollars and cents to spend today than two years ago and they simply will not pay the same prices as prevailed during those days of better times. They resent any attempt of their merchant, landlord, theatre, etc., to exact from them anywhere near the same prices for merchandise, rentals or services as under normal conditions.[15]*

Feature Presentation

● ●

**Grandview Theater
1830 Grand Avenue,
St. Paul
Opened 1933**

The Grandview, designed by full-time railroad employee and part-time architect Myrtus Wright, was the second new theater in the Twin Cities to incorporate elements of art deco design. (The first, the Boulevard in South Minneapolis, opened eight months earlier.) The theater's stepped façade, with its round, glass-block windows and horizontal stripes of contrasting brick, created a symmetrical backdrop for its jazzy, sunburst marquee. Originally a one-level theater capable of seating 750 moviegoers, the Grandview underwent a major renovation

The Grandview retained much of its original art deco charm into the 1970s and beyond.

in 1937 in which a balcony, with 350 seats, was added. It remained virtually unchanged until 1973, when owner Marvin Mann converted the balcony into a separate screening room.[1]

As the months went by and the Great Depression strengthened its grip, more and more theater owners reluctantly followed Steffes's lead. By the summer of 1931, nearly every neighborhood theater in the Twin Cities was charging ten cents for all shows before seven o'clock, even though they knew distributors might retaliate by making them wait even longer for the latest films.[16] Even some of the venerable downtown theaters, including the Shuberts in both cities, switched to dime picture runs in an effort to boost attendance.[17] The question was, would the tactic work? Mortensen was confident it would. "[The American public's] earning power has decreased an estimated average of 40 per cent," he reminded his readers. "It is well to analyze the meaning of that nickel to the person on the other side of the box office."[18]

Minneapolis's remodeled Rialto (designed by Jack Liebenberg) was one of many movie theaters in the Twin Cities that tried to lure customers with "Bank Night" cash giveaways and other promotional gimmicks.

Even as they squabbled over the advisability of reducing ticket prices, many Twin Cities exhibitors turned to creative marketing stunts in an effort to drum up bigger box office receipts. They were learning that they had to do more than simply put a movie on the screen. "It's getting to be that the local theatergoing public expects all sorts of inducements in the way of gifts," observed the Minneapolis correspondent for the show business weekly *Variety*. The RKO Orpheum gave away trips to Chicago. The Minnesota countered with trips to Alaska.[19] Many of Paramount-Publix's Twin Cities theaters, including the Aster in downtown Minneapolis, experimented with auction sales in which audience members bought clothes "off a live girl model" (who was wearing a bathing suit underneath).[20]

The most successful stunts were the ones that generated the most publicity. The trend spotters at *Variety* were particularly amused when a downtown St. Paul theater took a chance on what it called the "[Marlene] Dietrich gag."

After a girl walked through the loop dressed in men's clothing, evidently seeking personal publicity—and getting plenty—Publix sent out two of its boy ushers . . . dressed from head to foot in the latest spring fashions and smoking cigarettes.

Local rags gave the stunt a front page play, but the city attorney's office came to bat with an announcement that such antics in future would be liable to maximum of $100 fine or 90 days in the works, or both. Burg has had ordinance on the books since 1891 barring [one] sex from draping itself in the garments of the other.[21]

*O*n one of the first days of 1931, a wrecking crew began tearing apart the old theater on St. Paul's Seventh Street hill, just below Wabasha. The Princess—the first of Finkelstein and Ruben's many motion picture houses—had opened twenty years earlier to rave reviews. Now it was being demolished to make way for a new retail establishment. "In some lines and in some localities twenty years may not be a long span," a reporter with the *St. Paul Dispatch* mused, "but in the movie life of St. Paul it reaches to a time when attendance at a movie house was equivalent to a slumming party for anybody who 'was anybody.'"[22] The Princess was now a memory, just like the Finkelstein and Ruben theater chain to which it once belonged.

A few days later, on January 21, 1931, Moses Finkelstein died. A few months after that, on May 31, 1931, Isaac Ruben died. And then, a week and a half later, on June 10, 1931, William Hamm died.

Finkelstein, Ruben, and Hamm had once owned 150 theaters throughout the Upper Midwest. Now most of those theaters belonged to a Hollywood conglomerate. It seemed only fitting that F&R's first picture palace, the $1.5 million Capitol in St. Paul, was now known as the Paramount.

*T*he advent of sound gave defenders of public morality even more to worry about. It was bad enough when producers of silent motion pictures stuffed their films with inadequately clothed bodies and sexual innuendo. Now they had the ability to put objectionable words into the mouths of their actors. In 1930 Will Hays, Hollywood's nominally independent public watchdog, tried to calm the industry's critics by introducing a set of production guidelines known widely as the Hays Code. But the Hays Office had no power to enforce the code, even if it wanted to. Reformers, like Minneapolis's Catheryne Cooke Gilman, were convinced that the movies were getting worse, not better. "The consensus of opinion," Gilman wrote in 1931, "is to the effect that pictures are on the whole more obscene, more distasteful, more wanton in their violations of the April 1, 1930 Code."[23]

Gilman and her compatriots were most concerned with movies like Howard Hughes's *Hell's Angels* ("the marvelous photography [is] exploited by dragging in the objectionable sex phrases"), which pandered to audiences' more prurient tastes.[24] Others, including a reviewer at the *St. Paul Pioneer Press*, condemned the arrival of "gruesome thrill pictures" like *Frankenstein*. ("The picture serves no good purpose and its exhibition should be prohibited.")[25] But the Twin Cities' first major controversy of the talkie era concerned one of the most successful motion pictures of all time—one in which "sex phases" were not an issue—*The Birth of a Nation*.

During the final days of 1930, a talking version of *The Birth of a Nation* opened at the Garrick Theater in St. Paul. A few days later, it made its Minneapolis debut at the Lyceum. As in 1915, when the film first premiered in the Twin Cities, African American leaders were outraged. "The talking version . . . is said to be more objectionable to Negroes than the silent version," the *Northwest Monitor* reported. "Very little advance publicity was given to the film and it is believed that the promoters feared just such a protest as has developed."[26] The mayors in both cities tried to stop the film from showing, but their efforts stalled in the courts.[27] Like many other controversial films, *The Birth of a Nation* remained "a box office savior."[28] And as everyone in the business knew, saviors were in short supply during the early 1930s.

"*T*he bigger they are, the harder they fall!"

The editors of *Greater Amusements* didn't even try to hide their delight over the mounting troubles facing Paramount. In the two-plus years since it took over Finkelstein and Ruben, Paramount had watched its fortunes shrivel. A Depression-induced plunge in consumer spending and the company's "mad theatre grabbing orgy" of the late 1920s had combined to put Paramount in an untenable position. In the first fourteen weeks of 1932, its Publix theater chain, which included most of the old F&R houses, had hemorrhaged more than $1.2 million. "Somewhere in the annals of Paramount is an unpublished chapter relating to 'plans for domination of the film industry,'" *Greater Amusements* joked. "We doubt that this plan was the brain child of [Paramount founder] Adolph Zukor and he is perhaps having the last laugh, though it may be a wry one."[29]

Speculation was rampant that Paramount was on the verge of bankruptcy. It seemed obvious that the company would have to start shedding its least profitable theaters if it hoped to survive. In the spring of 1932, in a move that sent shivers through Twin Cities movie circles, Paramount-Publix shuttered the palatial Minnesota, which F&R had opened just four years earlier. "Our industry, like others, is passing through a transition period which necessitates adjustments in every department of operation to fit conditions created by general business decline," explained Publix's divisional manager John Friedl. "For many months the show business has been at ebb tide and despite every effort to reduce operating expense to offset reduced revenue, we have found it impossible to avoid a tremendous weekly loss in many of our theatres of which the Minnesota is an outstanding example."[30]

A few months later, Publix closed five more of its "lesser nabes," or neighborhood theaters, in Minneapolis and St. Paul.[31] In late January of 1933, its new Twin Cities–based subsidiary, the Minnesota Amusement Company (Maco), officially went bankrupt. The man named to oversee the company's restructuring was William Hamm Jr., son of Finkelstein and Ruben's partner and primary source of capital. The elder Hamm had negotiated a cash deal for himself and his brewery during the sale of F&R. Now Paramount owed the Hamm Brewing Company more than half a million dollars. As the court-appointed receiver of Maco, William Hamm Jr. would decide the fate of several dozen former F&R theaters, including many of the Twin Cities' most popular show houses.[32]

Suddenly, the movie business in both cities was competitive again. Paramount—through its Maco subsidiary—was discarding its least profitable theaters and letting others pick up the scraps. In St. Paul, Joseph Friedman reacquired the Tower and the Strand. In Minneapolis, Rubenstein and Kaplan bought back the Granada and the Arion, while the Uptown (formerly the Lagoon) reverted to the estate of its first owner, Joseph Cohen.[33] Competition increased even further when Al Steffes picked up the Shubert theaters in both cities—neither of which was a Paramount house.[34] Steffes renamed the Minneapolis Shubert the Alvin (his middle name) and the St. Paul Shubert the World. Paramount no longer controlled moviegoing in the Twin Cities. Many local exhibitors were eager to see what would happen next. As the opening night program at Al Steffes's new World Theater put it: "THE SHOW IS ON."[35]

The early 1930s was a lousy time to be a theater architect. Motion picture houses were closing, not opening. Only a financial masochist would consider adding another theater to the Twin Cities' already over-crowded cinema mix in the middle of an economic depression. Not that there weren't a few hardy souls willing to take a chance. In St. Paul movie veteran George Granstrom spent $15,000 to open the Grand-view Theater on Grand Avenue. In Minneapolis newcomer W. B. "Bill" Frank debuted the Boulevard, a theater-restaurant combo on Lyndale Avenue South. There weren't many, but those theaters that did open in the Twin Cities during the first years of the Great Depression provided a sneak architectural preview of what was to come—and a rejection of what had been.

The 1920s had proven to be a decade of excess as far as theater de-sign was concerned. Picture palaces like the Capitol in St. Paul and the State in Minneapolis were monuments of opulence. The obsession with extravagance continued through the decade, finding its final expression in the atmospheric style evident in Minneapolis's Granada and St. Paul's Uptown. But times had changed. Many of the people who had rushed

Yet another Depression-era publicity stunt: free movies and free popcorn for members of the school patrol.

to watch motion pictures in palatial surroundings during the 1920s were now in dire financial straits. Even if they could afford to take in a movie every once in a while, they didn't necessarily wish to do so in theaters that reminded them of better or more prosperous times. And it wasn't just decadence that made the picture palaces seem suddenly obsolete. For one thing, their operating costs were staggering. At the Minnesota, for example, it cost about $20,000 a week just to keep the staff paid, the lights on, and the doors open.[36] Sound was another problem. When films were silent, the chandeliers, ornamental plaster, and other decorative elements common to picture palaces and most atmospheric theaters caused few problems. But when the talkies arrived, and speak-

Feature Presentation

● ●

**Edina Theater
3911 West 50th Street,
Edina
Opened 1934**

Built on the site of an old dairy plant, the Edina was Jack Liebenberg's first all-new Depression-era theater. Liebenberg originally envisioned a 1,500-seat showplace done up in zigzag art deco style, but he eventually scaled back his plans. The auditorium shrank to 1,300 seats— 1,000 on the main floor and 300 in the balcony. Outside, the vertical sign blaring the theater's name—while eye-catching—did not flash its letters, E-D-I-N-A, as Liebenberg had planned. (Local residents disapproved of anything quite so gaudy.) The Edina featured art deco furnishings and several amenities—including a lobby fireplace, a nursery, and amplifiers for the hard of hearing—that were rare among Twin Cities theaters.[1] It remained largely unchanged until 1976, when its auditorium was split in

Although the Edina's vertical sign dominated the streetscape at Fiftieth and France, its letters did not flash—a concession to the neighbors.

two. A few years later, another subdivision turned it into an awkward three-screener. In 1988 Cineplex Odeon gutted the interior and built a new fourplex in its place. The reborn Edina featured two concession stands and two levels (and a mezzanine) and an elevator, an escalator, and a staircase.[2]

ers were installed, those same ornamental features sent dialogue bouncing in all directions throughout the auditorium. Economic realties and technological changes called for a new, simpler style. It was called "art deco."

The new style traced its origins to the Exposition Internationale des Arts Décoratifs et Industriels Moderne, which took place in Paris in 1925. The designs introduced at the exposition reflected a variety of recent artistic trends, including cubism and futurism. No longer satisfied to draw their inspiration from the past, artists set out to create new designs for the modern age. Simplified geometric patterns became the vogue. Soon the new style spread across the Atlantic and inspired the designs of countless American buildings—including movie theaters.[37]

George Granstrom's Grandview and Bill Frank's Boulevard were the first new theaters in the Twin Cities to incorporate art deco design. The Grandview in particular stood out as a prime example of an early deco movie house. Designed by local architect Myrtus Wright, its exterior featured two glass block porthole windows and long horizontal belts of contrasting brick. Its stepped façade peaked with two pillars of brick and internally illuminated glass block. The abstract sunburst of its horizontal marquee beckoned to the surrounding neighborhood.[38]

But the Grandview and the Boulevard were exceptions to the theater-building rule of the early 1930s: they were completely new. Most theater owners were unable or unwilling to sink great sums of money into new construction while the economy sputtered and movie attendance languished. Those who did invest usually were content to remodel their existing houses—or to tear down and rebuild. In the Twin Cities the architect that exhibitors turned to most often to make their old theaters more appealing was Jack Liebenberg.

In the first few years of the 1930s, Liebenberg abandoned the atmospheric style that had served him so well on the Granada and St. Paul Uptown projects and embraced art deco. His modern designs freshened several old movie houses that had begun to show their age. In at least two cases, he drew up plans for what were essentially replacement theaters. One of them, the St. Paul Strand, reemerged as a downtown deco house with a long, curving marquee that wrapped around the corner of Wabasha and Eighth and a towering neon sign that blared its name.[39] Over on University Avenue the Faust Theater was reborn as an odd amalgamation of old and new. On the outside the reimagined Faust looked something like an old English boardinghouse with a gaudy marquee jutting out from its façade. Inside, the modern décor represented

The new Strand Theater, at Eighth and Wabasha in downtown St. Paul, was among Jack Liebenberg's first art deco creations.

what Liebenberg called "the newest trend in theatrical architecture." Like most of the theaters he would design in the years to come, the Faust featured spring-cushioned seats, soothing indirect lighting, and the latest innovation in moviegoing comfort: air conditioning.[40]

Financial considerations limited the scope of Liebenberg's work during the first few years of the Great Depression, but money wouldn't always be so tight. Economic conditions were bound to improve. They could hardly get worse. Once the economy began recovering and theaters became more profitable, Twin Cities exhibitors would almost certainly open their wallets. Audiences were coming to expect modern amenities like comfortable seats and cooled air. New theaters would be needed to meet those higher expectations. And Jack Liebenberg was standing by at his drafting table, ready to design them.

Al Steffes had a choice to make. His Alvin Theater in Minneapolis (the old Shubert) and his World Theater in St. Paul (also previously known as the Shubert) both showed "foreign language and unusual pictures." The World, for example, had opened in early 1933 with *Ronny*, a Viennese operetta featuring the German motion picture stars Kathe von Nagy and Willy Fritsch.[41] German films in particular were quite popular among Twin Cities moviegoers who craved more sophisticated fare than that generally churned out by Hollywood. But events overseas were forcing exhibitors like Al Steffes to reconsider their policies. Adolf Hitler had risen to power in early 1933, about the same time that Steffes started showing foreign-language films at his theaters. As Americans learned more about Hitler and his anti-Semitic policies, theater operators had to decide whether to continue showing German films.

Al Steffes, who had grown up on Minneapolis's heavily Jewish north side, decided to take a stand. He declined to screen two German films that he had previously booked and refused to pay the films' U.S. distributors the $1,400 that he owed them for delivering the motion pictures. The distributors took Steffes to court, but he didn't budge. He had rejected the films, the trade press reported, to protest "the anti-Semitic campaign being waged in Germany by the Nazi government."[42] It was 1936, and no one—not even Al Steffes—had any idea how far that campaign would go.

*B*y the mid-1930s the rebound that Twin Cities exhibitors had been hoping for was well under way. Box office receipts, which had plummeted during the first years of the Depression, bounced back in 1934 and continued to climb. Attendance, which by some measures had never really fallen off (reduced ticket prices had apparently succeeded in drawing people to the box office even during the worst of times), was swelling, too.[43] There were plenty of reasons for the recovery. Lower ticket prices certainly helped. So, too, did the publicity gimmicks that many theater operators continued to employ. For example, bank night—a stunt in which each member of the audience was given an equal chance to win a cash prize—was proving to be wildly popular. There were other promotions as well: cooking classes, turkey raffles, and dish giveaways. "People would come every week to get a different piece," Martin Lebedoff recalled.[44] The handful of new theaters that had opened over the previous few years—with their spiffy modern décors, cushioned seats, and air conditioning—were still drawing crowds. And perhaps more than anything else, the movies themselves continued to offer a welcome distraction from the daily struggles of life during an agonizingly persistent economic crisis. Evelyn Fairbanks, for one, relished the evenings that she and her African American friends spent at St. Paul's Faust Theater.

> *The theater had three aisles, and we always sat in the fourth row on the right, not because of any law, but because that's where all of our friends were. The management tolerated lots of noise since the theater made most of its money on young people, so the Faust was a fun place to go. Besides, the movies they showed called for noise—cheering for the guys in the white hats during the cowboy movies, cheering when the girl*

got the boy in the musical comedies, cheering for the good ol' USA in the war movies, and laughing like crazy at Bud Abbott and Lou Costello. Not everyone sat in the fourth row, of course. When a couple began to be serious about each other, or more important, began to be serious about seeing the entire movie, they would sit in one of the other aisles with the quieter white people.[45]

For several years competition for the Twin Cities moviegoer's dollar (or dime, for that matter) had been wide open. Paramount and its regional subsidiary, Maco, had shed many of their theaters in Minneapolis and St. Paul in an effort to streamline their operations and pull themselves out of bankruptcy. Locally based independents like Al Steffes and Joseph Friedman had subsequently moved in. But now rumors were spreading that Paramount and Maco were itching to reestablish their dominance over the Twin Cities' market "on the theory that the box offices would again swell to their former size and intake."[46] As it turned out, the rumors were accurate. Maco began buying up picture houses, including some—like the Tower and Strand in St. Paul—it had jettisoned just a few years before. *Greater Amusements,* which had reveled in Paramount's misfortunes back in 1932, applauded the company for the "forward strides" it had made under reorganization. It attributed Paramount's recovery to better movies, better management, and a commitment to the "decentralization of theatre operations."[47]

Clearly, executives at Paramount believed the time was right to invest in movie theaters. They were not alone. By the fall of 1935, established theater operators in the Twin Cities were growing increasingly alarmed over a "threatened orgy of theatre building." In Minneapolis alone, seventeen new theater license applications were under consideration. The city's existing motion picture houses already had a combined seating capacity of more than 51,000, and about a fifth of those seats were in houses that were ten years old or less. Local exhibitors, still recovering from the tough times of recent years, were eager to head off any additional competition.[48]

But their efforts were mostly in vain. Theater construction continued, and most of the new and refurbished theaters that debuted during this period reflected the prevailing art deco architectural trend. Several Twin Cities architects, including Myrtus Wright and Perry Crosier, benefited from the uptick in theater building, but none was as consistently busy as Jack Liebenberg. Liebenberg had demonstrated through his previous work on the St. Paul Strand and the Faust that he knew how to apply art deco design concepts to movie houses. Now he was putting that skill to increasingly effective use.

For the first time since finishing his work on the Granada in 1928, Liebenberg was designing new theaters—not renovated ones. The first of his new movie houses, the 1,500-seat Edina, opened in the summer of 1934. The Edina was a suburban temple of sharp-angled zigzag deco style.[49] His second new theater, the Hollywood in Northeast Minneapolis, ranked as an art deco masterpiece. Opened in 1935 by Rubenstein and Kaplan, the Hollywood had a budget big enough to accommodate many of Liebenberg's most creative deco dreams. Unlike the Edina, with its zigzag patterns, the Hollywood was an early showcase of streamlined deco style: rounded corners, smooth surfaces, and asymmetrical balance.[50]

Liebenberg had found his calling. And just in time. Paramount, through its Maco subsidiary, was rebuilding its movie theater fiefdom in the Twin Cities and throughout the Upper Midwest, and it needed an architect who could handle the increasingly heavy workload. Liebenberg fit the bill. By 1935 Liebenberg had become, in effect, Maco's house architect, designing or redesigning theaters to the company's specifications. The arrangement was lucrative but stifling. "You are, no doubt, personally aware of the fact that the last month or two has kept me continually occupied with problems connected with the Minnesota Amusement Company and its various officers," he wrote to the venerable Theo Hays, now an executive with Maco. "I have had little or no time for myself, my family, or any other activity," Liebenberg continued. "If I knew how I could have divided my time, I certainly would have done so."[51] Over the next few years Liebenberg drew up remodeling designs for several important Maco houses, including the St. Clair in St. Paul and the downtown Grand (renamed the Gopher), the Rialto on Lake Street, and the Uptown in Minneapolis.

Liebenberg's emergence as the Upper Midwest's premiere theater architect coincided with (and depended on) Maco's resurrection as the region's dominant exhibitor. By the summer of 1938, Maco was operating more than one hundred movie theaters in twenty-five cities and towns in Minnesota, Wisconsin, and the Dakotas.[52] It already had revamped many of them using Liebenberg's designs. It planned to refurbish even more. But not even Jack Liebenberg could save every Maco theater.

On a cold day in February 1939, a wrecking ball punched a hole in Maco's President Theater in St. Paul. It was the first blow in what would turn out to be a quick death. The old theater at the corner of St. Peter and Fifth had opened as the Orpheum back in 1906. It had changed its name and converted to movies in 1929 with the advent of the talkies. But for those whose memories went back far enough, the President—or, if you preferred, the Orpheum—had always been a vaudeville house. *St. Paul Pioneer Press* critic James Gray was among those who couldn't help but "shed a sentimentalist's tear over its passing." Gray remembered conversing backstage with "assorted Marx brothers" when they were just an opening act and with George Burns and Gracie Allen when they were relegated to the "number 2 spot" on the vaudeville card. Now the President was being flattened to make way for a parking lot.

The following year, the Twin Cities' other original Orpheum—Minneapolis's Seventh Street Theater—suffered the same fate.[53] Old vaudeville houses apparently stood no chance when confronted by the growing parking needs of the area's automobile owners. "I once swore fervently that no matter how patriarchally [*sic*] old I might become I should never write wistfully about the 'good, old days.'" Gray wrote. "But, ah! Those were the good old days after all!"[54]

*I*n the two-plus decades that Twin Citians had been going regularly to the movies, there always seemed to be someone who wanted to keep them from seeing what they wanted to see. Sometimes it was child welfare activists, who believed movies were corrupting the nation's youth. (Henry James Forman's 1933 indictment of the motion picture industry, *Our Movie-Made Children,* was blasted by the *St. Paul Dispatch* for "trotting up and dumping at the studio door all the ills of society from crime to vanity that have at other times been blamed upon co-education, the bunny-hug, jazz music, French novels, high heels, the split skirt, [and] one-piece bathing suits.")[55] At other times it was black leaders, who objected to the racist depictions of African Americans in films like *The Birth of Nation.* And sometimes it was people like Catheryne Cooke Gilman, who believed Hollywood producers were exploiting the baser instincts of the moviegoing public. And in the mid-1930s the Legion of Decency, a new group of scandalized moral crusaders, joined the long parade of would-be motion picture reformers.

The Legion of Decency was the brainchild of a group of Roman Catholic bishops. It was a national organization committed to counteracting "the present tendency to immorality in the commercialized programs of recreation offered to our people by those who control the vast output of moving pictures."[56] Many church leaders were convinced that

Hollywood was crawling with unrepentant purveyors of depravity, and they hoped that the legion—by blacklisting offensive films—would force filmmakers to abandon their wicked ways. With the tacit approval of the Hays Office (cooperation burnished Hollywood's tainted image and diverted attention from the industry's questionable trade practices), the legion began passing judgment on dozens of films. In city after city, Catholics pledged to boycott any motion picture that the legion found morally objectionable.

St. Paul, with its large Catholic population, was a hub of legion

Feature Presentation

**Hollywood Theater
2815 Johnson Avenue,
Minneapolis
Opened 1935**

The Hollywood was a stunning package of streamlined art deco architecture—a built-from-scratch showcase of Jack Liebenberg's talent. With just under one thousand seats, it was a bit smaller than the Edina, but it was stuffed with the kinds of deco accoutrements that came to define Liebenberg's work: a soaring vertical sign; a patterned terrazzo floor; recessed lighting; simplified, gilded pillars; and acoustical tiles arranged in geometric patterns. From the street a mass of smooth, unadorned Kasota stone seemed to hold in check the curvilinear shapes that clustered around the main entrance.[1] Ads for the new show house claimed, with ample justification, that it was "the Twin Cities' most beautiful and modern neighborhood theatre." Still, the Hollywood's striking architecture did not readily translate

Jack Liebenberg bunched the Hollywood's entrance, marquee, and vertical sign to one side to balance the theater's expansive Kasota stone façade.

into financial success. Over the years its location in North Minneapolis—sparsely populated compared to other local theater districts—worked against it. The theater went through a series of ownership changes until 1987, when it finally closed. The Minneapolis Heritage Preservation Commission designated the Hollywood a historic land-

mark, and though that designation helped protect the building from demolition, it also created renovation restrictions that spooked potential developers. By the turn of the millennium, the Hollywood was a deteriorating historic structure facing shrinking odds of survival.

activism. In the summer of 1934, Archbishop John Gregory Murray called on all church members within the St. Paul archdiocese to stop patronizing theaters that presented "any immoral or indecent program." Parishioners signed pledge cards and handed them in to be filed with the legion's local chapter.[57] Within weeks theater operators throughout the Twin Cities were feeling the pressure. Louis Scott, the manager of the Metropolitan Theater in St. Paul, was among the exhibitors who received letters from "a group of interested persons."

> *Our object in writing this letter is merely to ask your cooperation in this movement and ask you to show only approved shows. As soon as a disapproved show is shown we shall stop our attendance; and until that time [we] intend to see them all if at all possible. Personally, we cannot see why you should spoil your good beginning by showing one or two condemned shows. We intend to give you all our patronage while you cooperate with this decency movement. This is merely a suggestion . . . to be accepted or rejected as you so desire. I am sure I am voicing the desire of many others interested in this good-clean-wholesome entertainment. If only one picture in a hundred is bad, we shall withdraw our patronage.*[58]

Like nearly every previous attempt to protect Twin Cities moviegoers from the offerings of morally suspect Hollywood, the campaigns of the Legion of Decency had little discernible effect. The ever-defiant Al Steffes, for one, refused to be cowed. In the summer of 1935, he booked a notorious film called *Modern Motherhood* at the Alvin in Minneapolis and the World in St. Paul. The movie featured, among other things, scenes of an abortion and a face-lift operation. *Modern Motherhood* was an immediate sensation. Its local distributor took out an ad with a photo of "crowds storming the doors" of the Alvin in hopes of seeing the movie. One trade publication noted, with apparent admiration, that several customers at the Alvin and the World fainted during screenings of the film.[59]

The Twin Cities were, in fact, developing a reputation for defying moral crusades. In February of 1938, the Lyceum in Minneapolis became the first theater in the nation to screen another highly controversial film, called *The Birth of a Baby*. Produced by the American Committee on Maternal Welfare, *The Birth of a Baby* was a bland dramatization of one couple's experiences during pregnancy. It probably would have faded quickly into obscurity if the producers had not spliced footage of an actual birth into the final reel. That addition ensured that *The Birth of a Baby* received plenty of publicity—both

Showings of *The Birth of a Baby* sparked protests in other cities, but not in Minneapolis.

positive and negative. "The picture is an absorbing example of dramatic visual education," a reviewer with *Time* magazine wrote. "For one breathless minute the camera, with its matchless eye for detail, watches the child's head emerge as the physician moves swiftly to support it, notes an infant arm fling heavenward as it comes into view, [and] shows the physician delivering the child at last from its laboring mother." But some were aghast that moviegoers might be exposed to such a scene. Squeamish censors in many states—most notably New York—delayed the film's opening, despite arguments that it promoted prenatal health. But in censor-free Minneapolis and St. Paul, hardly an objection was raised.[60]

Much of the credit for this measured response goes to the theater managers who first booked *The Birth of a Baby*. The Lyceum's Howard Feigley headed off potential trouble by arranging a private showing of

Feature Presentation

**Uptown Theater
2962 Hennepin Avenue,
Minneapolis
Remodeled 1939**

The Uptown was among Jack Liebenberg's most notable remodelings. Known originally as the Lagoon, the Uptown suffered substantial fire damage in 1938. It reopened the following year as a Liebenberg-designed art deco smorgasbord. On the outside, the theater called attention to itself with a dominating tower, a transitional glass base, and a dazzling marquee of fluorescent neon. Inside, its two-level foyer and lounge featured a bizarre mix of deco and baroque design elements. The auditorium, relatively plain in comparison, served in part as a gallery for two hulking murals carved out of acoustic Celotex and painted in fluorescent lacquers. The luminescent murals depicted two allegorical scenes: early explorers gazing on the modern city of Minneapolis; and the Father of Waters (the Mississippi River) kneeling beside a collection of water sprites symbolizing the city's five major lakes. "The compositions . . . are bas-reliefs in colored light," one critic wrote, "combining in a new technique, sculpture, painting and illumination."[1] In the years following its remodeling, the Uptown's location in Min-

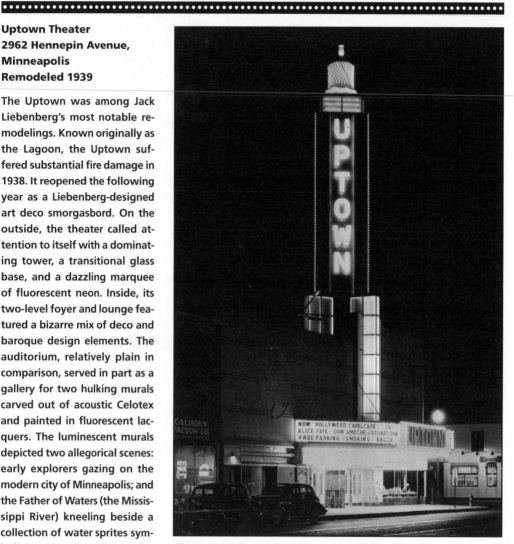

The Uptown's beacon-like sign tower quickly achieved iconic status in Minneapolis's Hennepin-Lake neighborhood.

neapolis's vibrant lake district helped it weather the movie business's ups and downs. It even avoided the subdividing, multiplex trend of the 1970s and 1980s. As the century came to a close, it was the only movie theater still operating in the Twin Cities with a full balcony.

the film for local physicians, nurses, and medical students from the University of Minnesota. After the screening he asked the audience to vote on whether they thought the movie should be shown to the public. The results were overwhelming. Only forty out of the more than two thousand medical professionals and students in attendance considered the film inappropriate for public viewing. Feigley followed up that publicity coup by convincing the Hennepin County Medical Society to publicly endorse the picture.[61] When *The Birth of a Baby* opened at Al Steffes's World in St. Paul, advertisements announced that the film was "approved by the executive council of the Ramsey County Medical Society."[62] With the backing of the local medical establishment, the film did "top box-office" in Minneapolis and St. Paul, while censors in other major cities hemmed and hawed.[63]

The Twin Cities' aversion to film censorship resurfaced two years later with the release of *Strange Cargo*, a major Hollywood production starring Clark Gable and Joan Crawford. *Strange Cargo* was, on its most basic level, the story of a group of escaped convicts from an island prison, but the way it handled its underlying themes of sin and redemption did not sit well with some religious leaders. The Legion of Decency slapped a condemned rating on the film for the rare trifecta of presenting "a naturalistic concept of religion contrary to the teachings of Christ, irreverent use of Scripture, and lustful complications." Censors in several cities, including Detroit, Boston, and Providence, responded by banning the film. Catholics in other cities picketed theaters where the movie was shown.[64] But it was a different story in the Twin Cities. When *Strange Cargo* arrived in St. Paul for a one-week run at the RKO Orpheum, more than one hundred legion members called the theater's manager, Lou Golden, to register their disapproval. Most of them reminded Golden that St. Paul was "a strong Catholic town" and that they intended to boycott the Orpheum until he publicly apologized for booking the film. Golden refused to back down. "When the storm blew over," *Variety* reported, it turned out that the Orpheum's receipts for *Strange Cargo* "tallied up to good biz."[65]

*T*he box office rebound of the mid-1930s proved to be short lived. Maybe all those new and remodeled theaters—many of them designed by Jack Liebenberg—had produced an overabundance of seats. Maybe theater operators had erroneously assumed that the creative marketing gimmicks they used during the early years of the Depression were no longer necessary. Maybe the movies weren't as good as they used to be.

The Tower in St. Paul was among the many Twin Cities theaters that began booking double features during the 1930s. It continued to show twin bills even after business picked up during World War II.

But whatever the reason, theater operators were feeling the pinch. "Business in the loop houses in the Twin Cities is [way] off," Al Steffes complained in the summer of 1938. "This is true of nearly every large city in the country."[66]

As they had in the first years following the stock market crash, exhibitors slashed prices in hopes of attracting bigger audiences. Maco dropped its top ticket price in Minneapolis from fifty-five to forty cents, and many independent operators quickly followed suit.[67] The discounting trend expanded even further as more and more theaters switched to two-for-one movies, or double features. Duals, as they were often known, were especially popular at smaller neighborhood houses that were unable to book high-quality first-run movies. By pairing two lower-tier films, managers convinced many penny-pinching customers that they were getting more for their money. Among the most popular double bills was the combination of *Dracula* and *Frankenstein* (both were pushing ten years old by then).[68]

Exhibitors, desperate for bigger box office receipts, resorted to every marketing trick they could muster. Bank nights and other cash promotions remained potent draws. Dishes and cookware were big, too—so big that, on at least one occasion, the ads for the Empress Theater in Minneapolis didn't even bother to mention the movie that was showing there on hot ovenware giveaway night.[69] Sometimes the stunts worked. Sometimes they didn't. When the manager at the State in Minneapolis announced that he was giving away free tickets to the movie *Lucky Night* to anyone who brought in a four-leaf clover, an overflow crowd of twenty thousand clover-carrying patrons showed up. (The manager didn't realize how common four-leaf clovers were.)[70] In 1940 the Minneapolis Orpheum tried an even more audacious promotion involving a Laurel and Hardy movie and the giveaway of a live monkey. As *Variety* gleefully reported, the stunt failed miserably.

> *The animal was purchased and brought to the theatre where it ran amuck. It attacked and scratched up [the manager] and escaped into the recesses of the empty space among the rafters over the theatre balcony. After three days, the monkey is still at large somewhere in the theatre and without food or drink. The opening into the rafter space is being constantly guarded so that the animal cannot dash into the auditorium proper.[71]*

Monkeys, four-leaf clovers, dishes, and cash all attracted their share of otherwise reluctant moviegoers, but they rarely added as much to the theater operator's bottom line as another Depression-era phenomenon: the concession stand. Candy had always been part of the moviegoing experience, but it was almost always sold at a nearby confectionary—not in the theater itself. In Minneapolis, for example, Theo Hays's Bijou sat next door to a candy shop run by his brother. But now, with box office receipts slumping again, theater operators began eyeing the tantalizing profits that could come from the sale of sweets. By 1936 candy sales at the nation's movie theaters—which had accounted for virtually nothing a decade before—exceeded ten million dollars.[72] Four years later, Paramount officials claimed that candy profits had paid off all the company's debt financing.[73] By the end of the 1930s, Twin Cities theater operators were beginning to cash in on what would soon become an even bigger moviegoing staple: popcorn. Popcorn—which was cheaper than other treats—was one food that Americans actually ate more of during the Great Depression, and movie theaters were largely responsible for feeding the habit. And with more demand came more supply. Between 1934 and 1940, the nation's popcorn harvest grew from 5 million pounds to more than 100 million pounds.[74]

Janet Gaynor look-alike contest during the Paramount Theater's showing of *A Star Is Born*, 1937.

Theater managers were doing everything they could to drum up business, but they kept falling further and further behind. In early 1939 the Minnesota Theater—which had served as an economic barometer for the local film industry since opening a decade earlier—again succumbed to economic realties. The Minnesota was the jewel of Maco's top-notch movie houses, but not even Maco (and by extension, Paramount) could turn a profit there. The Minnesota was "a nut which can't be cracked," industry analyst T. E. Mortensen observed. "There is, supposedly, the question of pride, glory and all the trimmings, which should make [Maco] determined to keep its principal show window open," he wrote, "but when the matter reaches a point where the financial well-being of the entire circuit is threatened, that's something else again, for pride hardly is an asset when immersed in a sea of red ink."[75] The local exhibitors who took over the Minnesota lease were even less successful than was Maco. In "one of the most unique appeals ever made by a Minneapolis theatre," the managers of the Minnesota ran a trailer before each motion picture admitting that they had been unable to book high-quality films. Without naming names, they intimated that Maco, as the Twin Cities' most powerful theater chain, kept all the good films to itself.

*Because of the fact that the Minnesota theatre is the only theatre oper-
ated by its owners, we have been experiencing difficulty in obtaining
good pictures in competition with other Minneapolis theatres that are
part of theatre chains. It always has been our honest endeavor and
desire to give you the best possible stage shows and talent and motion
pictures, and we urge those who would like to see this theatre continue
in operation to attend regularly. Without your support and with the
lack of screen product, the operators of this theatre may be forced to
close it.*[76]

It was no empty threat. Eight months later, the Minnesota closed
down once again—the victim of relentlessly depressed consumer spending, ridiculously high overhead, and a film distribution system rigged in
favor of studio-controlled theater chains like Maco.[77] If the Minnesota
couldn't make it, how could the Twin Cities' other theaters—especially
the independents—hope to survive? If the economy didn't turn around
soon, audiences in Minneapolis and St. Paul would have to make do
with many fewer movie choices.

*A*lthough some things had improved, the U.S. economy remained
mired in the Depression as the 1930s came to a close. But the nation's
outlook—at least its economic outlook—was about to change. Europe
was at war again. Japan's military was running roughshod over many of
its neighbors in Asia and the Pacific. The United States, aware of the
growing military threat, was waking from its isolationist slumber. By
late 1941 the federal government was pumping more than half a billion
dollars into Minnesota through defense contracts. The number of Minnesotans employed in manufacturing jobs was up nearly 30 percent.[78]
For the first time in years, business owners throughout the state—
including the Twin Cities' struggling theater operators—had reason
to believe that the worst was over. Among the most hopeful were the
brothers Abe and Louis Engler, a pair of established exhibitors who
decided it was time to expand. Their new Hopkins Theater, opened in
the summer of 1941, was the last new cinema to open in the Twin Cities
until after World War II.

Optimism turned briefly to pessimism when the Japanese attacked
Pearl Harbor on December 7, 1941. With the nation at war, theaters and
other businesses suffered a sudden blow. *Greater Amusements* reported
that box office receipts dropped to "all-time lows" because of "the wild
radio accounts of action, rumors, blackouts and other elements that
naturally would cut into entertainment receipts." When a Minneapolis

psychiatrist named Alexander Dumas recommended motion pictures—"especially comedies and musicals"—as a remedy for "war jitters," theater operators put his comments to immediate use. An advertisement for the State Theater in Minneapolis claimed that the new movie *Louisiana Purchase* "would fill Dumas' prescription for the city's war-worried populace to a 'T.'"[79]

As it turned out, Dumas may have been onto something. Within months Twin Cities exhibitors began seeing a noticeable upsurge in attendance. Among the biggest winners was the Newsreel Theater in downtown Minneapolis. The Newsreel had opened seven years earlier as the Time and had later been rechristened the Esquire, but no matter its name, it had always been a flop. But then, with the coming of war, the owners renamed the theater again—this time to the Newsreel—and switched to a policy relying almost exclusively on war dispatches. The change was successful beyond the owners' wildest hopes. "Wiseacres here didn't give the policy a chance in this town," *Variety* reported, "and [now] they're dazed by the fact that [the] house has been a constant winner."[80]

The war finished off the Depression once and for all, and for that, theater operators were grateful. The movies provided an escape for millions of people looking to take their minds off war—however briefly. And besides, where else were Americans going to spend all that money they were making in the booming wartime economy? "All down the line the average person has more spending power today than at any time since 1929 and perhaps even more than in those lush days," *Greater Amusements*'s T. E. Mortensen noted. "Older people and adolescents are going to theatres in droves, easily offsetting the shift in population to the armed forces and defense industries."[81] Nationwide, box office receipts increased steadily from a low of $809 million in 1941 to a high of $1.45 billion in 1945. By the end of the war, around 70 million Americans were going to the movies every week.[82]

As moviegoers returned in ever-greater numbers, theaters emerged as hubs of patriotic expression. War films such as *Wake Island*, *Guadalcanal Diary*, and *Thirty Seconds over Tokyo* appealed to audiences' flag-waving impulses. Propagandist crowd-pleasers like James Cagney's *Yankee Doodle Dandy* served as unapologetic morale boosters. On several occasions Twin Cities theater operators used "glamour and ballyhoo" to raise money for the war effort. They set up booths outside their box offices and offered free admission to anyone who pur-

chased a war bond.[83] And once, in May of 1942, they helped arrange what may have been the largest gathering of Hollywood stars the Twin Cities ever saw. About two dozen famous actors, including Bing Crosby, Cary Grant, Claudette Colbert, Joan Bennett, Bob Hope, Groucho Marx, and Laurel and Hardy, played two sold-out shows—a matinee at the St. Paul Auditorium and an evening performance at the Minneapolis Auditorium. The Twin Cities appearances of the Hollywood Victory Caravan raised about $65,000 (minus expenses) for army and navy relief organizations.[84]

When word came of Japan's formal surrender on August 14, 1945, Minneapolis and St. Paul burst into spontaneous celebrations, and for one brief moment moviegoing screeched to a halt. "It summed up to one of the lowest 'gates' for any single day in several years," the trade press reported. But the V-J Day drop-off turned out to be a minor blip. The following day, business at Twin Cities box offices rebounded to holiday levels. By the end of the week, attendance was even better than usual. "Some circuit executives see in this quick recovery a tendency on

The Hollywood Victory Caravan arrives in Minneapolis. Front row: Charlotte Greenwood, Joan Bennett, Joan Blondell, Claudette Colbert, Charles Boyer, Cary Grant, and Pat O'Brien. Back row: Eleanor Powell, Bert Lahr, Ray Middleton (partially hidden), Frank McHugh, Groucho Marx, Risë Stevens, Desi Arnaz, Stan Laurel, and Oliver Hardy.

the part of the public to 'get their full share' of motion picture entertainment over a given period," *Greater Amusements* noted. "[They] believe it augurs well for theatre biz in the changeover from war to peacetime operations."[85]

*O*n May 5, 1945, three days before the United States and its allies officially defeated Nazi Germany, Theo Hays died at the age of seventy-eight. Hays was the grand old man of show business in the Upper Midwest. He had built his reputation as the successful manager of the Bijou in Minneapolis. He had been among the first to bring projected motion pictures to the Twin Cities. He had worked side by side with Finkelstein and Ruben and had moved over to Paramount's Publix and Maco subsidiaries when F&R sold out. Over the years he had had several opportunities to leave the Twin Cities and assume executive positions in the film industry, but he had always turned them down. Leaving the Twin Cities had never been a real option for Hays. As *Greater Amusements* noted in his obituary, he preferred to "remain with 'his boys' in the territory."[86]

Feature Presentation

**Highland Theater
760 Cleveland Avenue
South, St. Paul
Opened 1939**

Six years after opening the Grandview, George Granstrom debuted the Highland—another art deco show house designed by Myrtus Wright—a couple miles away, in St. Paul's Highland Park neighborhood. The Highland was similar in size to the Grandview. Its auditorium was bowl shaped, with an arched ceiling, balcony, and walls of turquoise and silver damask. The lobby and lounge were heavily streamlined, with circular mirrors and curvilinear furnishings. Like the Grandview,

The Highland's lounge was a showcase of art deco chic.

the Highland underwent an extensive remodeling in the 1970s, when its balcony was sealed off to create a small "screening room."[1]

Business had been sluggish during the war for Jack Liebenberg, as it had been for most architects. Shortages of building materials and government-imposed restrictions had brought most construction projects—except those directly related to the war effort—to a halt. Most of Liebenberg's theater jobs during the war involved minor improvements to existing structures. With nearly every project he found himself having to navigate the treacherous waters of wartime government bureaucracy. The War Production Board (WPB) had ordered in the spring of 1942 that all construction projects costing more than five thousand dollars be suspended. But even those projects that fit under the five-thousand-dollar cap often ran afoul of other arcane wartime rules. At the Granada, for example, Liebenberg convinced the WPB to approve acoustical ceiling work under the heading of "insulation." But at the Minneapolis Lyric, where the ceiling had no existing acoustical treatment, the WPB determined that the addition of such treatment would constitute prohibited "new construction."[87]

Moviegoers pack the lobby of the recently rechristened Radio City Theater (formerly the Minnesota), 1945. Twin Cities theater managers hoped that big crowds would continue to show up once the war was over.

As the war progressed and the prospects for victory improved, Twin Cities exhibitors began planning for what many assumed would be a postwar theater-construction boom. In the spring of 1945, the WPB began slowly easing its restrictions on construction. When the war ended a few months later, many of the old rules remained temporarily in place, but that didn't stop theater operators from making plans. Liebenberg, for one, expected "everybody to run in at one time" now that the government was easing up.[88]

Many existing theaters in Minneapolis and St. Paul needed significant updating after years of heavy wartime use and restricted wartime maintenance. Maco, for example, planned major renovations at the Paramount and Riviera in St. Paul and the Aster and Lyric in Minneapolis.[89] But renovations were just part of the immediate postwar story. Several local exhibitors—most of them relative newcomers to the Twin Cities' movie business—had shelved proposals for new theaters when the nation went to war, and now they were eager to resurrect their plans. Ben Berger wanted to build a 1,200-seat house in North Minneapolis. Ted Mann was eyeing St. Paul's east side. And the brothers Sidney and William Volk hoped to build a new 1,000-seater in Robbinsdale.[90] Jack Liebenberg had already sketched out designs for a few projects, including the Volks' theater in Robbinsdale and Maco's proposed Victory Theater in Roseville. Now he was just waiting for the go-ahead.

DESPERATE MEASURES

*T*win Cities moviegoers who wanted to see the latest films as soon as they came out had little choice in the matter: they had to go downtown. It was the way the movie business had always worked. The best first-run films opened at the best downtown theaters, and they stayed at those theaters as long as they continued to draw big crowds. When a film finished its initial downtown run, it moved to another venue— either a lower-tier downtown theater, known as a "move-over house," or a subsequent-run cinema in a neighborhood or suburb beyond the downtown loops. But the downtown ace houses, with their first-run motion pictures, remained the glamour spots of the local movie trade. They tended to be big, fancy, and well kept. And because they were so expensive to own and operate, they almost always belonged to well-financed companies or individuals. By the end of World War II, nearly all of the first-run movie theaters in the Twin Cities were owned by one of two national motion picture firms. Paramount, through its Maco subsidiary, controlled the State, Radio City (the former Minnesota), and Lyric in Minneapolis and the Paramount, Strand, and Tower in St. Paul. Radio-Keith-Orpheum (RKO) owned the Orpheums in both cities as well as the Pantages (soon to be renamed the Pan) in Minneapolis. The first-run movie business was a game for players with deep pockets and plenty of experience. Or so it seemed.

In the first week of 1947, a group of local exhibitors purchased two downtown Minneapolis theaters—the Alvin and the World—from the estate of Al Steffes, who had died a year earlier. The first reports of the sale indicated that longtime St. Paul theater operator George Granstrom was the primary investor. But it soon became clear that someone else was in charge.

Over the previous twelve years, Ted Mann had earned a reputation as an up-and-comer among the Twin Cities' more established theater operators. He was part of a new generation of local exhibitors, many of whom came from the same area that produced Al Steffes, Sol Lebedoff, and other early theater men—the largely Jewish neighborhoods of North Minneapolis. Mann got his first taste of the movie business in 1934 when, at the age of eighteen, he became manager of the Metro, a small South Minneapolis theater owned by his new mother-in-law, Esther Charon. Two years later, he bought his first theater, the Selby, on Selby Avenue in St. Paul. The purchase of the Selby was a huge gamble for a young man with little experience and even less money. One neighborhood newspaper described the theater as "a graveyard of ambitions and fortunes."[1] But Mann was a tenacious worker. He renamed his the-

Previous page:
Ted Mann transforms the old Alvin Theater (previously the Shubert) into a top-notch show house called the Academy— with help from Miss Downtown Minneapolis, Pati Olson.

ater the Oxford, handled every part of the business himself, and pinched every penny that came his way. He wouldn't even pay to have heating coal delivered to the theater during the winter. Instead, he loaded chunks of the dusty black rock into the back of his car and made the deliveries himself.[2] With dogged effort he turned the notoriously unsuccessful Oxford into a modest moneymaker and used his profits to purchase two more theaters—the Gem, on West Seventh Street in St. Paul, and the Metro, his former haunt in South Minneapolis.

Like most other exhibitors, Mann put many of his plans on hold during the war. Following the attack on Pearl Harbor, he leased out the Oxford and the Gem and went to work at a Minneapolis defense plant.[3] But in the weeks after the war ended, he jumped back into the movie business with characteristic determination. First, he purchased another theater—the Bluebird on Rice Street in St. Paul. Then, he formed a partnership with Don Guttman, a fellow theater operator who, like Mann, had grown up in the neighborhoods of North Minneapolis. Together, Mann and Guttman controlled eight movie houses in the Twin Cities: the Metro, Alhambra, and Northtown in Minneapolis and the Oxford, Gem, Bluebird, Roxy, and Arcade in St. Paul.[4] Their chain of neighborhood theaters now ranked among the largest in the area. Guttman, however, was tiring of Minnesota. About a year after teaming up with Mann, he moved to California and left his partner in charge of the Twin Cities operation.[5] Ted Mann once again was on his own, and he didn't seem to mind one bit.

All this time, Mann had limited his operations to neighborhood theaters outside the downtown areas of both cities. But when it became clear in the fall of 1946 that the administrators of Al Steffes's estate intended to dispose of the Alvin and the World, Mann scrambled to put together an offer. Maco, which already controlled most of the first-run theaters in the Twin Cities, submitted an offer as well, but it failed to impress the Steffes estate's trustees. Ted Mann landed the Alvin and the World for a price tag reportedly topping $200,000.[6]

Mann was now in direct competition with Maco and RKO, and he had to tread lightly—at least where the World was concerned. The Alvin was not much of an issue. It had been operating as a burlesque house for several years and would continue to do so for the time being. But the World was a different story. It played first-run movies, just like the downtown ace houses belonging to Maco and RKO. Sometimes it also ran move-overs—the not-quite-new first-run films that Maco and RKO gave up to accommodate even newer movies. Now Mann had to figure out how to continue showing first-run motion pictures at the World without stepping on the toes of his much larger competitors. When asked about his plans, he demurred, saying he was "just getting his feet on the ground."[7]

But as events would demonstrate, Ted Mann was not one to avoid confrontation. He was a Diamond Belt boxing finalist and an avid handball player. He seemed to thrive on competition.[8] If the executives at Maco and RKO—or anyone else for that matter—suspected that the new owner of the World was a pushover, they would soon learn otherwise.

The war had papered over the increasingly acrimonious relationship between Hollywood and those who believed movies were gnawing holes in the nation's moral fabric. The film industry had served as a virtual propaganda arm of the U.S. government during the war, producing motion pictures that both appealed to Americans' patriotism and distracted them from wartime hardships. With fewer controversial films being produced, reformers kept mostly to themselves. But when the war ended, Hollywood went back to its give-the-people-what-they-want ways. And it wasn't long before the self-proclaimed guardians of public morality were mobilizing to cleanse Twin Cities movie theaters of perceived wickedness.

In the spring of 1947, Minneapolis emerged as one of the early skirmish sites in the battle over the Howard Hughes film *The Outlaw*. Hughes had released *The Outlaw* during the first few months of the war, but few people had seen it. It was too controversial. The problem, most everyone agreed, was the movie's female star, Jane Russell—or, to be more specific, Jane Russell's breasts. Hughes had gone out of his way to showcase the Minnesota-born actress's physical attributes in the film and in its advertisements, and his decision to do so had immediate consequences. The Hays Office refused to give the movie its stamp of approval. The Legion of Decency officially condemned it. As a result only a few exhibitors around the country booked it. *The Outlaw* disappeared for the duration of the war. But now the war was over. Hughes released a slightly altered version of the film, and the controversy erupted again. Maco, which had previously banned the film from its Twin Cities theaters, refused to change its policy. United Artists, the movie's distributor, responded by making it available to "anybody who wants to buy it." In April of 1947, the Lyceum Theater in downtown Minneapolis booked *The Outlaw* for an extended run.[9]

For the first time since the release of the sound version of *The Birth*

This quarter-page ad in the *Minneapolis Tribune* announced that *The Outlaw* had finally made it to the Twin Cities.

of a Nation in 1930, the mayor of Minneapolis was forced to decide whether to prohibit the showing of a film. On the morning before *The Outlaw* was scheduled to open at the Lyceum, Mayor Hubert Humphrey and "a broadly representative committee of 31 Minneapolis citizens" gathered to watch the film and pass judgment on it. Many people, including leaders of several local parent-teacher groups, applauded Humphrey's decision to consider a ban, but others, including *Minneapolis Tribune* columnist Will Jones, were aghast at the prospect of community censorship.

> *From all I've been able to gather without actually seeing the thing, "The Outlaw" is a stinker of a movie.*
>
> *Wherever it has been shown, the reviews have been bad.*
>
> *But whether I go see the picture or not is a decision I'd like to make myself.*

It bothers me to know there are people around town who want to decide for me that I'm not going to see it.

If those people succeed in getting "The Outlaw" banned, in effect they'll have succeeded in telling me and every other adult moviegoer in town that they don't think we're intelligent enough to choose what movies we see.

Whether it's true or not, it distresses me to be told directly, or by implication, that I'm dumb.[10]

The city's would-be censors emerged from the special screening looking rather sheepish. Calling *The Outlaw* a "Class Z picture," Humphrey announced that he saw no reason to stop its showing at the Lyceum. "It is mediocre, and in many judgments a poor production," he

Feature Presentation

**Rose Drive-in
Snelling Avenue and
County Road C, Roseville
Opened 1948**

The Rose was the first Twin Cities drive-in built by Minnesota Entertainment Enterprises, a consortium of local theater owners. (The Bloomington Drive-in, which had opened the previous summer, was owned and operated by an out-of-state firm.) The Rose was one of the few drive-ins designed by Liebenberg and Kaplan, and as such, it was something of an experiment. While the drive-in was primarily a bulldozed lot, it also included several structures, including a concession building (with restrooms), a box office, and a screen. The back side of the Rose's screen was its most striking feature. At dusk it lit up with a line of porthole-style lights, red and pink block lettering, and an eye-popping, 36-by-18-foot green-stemmed rose.

The Rose Drive-in, the first outdoor theater built by Minnesota Entertainment Enterprises.

Worried that it would be nearly impossible to change the light bulbs on such a tall structure, the Rose's owners asked Liebenberg to make sure that hooks were installed on top of the screen so that workers could reach the lights using ropes and scaffolds.[1]

said of the film, "but there is nothing in it that calls for the exercise of police powers." Hugh Flynn, a local PTA leader, apologized to Humphrey for creating a commotion over such an innocuous movie. "As far as I am concerned, you can forget all those letters from teachers and PTA officers," he wrote. "I'll have to apologize for them too."[11]

The efforts to protect Twin Cities moviegoers from the sight of Jane Russell's ample bosom had failed, but the episode suggested that the struggle to determine which films would be shown in Minneapolis and St. Paul was not going to end anytime soon. "It was only a temporary victory for a single production," wrote *Greater Amusements*'s T. E. Mortensen. "There is a bitter fight in the making over the encroachment of public rights by minority groups and the motion picture industry must prepare to face it with all the resources at its command."[12]

Mortensen was right about at least one thing: reformers were not about to quit. When the Legion of Decency condemned the nuns-in-peril drama *Black Narcissus* later that year, local exhibitors again had to decide whether to risk the legion's wrath. Maco passed on the film, but as was the case with *The Outlaw*, an independent exhibitor quickly picked it up. This time it was Ted Mann. Mann booked *Black Narcissus* at the World, determined that "the ticket-buying public should be the final judge of the theatre's entertainment." In the end, the film did "terrific business"—thanks largely to the publicity generated by the Legion of Decency's objections—and was held over an extra week.[13]

*I*t was the Friday before Labor Day 1947, and Seventy-eighth Street, separating Bloomington from Richfield, was a snarled mess. Long lines of automobiles were converging from east and west on the metropolitan area's first drive-in theater, the Bloomington. Highway patrol troopers did what they could to keep the traffic moving. Inside the theater complex harried attendants, armed with flashlights, tried in vain to slow down drivers as they took off in search of prime parking spots. Slowly, the lines dwindled and each car took its place. Mosquitoes feasted on the unsprayed. As dusk turned to darkness, an uninspired musical called *Carnival in Costa Rica* flickered to life on the Bloomington's big outdoor screen. Dozens of patrons, unaware that the little speakers on the poles next to them were meant to go *inside* their cars, complained that they couldn't hear the movie's soundtrack. Cab driver William Johnson, treated to a night at the movies by newspaper columnist Will Jones, knew what to do with the speakers, though, and he was impressed. "I'm going to bring my family out here," Johnson said.

"Even on my days off I have to take them out for drives. I might as well get them out here and get a little rest."[14]

The Twin Cities area was a late convert to drive-ins. By the time the Bloomington opened in the summer of 1947, more than two hundred drive-in theaters were operating nationwide, and many more were in the planning or construction phases.[15] But for the moment the Twin Cities had only the Bloomington. The Minnesota climate, with its harsh winters, was largely to blame for the dearth of outdoor screens. Industry experts estimated that a drive-in theater in Minneapolis or St. Paul would be able to stay open only about 150 days a year. It was anyone's guess whether Twin Citians would turn out in great enough numbers during such a short season to make outdoor theaters profitable.[16] But there was at least one other reason that drive-ins were slow to arrive in the Twin Cities: local theater owners had worked diligently to keep them out.

Many established exhibitors considered drive-ins a major threat to their business—and with good reason. The trends working against traditional theaters were undeniable. Car ownership was increasing rapidly now that the nation had converted to a peacetime economy, and Americans were spending much of the money they had saved up during the war. As the population became more mobile, it was migrating from the cities (where most of the movie theaters were) to the mushrooming suburbs. And young couples were having babies at a phenomenal rate,

The Twin Cities' first drive-in theater, the Bloomington.

which meant they were spending more time at home and less time going out. Drive-ins, unlike traditional cinemas, catered to automobile owners, suburbanites, and young families. The owners and operators of what were now whimsically known as "hardtops" worried that their theaters—especially those in the suburbs—might soon become obsolete.

Local theater owners had begun mobilizing against proposed drive-in projects soon after the war ended. At first it appeared their efforts would pay off. Several Twin Cities suburbs, including Richfield and Golden Valley, rejected plans to build drive-ins within their city limits.[17] But the opening of the Bloomington—orchestrated by a national firm, Flexer Drive-In Theatres—seemed to signal the beginning of a drive-in building binge. The informal Twin Cities drive-in blockade was over. *Greater Amusements* reported that local exhibitors now were "frantically searching for a means to halt the [drive-in] 'invasion' as rumors reach[ed] film row of more impending outdoor show houses for the district."[18]

But halting the invasion was out of the question. The first drive-in had arrived. More were sure to come. The only question was, who would own them—outsiders or insiders? Two months after the Bloomington opened, seventeen Twin Cities theater owners, including Bill Frank, Ben Berger, George Granstrom, Sidney Volk, and Ted Mann, pooled their resources to create a new company, Minnesota Entertainment Enterprises (MEE). The company's incorporators had one goal: to control the drive-in movie theater business in Minneapolis and St. Paul.[19]

As it turned out, that goal proved easier to achieve than anyone associated with MEE suspected it would be. The following spring, Flexer Drive-In Theaters suddenly abandoned the Twin Cities' market. It sold the Bloomington to MEE and relinquished its claim to a drive-in site in Rose Township (soon to be known as Roseville). With Flexer out of the picture, MEE launched an aggressive campaign to "envelop the Twin Cities area with a network of outdoor theatres."[20] It reopened the Bloomington, built a new "ozoner" (the Rose) at the old Flexer site in Rose Township, and mapped out plans for two more drive-ins—one in West St. Paul (the Corral) and another in Robbinsdale (the Starlite). Several MEE members fretted that the new drive-ins would siphon customers away from their indoor theaters, but the company's general manager, Bill Sears, told them not to worry. In a letter to Ted Mann, Sears insisted most drive-in patrons were not regular moviegoers anyway. "We are going to do far more business in Minneapolis than any of us realize," he wrote, "providing we have proper facilities and a first class set-up."[21]

$\mathcal{M}$ost Twin Cities moviegoers didn't care who owned the theaters they patronized—so long as they were able to watch the movies they wanted to see. Few were aware that Minneapolis and St. Paul were at the center of a long-running struggle to remake the movie business. Even those who were aware of it had a hard time understanding what it meant to them. They were about to find out.

The small fraternity of Twin Cities movie exhibitors had, over the years, produced several nationally known firebrands—most notably Al Steffes—who rejected the legitimacy of the system that brought motion pictures from the studio to the screen. These independent theater owners objected to many of the practices they had to follow to secure films. They especially despised block booking, a practice that forced them to purchase movies—many of them subpar productions—in bundles, instead of on a film-by-film basis. Many exhibitors believed the root of their problems lay in the fact that five major Hollywood studios—Paramount, MGM, RKO, Twentieth Century-Fox, and Warner Brothers—dominated the motion picture industry at each level: from production to distribution to exhibition. Because the studios produced most of the best pictures and owned many of the best theaters, they were able to dictate terms to independent exhibitors. The independents, having little leverage in negotiations, were forced to play by the studios' rules.

In the mid-1930s Al Steffes and his colleagues at the regional trade group Allied Theatres of the Northwest began lobbying state governments to prohibit movie producers from owning theaters. The effort to divorce film production from film exhibition produced few lasting successes (the North Dakota legislature, for example, repealed the nation's only divorcement law a year after passing it), but the idea gradually caught on.[22] In 1938 the federal government went to court, accusing Hollywood's biggest producers and distributors of dominating all aspects of the movie business, "from selection of the story to final showing at the theater."[23] It asked, among other things, that the studios be required to divest themselves of their theaters. The case slogged through the courts for ten years, until finally, in 1948, the U.S. Supreme Court ruled in favor of the government. The studios would have to get rid of at least some of their theaters.

Most independent theater owners in the Twin Cities rejoiced at the Supreme Court's decision. After years of battling against the studios, they had finally won. Ben Berger, the Minneapolis-based exhibitor who had assumed the combative-leadership role once filled by Al Steffes, relished the opportunity to declare victory. "I am very elated over the

Feature Presentation

•••

**Terrace Theater
West Broadway and 36th
Avenue North, Robbinsdale
Opened 1951**

Few, if any, Twin Cities movie theaters ever attracted the kind of national attention that the Terrace received when it opened in 1951. Set on a ten-acre tract above Robbinsdale's Crystal Lake, the Terrace was a true trendsetter of early baby boom design. The *Minneapolis Star* was among the theater's many breathless admirers. "It has a soundproof nursery where parents can watch the show with their baby," it reported. "There's a snack bar and a refreshment bar, there's a room where parents can bring their children for parties, there's coffee in a country club lounge, and there's a soundproof room where you can, if you wish, watch television."[1] With 1,300 seats and a 1,000-car parking lot, the Terrace could easily accommodate the large crowds that it initially attracted. But over the years, the ultramodern theater on the hill began to lose its luster. A strip mall moved in next door, obliterating its charming lake view. Other, more conveniently located cinemas siphoned off suburban moviegoers. In 1988 the Terrace's auditorium—the largest still operating in the Twin Cities—was partitioned and turned into a threeplex.[2] The old atomic age show house showed its last movie in 1999 and was still awaiting its fate eight years later.

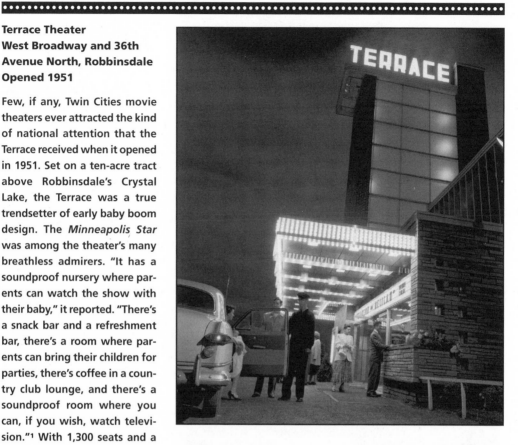

Top: the striking exterior of the Volk brothers' Terrace Theater in Robbinsdale. Bottom: the Terrace's refreshment counter was a popular hangout for teenagers during the 1950s.

Supreme Court decision which told the producers and distributors in no uncertain terms that their operations have been illegal all along and that they must begin abiding by a decent and legal set of rules and regulations. The combination of production, distribution and exhibition in the same monopolistic hands is inconsistent with the American way of life."[24] Berger and other supporters of the Supreme Court decision were convinced that the motion picture business was entering a new era of tough but fair competition. But it still was unclear whether the moviegoing public would benefit.

In most major cities the movie exhibition business was controlled by one or two of the big studios. In Minneapolis and St. Paul, Paramount—acting through its Maco subsidiary—was the dominant force. But now that the courts had approved divorcement, speculation was rampant that Paramount and Maco would lose control of the Twin Cities' market. When Paramount agreed in a 1949 consent decree to shed dozens of theaters nationwide, Twin Cities exhibitors began debating which properties the company would let go. Would it jettison its perennial money pit, the Radio City? Or would it, perhaps, give up its more profitable picture palaces, the State in Minneapolis and the Paramount in St. Paul? Or would the government be satisfied with a few smaller theaters?

When Paramount finally made its decision, the results were less than momentous. In accordance with the consent decree, Maco sold two of its lower-tier first-run theaters—the Gopher in downtown Minneapolis and the Strand in downtown St. Paul—and kept nearly everything else.[25] Many local exhibitors had hoped that divorcement would loosen Maco's grip on the Twin Cities' market, but in the end the company gave up just two properties that it probably would have dumped anyway. It continued to dominate the local movie trade.

But that didn't mean divorcement was pointless. Now that Paramount and the other studios had agreed to disconnect their theater holdings from their production and distribution arms, all movies were, in theory, available to all theaters—even new theaters. Suddenly, would-be cinema operators, who previously would have blanched at the thought of competing with studio-owned theater chains, now saw an open field. They began inundating city councils throughout the Twin Cities area with building permit applications. Established theater operators, most of whom had supported divorcement, now wondered what they had gotten themselves into. "The theatre-building orgy planned for the [Twin Cities] has established exhibitors gulping hard," *Greater Amusements* reported. "Several spokesmen [are] blaming the building craze on divorcement's consent decree, which makes pictures available 'for every building and vacant lot in America.'"[26] Divorcement was spawning a new era of competition in the Twin Cities' movie trade—it just wasn't the kind of competition that many established theater operators were counting on.

*B*ill and Sidney Volk were, like Ted Mann, members of the new guard of Twin Cities movie men. Born in Lithuania, they had immigrated to Minnesota in the early 1920s. And though they knew almost nothing about movies when they arrived, their movement into the theater business seemed practically preordained. Their uncle and sponsor, Max Kaplan, was a brother-in-law of Moses Finkelstein.[27] Their neighbors on Minneapolis's north side included Ted Mann, Don Guttman, and Saul Lebedoff. The Volks launched their careers as movie exhibitors in the early 1930s when they took over two Minneapolis neighborhood theaters—the Camden on the north side and the Nile on the south side. Unlike many other local showmen, they expanded their operations during the years of the Great Depression, adding the New Ray in St. Paul, the Falls in Minneapolis, and the Robin in suburban Robbinsdale.[28] Their chain of theaters ranked among the Twin Cities' largest.

The Volks had never fit comfortably into the tight-knit society of Twin Cities theater owners, and in 1946 they set themselves apart even further when they initiated the "theatre-building orgy" that so upset the editors of *Greater Amusements*. Minneapolis had gone twelve years without a new movie theater, and many established exhibitors wanted to keep it that way. But the Volks had other ideas. They wanted to replace their aging Falls Theater with a new cinema less than a mile away, and with that in mind, they asked the city council to transfer their Falls license to the new project. Many, if not most, Twin Cities exhibitors were irate. They were sure that if the Volk project were allowed to move forward, it would "split the town wide open" and lead to a glut of new theaters.[29] They made their case to the city council, but it did no good. The Volks got their license. After the long twelve-year drought brought on by economic depression and war, Minneapolis finally got a new movie theater. The Riverview, as the new cinema was known, opened in December 1948.

In the years that followed, Bill and Sidney Volk earned a national reputation as innovators in postwar theater design. In the spring of 1951, they opened a new theater in Robbinsdale called the Terrace. Designed by Liebenberg and Kaplan, the Terrace was one of the first ultramodern theaters in America—a cross between a movie house and a country club. It boasted a large parking lot, a sunken lounge with coffee service, a snack bar, a soundproof nursery, a television room, and a spacious lobby overlooking a landscaped terrace. Ticket sales were phenomenal despite an industry-wide attendance slump. Exhibitors from around the country flocked to Robbinsdale to see what the Volks had done. "Let's face it," Sidney Volk said, "the theater business has changed, and we've built a place to take care of the needs of today. We now have what the public wants. The box office tells the story."[30]

A few years later, the Volk brothers again hired Liebenberg and Kaplan to remodel the Riverview along the lines of the Terrace. They now had two theaters done up in ultramodern design, and many people, including *Minneapolis Journal* columnist Cedric Adams, were impressed.

> *If you're refurnishing your living room or maybe your amusement room, let me give you a suggestion. Skip out to the newly-done Riverview theater on Thirty-Eighth street and Forty-second avenue S. Sounds odd, doesn't it? But the Volk brothers, William and Sidney, have done it again . . . they've done over the Riverview to make it, in some respects, a sister theater of the Terrace. It's breath-taking, believe me. You think you're walking into a beautiful modern living room the minute you step into the lobby—Dunbar tables, McCobb stools, Herman Miller divans and chairs, walnut panels imposed on light wood, graceful modern lamps, stunning draperies. The bar stools at the little snack bar in the lobby are the most attractive I've ever seen. I'm sure you'll get some ideas. . . . Drop by sometime, it's a gasper.[31]*

By this time some industry analysts had come to believe that trends—particularly the growing popularity of television—were working against the motion picture industry. But the Volks thought otherwise. They remained confident that their luxurious atomic age picture houses would continue to draw plenty of customers—especially women. "If a woman has been at home tending her kids all day, washing, ironing, and cooking, it's going to take more than television to keep her there at night," Sidney Volk observed. "As long as we have women in this world, people are going to go out. Nobody ever bought a mink coat for his wife to keep warm."[32]

$\mathcal{S}$idney Volk's optimism notwithstanding, the movie business was in serious trouble. Moviegoing had peaked nationwide in 1946 and had been declining ever since. Box office receipts were down. The amount of money that the average American spent on the movies was down.[33]

And the Twin Cities were not immune. In an eighteen-month period beginning in 1951, a dozen theaters in Minneapolis and St. Paul shut down "rather than continue the fight against dwindling attendance."[34] The perpetually pessimistic Ben Berger seemed virtually inconsolable. "The truth is not known to the rank and file of the exhibitors," he wrote, "[but] the situation is positively more serious than at any time in the history of our business."[35]

Industry insiders argued about the causes of the postwar downturn, but some reasons seemed more plausible than others. From an eco-

Feature Presentation

**Riverview Theater
3800 42nd Avenue South,
Minneapolis
Remodeled 1956**

The Riverview was only seven years old when the Volk brothers hired Jack Liebenberg to turn it into a postwar entertainment getaway reminiscent of the Terrace. The lobby of the reimagined Riverview was living-room-like, with marble coffee tables, imported lamps, potted plants, floral-print carpeting, wood wall paneling, and a separate TV lounge. Room dividers split up the space and guided patrons toward the auditorium without relying on ropes and posts.[1] The auditorium, with its backlit proscenium and rear-section stadium seating, remained largely unchanged. Unlike many vintage Twin Cities show houses, the Riverview survived into the new millennium as a single-screen theater.

The Riverview's redecorated lobby, worth the price of admission.

nomic standpoint Americans were now spending large amounts of money on washing machines, refrigerators, and other pricey consumer items that had been unavailable during the war. With wages holding steady, that left fewer dollars to spend at the movies. And there were sociological factors, too. Young men and women between the ages of nineteen and twenty-five had always been the most reliable moviegoers. But when the war ended, millions of Americans in that age group got married and got pregnant. Suddenly the very people that exhibitors were counting on to show up at the box office were spending evenings at home with their spouses and their kids. And to make matters worse, many of those young families were buying homes in the suburbs, miles away from the big-city theaters with their aging facilities and lack of parking.[36]

But of all the factors that might explain the slump, none haunted the dreams of theater owners as relentlessly as television. As early as 1948, local exhibitors were fretting that the advent of television would significantly reduce their chances of "knocking out a happy living."[37] By 1951 their fears seemed to be realized. "No one familiar with what is going on can deny that television is the villain of the piece," commented Ted Mann. "I've seen enough statements of theatres in television areas to know that many independent exhibitors are hanging on by the skin of their teeth."[38] Although nearly everyone in the business acknowl-

In a nod to the growing popularity of television, the Volk brothers put a TV lounge in the lobby of their new Terrace Theater.

edged that television was taking a bite out of revenues, the fact was that the downturn in the movie trade had begun several years before television truly caught on. It was just one factor among many that contributed to the industry's problems.[39] Still, those problems were real, and they demanded solutions.

As the lines at the box office began shrinking, local theater owners turned to marketing gimmicks—some old and some new—in an effort to drum up business. Bank nights made a comeback after a wartime hiatus.[40] Chewing gum emerged as a new and important source of revenue at the concession stand.[41] And to the consternation of many exhibitors, profit-draining double features returned with a vengeance. During the war, when business was good, local theater operators had found it unnecessary to book twin bills, but now that attendance was slumping, they were willing to try almost anything—even if it meant incurring the wrath of their fellow exhibitors. In 1947 Rubenstein and Kaplan's Faust and Dale theaters in St. Paul instigated what the trade press called a "war" when they began showing double features of top-flight pictures. By the end of the decade, a large proportion of the Twin Cities' smaller theaters were booking twin bills.[42] It wasn't long before several deluxe first-run houses, including the RKO Pan in Minneapolis and the Tower in St. Paul, were resorting to showing double features of horror movies.[43]

When it became clear that none of the old gimmicks were solving the attendance problem, theater operators began grasping at whatever new marketing straws might come their way. In 1953 many of them put their faith in a new type of motion picture: the three-dimensional film. The 3-D process had been around since the 1920s, but Hollywood had never fully embraced it. Now, with box office receipts continuing to lag, the studios gave it another try. The first major 3-D feature film, *Bwana Devil* ("A lion in your lap! A lover in your arms!"), set box office records at the Maco-owned State in Minneapolis and Riviera in St. Paul.[44] Soon other local exhibitors were clamoring to install the extra projectors and special screens needed to take full advantage of the technology. Hollywood followed up *Bwana Devil* with additional 3-D features, including *House of Wax, Kiss Me Kate,* and *It Came from Outer Space,* but the fad did not last. The box office bump that 3-D provided barely covered the additional expenses that exhibitors had to incur. The special cardboard spectacles needed to view the movies cost five to ten cents apiece, and most people—especially those who already wore

Audience members experience the 3-D wonders of *Bwana Devil* at the Riviera in St. Paul.

glasses—detested them. By the middle of 1954, the 3-D craze had burned itself out.[45] In the words of *Greater Amusements,* it was "deader than a dodo."[46] Theater operators began looking for a new savior.

On an unseasonably cold evening in April of 1954, hundreds of well-bundled moviegoers lined up outside the old Century Theater in downtown Minneapolis to experience the latest innovation in motion picture entertainment: Cinerama. Cinerama was one of several wide-screen formats to hit Twin Cities theaters during the 1950s. Three synchronized projectors cast images on a seventy-two-foot-wide semi-circular screen that virtually wrapped around the audience. Multitrack stereo sound added to the spectacle. The idea was to make audience members feel as though they were in the middle of whatever action was projected on the screen.

The 1,100-or-so patrons who packed the Century that evening gasped, screamed, and dug their fingernails into their armrests as the first scene of *This Is Cinerama* unfolded around them. They knew it was just a movie, but it didn't matter. The opening sequence, shot from the front car of the rollercoaster at New York's Rockaway Amusement Park, made them feel as though they were actually on the ride. Later scenes, including an aerial excursion through the Grand Canyon and a water ski show at Florida's Cypress Gardens, provoked similar sensations. Audiences loved it. The Century had a hit on its hands. *This Is Cinerama* would go on to run for sixty-seven consecutive weeks, a Twin Cities record. More than 800,000 people—many of them from rural towns beyond Minnesota's borders—would see the film.[47]

Cinerama was a success, but it was a very limited one. The Century was the only Cinerama theater in the Twin Cities. Its big take at the box office was an exception to the prevailing—and depressingly persistent—movie business rule. Still, Cinerama's success proved there was a market for widescreen motion pictures. And Cinerama was not the only widescreen format available.

Of all the new projection systems introduced during the 1950s, CinemaScope had the biggest impact. CinemaScope projected an extra-wide image on the screen, just as Cinerama did. But unlike Cinerama, it utilized one standard projector equipped with a special anamorphic lens and a slightly curved screen that was relatively easy to install. CinemaScope made its Twin Cities debut in the fall of 1953 when Twentieth Century-Fox's *The Robe* opened to sellout crowds at Maco's Radio City in Minneapolis.[48] Once it became clear that *The Robe* was a smash, other local exhibitors rushed to install the new system at their theaters. "CinemaScope seems to have set a new standard for the manufacture and showing of motion pictures," Ted Mann wrote. "If but one more company [besides Twentieth Century-Fox] goes for it, every exhibitor is going to have to have it in order to assure himself of a ready supply of [films]."[49] Within a year of *The Robe*'s opening at the Radio City, forty Twin Cities theaters were equipped for CinemaScope.[50]

Unfortunately for theater operators in the Twin Cities, nothing they tried—not bank nights, not 3-D, not CinemaScope—could change the bleak picture at the box office. Attendance continued to languish. Theaters continued to close. U.S. census figures showed that between 1948 and 1954 the number of movie theaters operating in Minneapolis and its surrounding suburbs dropped more than 13 percent.[51] Maco, which along with its predecessor, Publix, had dominated the Twin Cities' market since the Finkelstein and Ruben buyout, began pulling out. By the summer of 1956, Maco was down to two theaters in St. Paul (the Paramount and Riviera) and five in Minneapolis (the Radio City, State, Lyric, Uptown, and Rialto).[52] With the Twin Cities' dominant theater circuit cutting back its operations, many local independent exhibitors wondered whether they should cut back, too.

*W*ith so many young adults sidestepping the movies to spend time at home with their families, Hollywood turned its attention to another segment of the moviegoing public: teenagers. High school–aged kids had always accounted for a fair share of each exhibitor's box office take, but the movies they watched were rarely made with their specific tastes in mind. That all began to change in the mid-1950s with the rise of the exploitation film. Producers of exploitation fare, including Roger Corman of American-International Pictures (AIP), believed "sensational and thrilling—but not necessarily sexy—subject matter" would attract teenagers in droves. In 1957, after producing just four pictures in its first year, AIP churned out twenty-four low-budget films aimed at the teenage crowd. It released many of its films in pairs, suitable for showing as double features. In the summer of 1957, for example, the Tower Theater in St. Paul chalked up impressive box office receipts during a two-week run of AIP's *Girls in Prison* and *Hot Rod Girls*. "The youngsters still love movies," explained AIP's James Nicholson, "but they're looking for kicks. That's why today's heads-up exhibitor is buying exploitation pictures in greater numbers than before. They fit the needs of competition and audiences."[53]

Finally, local theater operators had something to celebrate. "The joyous shouts you have been hearing are the happy voices of smalltown as well as big city exhibs over the sudden 'teen-age attendance boom,'" *Greater Amusements*'s T. E. Mortensen wrote. "Having weaned the youngsters away from their television sets both the distributors and the exhibitors are looking for ways and means of making the boom permanent."[54] More and more Twin Cities theaters began booking films aimed at teenaged moviegoers. And it wasn't just double feature houses that were riding the wave. First-run theaters in the downtown loops were now joining in the chase for the teenage entertainment dollar, as well. Big-studio productions with appealing young stars like James Dean and Elvis Presley were drawing huge crowds. At the RKO Orpheum in Minneapolis, off-duty police officers stood by to make sure the audience at the opening night of Presley's *Love Me Tender* didn't get too enthusiastic. As it turned out the crowd was "orderly if a little on the noisy side."[55]

Not all teenagers were quite so well mannered, though, and their behavior did not always sit well with older moviegoers. Drive-ins, in particular, tended to attract crowds of youngsters whose interest in movies was fleeting at best. Nearly a dozen drive-ins—half of them owned by Minnesota Entertainment Enterprises—had sprouted around the Twin Cities in the decade since the Bloomington opened in 1947, and all of

them were popular with young people. Some older Twin Citians, including an unidentified reader of the *East Minneapolis Argus*, complained that teenagers were turning the area's drive-ins into "passion pits" where "heavy petting" and "immoral acts" were on display for everyone to see.

> It is getting so a family cannot go to the drive-in theaters with their children anymore. . . . I was so shocked to see these young [people]—and I mean kids—doing this. I am boiling mad. It is no fun taking your kids out for a movie when they ask what the people in the next car are doing. . . . The police do check parking spots, I know, for this sort of thing, but where they should really check is the drive-in theaters.[56]

The police preferred, however, to let the drive-ins manage their own affairs. And most managers, including Gerry Herringer of the 100 Twin in Fridley, adopted a live-and-let-live approach to drive-in morality. "We had a policy," Herringer explained. "As long as the customer didn't bother anybody and we didn't get a complaint from the car next to him, we wouldn't take action. We didn't gratuitously peak in windows."

Still, there were some things that drive-in managers could not abide—especially when money was involved. Herringer remembered

During the 1950s many theaters, including the Gopher in downtown Minneapolis, catered to young audiences with spoofs like *Abbott and Costello Meet the Mummy* as well as with racier exploitation films.

when, one evening, neighbors living along the access road to the 100 Twin called the box office to warn him that two girls had climbed into a car trunk in hopes of sneaking into the theater. Herringer stopped the car at the entrance and asked the boys in the front seat to pop the trunk. After a brief protest they complied, and the girls climbed out. At that point Herringer could have evicted the kids, but instead, he resorted to one of the most effective weapons in his arsenal: humiliation. "You're good-looking girls," he told the pair of sheepish trunkmates. Then he gestured to the boys. "You certainly could find dates who aren't as cheap as these two guys." Herringer was pretty sure the two young men never again tried to stash their dates in the trunk.[57]

Ted Mann had muscled his way into the first-run movie business in 1947 with his acquisition of the World Theater in downtown Minneapolis. In the years since then, he had developed an even greater taste for top-of-the-line motion pictures and upper-tier theaters. He had shed his small neighborhood houses and replaced them with four larger cinemas in high-traffic areas: the World and Lyceum in downtown St. Paul, the Granada (renamed the Suburban World) in Minneapolis's Uptown

The Alvin, until recently a burlesque house, finds God.

district, and the Westgate in Edina. With five important theaters in the metropolitan area, Mann now ranked as the Twin Cities' most successful independent exhibitor. All he needed to cement the title was a true ace house—a theater that would rival Maco's Radio City, State, and Paramount in size and elegance.

In 1957 Mann made his move into the big time. For the better part of a decade, he had struggled to figure out what to do with the Alvin Theater—the legitimate playhouse formerly known as the Shubert—which he had acquired in 1947 along with the Minneapolis's World. For the first six years he owned the Alvin, it continued to operate as it had for many years—as a burlesque house. In 1953 a local minister named Russell Olson took over the lease and turned it into a religious revival center called the Minneapolis Evangelical Auditorium. (*Minneapolis Star* columnist Barbara Flanagan recalled that Mann acted uncharacteristically awkward when, during the church's opening service, Olson called him out on stage to thank him and pray for him.)[58] Three years later, Olson moved his church to the Loring Theater on Nicollet Avenue, and the Alvin reverted briefly to burlesque. But by that time Mann already was making bigger plans for the old theater. With design help from Liebenberg and Kaplan, he transformed the Alvin into a modern movie house worthy of first-run motion pictures. He renamed it the Academy.

Mann was determined to make the grand opening of the Academy one of the biggest entertainment spectacles the Twin Cities had ever seen. But to succeed, he needed a big motion picture. And big is what he got. The opening night feature at the Academy was *Around the World in 80 Days*.

Around the World in 80 Days was the pride and joy of producer Mike Todd, a Twin Cities native who had spent his earliest years in the same North Minneapolis neighborhoods that produced Mann and so many other local theater men. (In those days he was known as Avrom Hirsch Goldbogen.) The movie had had its world premiere in New York the previous December and had since won five Oscars, including Best Picture. But it had yet to make its way to the Twin Cities. It had been shot in the latest widescreen format—Todd-AO—and only Todd-AO-equipped theaters could show it. Mann had secured the rights to show the film at the Academy by agreeing to install all the necessary Todd-AO equipment, including a forty-five-foot curved screen and special 70 mm projectors.

The Upper Midwest premiere of *Around the World in 80 Days* gen-

Twin Cities native Mike Todd, in town for the local premiere of *Around the World in 80 Days*, gets a street named after him in Bloomington.

erated just the kind of publicity that Mann was hoping to receive. And Mike Todd—master showman that he was—deserved much of the credit. Todd played the hometown-boy-makes-good angle for all it was worth. He flashed a huge smile as a crowd of about three thousand fans cheered him when he arrived at the Minneapolis airport. He showed good-natured patience as a pack of reporters trailed him on a visit to suburban Bloomington. (His family had moved there from North Minneapolis when he was a young boy.) And he created a considerable buzz when he disappeared for twenty minutes during a preshow backstage banquet at the Academy. On his return he explained his absence to his tablemate, Senator Hubert Humphrey. He had, he said, been on the phone with his wife, actress Elizabeth Taylor. "That was Liz," he told Humphrey. "We had another fight. She told me, 'If you're not back here tomorrow morning, I'll be on a plane tonight.' I told her to stay put. I hope all couples fight like Liz and I do. It's so nice to make up."[59] Many fans were disappointed that Todd did not bring Taylor with him to Minneapolis, but this gossipy tidbit, published the next day in the *Minneapolis Tribune*, helped make up for her absence.

In the end *Around the World in 80 Days* was more of a sideshow than a main attraction. It was, after all, more than half a year old by the time it finally arrived in Minneapolis. But that was fine by Ted Mann. He had hoped all along to turn the opening of the Academy into a major event, and Mike Todd and his movie had helped him do just that. Few, if any, Twin Cities theater openings had ever received the kind of news coverage that the Academy's opening received. And in nearly every story that ran, Mann's name appeared next to Todd's. Mann's days as a small-time Twin Cities theater operator were now officially over. He was a player.

*E*ver since the flap over *The Outlaw* during the late 1940s, the self-appointed defenders of morality had been trying with little success to influence Twin Citians' moviegoing habits. A 1950 boycott of local theaters had crumbled just a few weeks after it was initiated by Roman

Ted Mann's Academy Theater opens with a bang.

Feature Presentation

**Cooper Theater
5755 Wayzata Boulevard,
St. Louis Park
Opened 1962**

Top: a private airplane serves as a promotional prop during the Cooper's local premiere of Airport, *March 18, 1970. Bottom: interior view of the Cooper's construction, 1962.*

The round, orange Cooper Theater in St. Louis Park was the second of three nearly identical Coopers that were built in the United States during the early 1960s. (The other two were in Denver and Omaha.) Built and operated by a national theater chain called the Cooper Foundation, the St. Louis Park Cooper—like its two namesakes—was constructed specifically to show Cinerama films. Its 105-foot curved screen stretched 146 degrees along the auditorium's circumference, and its three projection booths hid within the auditorium's back wall instead of poking into the audience, as was the case in most older, converted Cinerama theaters.[1] The Cooper was a destination for movie lovers throughout the Midwest—and not just because it was the only Cinerama theater in the region. The theater itself was worth the trip. Motorists dropped off their passengers at a covered drive and proceeded to the roomy, 400-car parking lot. The 3,000-square-foot lobby was a snazzy place-to-be-seen, done up in walnut paneling, black brick, burnt orange furnishings, and blue acoustic ceiling tiles. The main floor and balcony of its auditorium contained nearly one thousand comfortably spaced seats upholstered in blue mohair. Its five refreshment stands were open only during intermission and, in keeping with Cinerama tradition, served only drinks and Swiss chocolate—no popcorn.[2] But if Cinerama was the Cooper's main attraction, it also was a serious drawback. The paltry selection of Cinerama films was a constant source of frustration for the Cooper's management. In 1970, with Cinerama all but dead, the Cooper switched to standard-format Hollywood films. It remained a top-notch, first-run theater, but it slowly lost its cachet. In 1975 its owners built a 300-seat appendage theater alongside it called the Cooper Cameo. It limped along through the 1980s, steadily deteriorating due to corporate neglect. The Twin Cities' only movie-theater-in-the-round showed its last film in 1991 and was demolished the following year.

Catholic archbishop John Murray of St. Paul.[60] Efforts to prevent the showing of another spicy Jane Russell film, *The French Line*, had disintegrated when Gerry Herringer's 100 Twin Drive-in booked the movie for what turned out to be a lucrative thirty-one-day run.[61] ("We didn't think it was shocking," Herringer recalled. "My dad said a priest was in the front row.")[62] And to make matters worse for supporters of motion picture censorship, the U.S. Supreme Court had ruled in 1952 that the constitutional guarantees of free speech and free press applied to movies just as they did to other forms of expression.[63] (The case involved *The Miracle*, a film directed by Robert Rossellini that had been banned in several cities, including St. Paul.)[64] Trends seemed to be moving against the would-be censors. But the fight wasn't over.

On a Tuesday evening in August 1956, the projectionist at Bill Frank's West Twins Theater in West St. Paul made a fateful mistake. The theater was filled with kids who had come to see an innocuous family film called *The Birds and the Bees*. But when the lights went down and the projector came to life, the young audience members saw something they didn't expect: a preview—including several shots of a naked woman—for a Finnish motion picture called *The Witch*. The projectionist's blunder triggered an uproar. A fourteen-year-old boy who was in the audience started a petition drive protesting the West Twins's penchant for screening adults-only fare. Parents quickly picked up the cause, pressuring the city council to take action. A few weeks later, West St. Paul became the first community in Minnesota to pass a motion picture censorship law. Under the new ordinance a special police commission was given the power to approve or disapprove every film the West Twins planned to show. The council also doubled the theater's annual license fee.[65]

Twin Cities exhibitors were appalled. If West St. Paul was willing to stoop to censorship, what was to stop other communities in the metropolitan area from doing the same? As if to confirm their fears, a poll conducted for the *Minneapolis Tribune* suggested that most Minnesotans would support a state law similar to the West St. Paul ordinance.[66] Theater owners braced for what might happen when the next controversial film came to town. They didn't have to wait long.

On the Saturday before Christmas 1956, a small group of St. Paul city officials attended a special screening of a new film called *Baby Doll*. The movie starred Carroll Baker as a childish but conniving young woman at the center of a sexually charged rivalry, and it promised to cause plenty of trouble. The Legion of Decency had already condemned the film, declaring that it "dwells almost without variation or relief upon carnal suggestiveness." *Time* magazine called it "just possibly the dirtiest American-made motion picture that has ever been legally exhibited."[67] *Baby Doll* was scheduled to open on New Year's Day at the RKO Orpheum theaters in both Minneapolis and St. Paul, and the manager of the St. Paul Orpheum had scheduled the special screening in hopes of muting the protests that were sure to come. He had invited the mayor, the entire city council, the police department, and all the local movie critics. But only four people—a council member, two police officers, and the *Minneapolis Tribune*'s Will Jones—bothered to show up. In his review Jones seemed genuinely befuddled that the movie was creating such a ruckus. "But for the fuss, it might have played a couple of weeks at a small downtown theater, and maybe stirred up some bridge-table conversation in passing," he wrote. "Now there's no telling what will happen."[68]

The opening of *Baby Doll* initiated a barrage of letters to newspaper editors in both cities. A professor at the University of Minnesota accused the Legion of Decency and its allies of "flagrantly [disregarding] the rights of those who do not accept their judgment."[69] Others rejected the professor's conclusions. "Many speak with learned tongues but are spiritually ignorant," one reader wrote. "We, as Christians, do not put up with evil for the people to decide but carry forward good for the people."[70] Still others found the entire debate absurd.

> *"Baby Doll" is about as lascivious and corrupting as a Roman orgy led by Donald Duck. It is, perhaps, as brilliant a thing of its kind as has come to town since "Richard III" (which, thanks to our notorious attitude toward artistic masterpieces, stayed one whole week). But an adult picture must occasionally be produced, and great shriekings and cryings must perforce be made.*[71]

Predictably, as with previous movie controversies in the Twin Cities, the furor over *Baby Doll* died down quickly. The movie finished successful runs at both Orpheums without ever generating the kind of organized protests seen in other major cities. The theaters received a few angry phone calls and letters, but that was it.[72] Even the new archbishop of St. Paul, William Brady, found it difficult to get too worked up about the film. He had not seen the movie, he said, and had no plans to do so. His advice was simple: "Save your money for some other real good show."[73] The Legion of Decency continued to pass judgment on movies well into the 1960s, but after *Baby Doll*, moviegoers in the Twin Cities stopped paying much attention.

Baby Doll and many of the other mainstream motion pictures flagged by the legion were tame, however, compared to the new adults-only films being produced on the West Coast and overseas. The Twin Cities got its first adults-only movie house in late 1957 when Ingmar Bergman's *Illicit Interlude* opened at Bill Frank's Avalon Fine Arts Theater on Lake Street in Minneapolis. Whereas *Illicit Interlude* clearly had artistic merit, most of the films that followed its run at the Avalon failed to approach Bergman-like standards. One typical double bill featured *The Flesh Is Weak* ("The life and loves of a girl for a deceitful, ruthless man!") and *Blonde in Bondage* ("A young girl becomes a puppet for the man she loves!").[74]

In 1963 the Avalon enjoyed a long and successful run of *Babes in the Woods,* a locally produced nudie financed by a group of Twin Cities exhibitors including Harold and Marvin Engler, who had taken over the local chain started by their father, Abe, and Louis Engler.[75] *Greater Amusements* reported that *Babes in the Woods* was the story of "three winsome babes who arrive in a polka dot jeep to spend a vacation 'roughing it' in the northwoods." With a budget of $35,000, the film had to be shot in four days "because a longer schedule would have resulted in unhidable skin blemishes inflicted by voracious mosquitoes and horseflies operating on unprotected flesh." The Englers and their partners hid their involvement with the film behind a list of fictional credits. One unnamed producer told the *Minneapolis Tribune*'s Will Jones that he had "been regretting this thing ever since we did it." The participants' postproduction remorse suggested that, while the screening of adults-only films was becoming more socially acceptable, the production of such films still carried a mighty stigma. "My wife knows about it . . . but not even my close relatives know," the anonymous producer admitted. "It's frightful what you'll do for money, isn't it?"[76]

*M*ovie exhibitors hated daylight saving time. The federal government had adopted fast time, as it was often called, twice during the previous half century—during World War I and World War II—on the theory that the switch would help the country conserve energy. But exhibitors, among many others, believed that daylight saving was bad for business. Under fast time the sun rose an hour later in the morning and set an hour later in the evening. And since exhibitors assumed that many of their customers would find other things to do with their evenings if the sun was still out, they naturally opposed any efforts to make daylight saving time a permanent fixture of daily life.

The threat posed by the concept seemed to diminish after World War II, when most states—including Minnesota—went back to regular time. But in 1957 the Minnesota legislature took up a bill to push forward the state's clock one hour during the summer. Local exhibitors sounded the alarm. This time, as the editors of *Greater Amusements* pointed out, the stakes were higher than ever. The problem was the drive-in theater.

> *At the height of the summer season (June 21) in the twin cities area, it is impossible to start screening before 8:30 PM. Daylight savings will push that back to 9:30 PM, limiting the drive-ins to a single show nightly and almost certainly eliminating the popcorn-and-pajama set and their parents as patrons. . . .*
>
> *There's only one way to beat this threat and that is to alert your local legislative representatives to what the loss of a motion picture theatre means to your community.*[77]

North Central Allied, the organization that represented most of the area's independent theater operators, circulated a petition urging lawmakers to defeat the measure on the grounds that it would force "many already hard-pressed theatre owners out of business."[78] But the effort went for naught. The legislation became law.[79] In the years that followed, local exhibitors continued to fight for repeal, but the law stayed on the books. It wasn't until 1966 that the federal government, fed up with the hodgepodge of state laws, made daylight saving time a nationwide rite of summer. Coincidentally or not, it was about that time that many of the Twin Cities area's drive-ins began falling on hard times.

*M*inneapolis and St. Paul, like many other major cities of the late 1950s and early 1960s, were due for makeovers. The urban cores of both cities looked shabby from years of neglect. (Money to repair and maintain aging buildings and infrastructure was in short supply during the Great Depression and World War II.) People and businesses were abandoning the old downtowns and moving to the suburbs. In downtown St. Paul annual retail sales had plummeted by about fifteen million dollars between 1948 and 1954. Property values had dropped even faster.[80] In Minneapolis civic leaders worried that the city was turning into a "doughnut with a hole of blight." With their futures in doubt, both cities set out to reinvent themselves. They put their faith in the healing powers of federally funded urban renewal programs and drew up plans to "sanitize, reorganize, and modernize" their deteriorating downtowns.[81] Wrecking balls and bulldozers moved in. Hundreds of old buildings—

many of them architectural treasures—came down. Among the casualties were some of the Twin Cities' most revered movie theaters.

The Radio City was one of the first to go. Ever since it opened as the Minnesota in 1928, it had been something of a problem child. It was just too big and expensive to operate. The Minnesota had endured four extended closings, including a six-year shutdown beginning in 1938. Its 1944 rebirth as the Radio City had raised hopes that its luck would change, but the movie business's protracted slump sealed its fate. The owners and operators of WCCO radio and television bought the old picture palace from Maco in the summer of 1958. They sent in wrecking crews the following winter. A parking deck replaced the theater.[82]

While the Radio City succumbed to its own excesses, other Minneapolis theaters fell victim to the bulldozing progress of urban renewal. For seventy years Theo Hays's old Bijou Theater had provided popularly priced entertainment to the people of Minneapolis. But now the city was flattening large swaths of real estate, including the nearby Gateway district, in the name of progress. The dusty old Bijou did not fit Minneapolis's new self-conception. In the summer of 1960, *Minneapolis Tribune* columnist George Grim wrote its elegy.

> *These days, 25 cents gets you in anytime and you can stay as long as you like. The Bijou became a home for those whose funds had run low.*

The Radio City, once the grandest theater in the Twin Cities, makes way for a parking deck.

It was a no nonsense movie grind, playing all the pictures, later, of course. But it stayed in show business.

Now, the contract for its demolition has been signed. With the old barber college, several missions, hotels, bars, and the unique establishment of the Danish Seed company, the Bijou will be swept away by progress.

You can still pay a sentimental visit to the old theater. The people who run it say they'll keep the show on until the bulldozers start nudging the walls.

Fancier theaters have opened and closed, gone bankrupt, dark.

But the Bijou's going to keep the show on until the very last minute. It won't turn into a supermarket or a garage either. When the show stops, the wrecking begins.[83]

Four years after the Bijou disappeared, the fifty-six-year-old Century showed its last motion picture, *The Unsinkable Molly Brown.* Opened originally as a vaudeville house in 1909, the Century (or the Miles, as it was first known) was recalled by many old-timers as

Feature Presentation

Southtown Theater
I-494 and Penn Avenue
South, Bloomington
Opened 1964

Unlike most of the shopping mall theaters that eventually sprang up around the Twin Cities, the Southtown was a classy, comfortable cinema that rose above its bland surroundings. Ted Mann's first built-from-scratch show house was, in the words of its grand opening advertisements, "your comfort theatre of tomorrow." Its sprawling, wrap-around marquee beckoned film fans from across the Twin Cities area. Its lobby featured a futuristic red box office, floor-to-ceiling red draperies, and an expansive oval concession stand. In the auditorium, rows of rocker-back

Opening week at the Southtown, August 1964.

seats, spaced 42 inches apart, allowed moviegoers to stretch out in "livingroom comfort." The 70-by-32-foot screen was purported to be the largest in the Upper Midwest. Overwhelmed by the multiplex trend of the 1970s, the Southtown was subdivided into two 520-seat auditoriums in 1980. Without its massive screen, it lost much of its original appeal. The Southtown was torn down in 1995.[1]

the home of "crying matinees"—weepy melodramas favored by the "women's luncheon-shopping crowd."[84] The Century had achieved its greatest success as the Upper Midwest's only Cinerama theater, but it had gone back to regular motion pictures in 1962 after losing its Cinerama lease to the new Cooper Theater in St. Louis Park. The death of the Century provoked outpourings of nostalgia from moviegoers throughout the Twin Cities. "It isn't probable that the present generation will ever have the same affection for the cinema palaces of today that those of us in our middle years have for the old, ornate palaces now darkened or gone," one writer lamented. "Somehow, we suspect, ours was an era of opulence which has vanished, an era that had the same relationship to the present that a paddle wheel steamer on the Mississippi has to an atom powered vessel."[85]

St. Paul did not lose as many theaters during the 1950s and 1960s as Minneapolis did (it didn't have as many theaters to start with), but in 1965 it did say farewell to its only true picture palace: the former Capitol Theater, now known as the Paramount. Like the Radio City, the Paramount was just too big. The cavernous auditorium, with its main floor, mezzanine, and balconies, seated more than 2,200 people. It was a rare day that the theater ever came close to selling out. One day in the late summer of 1965, *St. Paul Dispatch* columnist Gareth Hiebert toured the inside of the old movie palace as demolition crews pounded it into dust. "I wondered what Moses Finkelstein would have thought," he later wrote.

> *Was I standing now on the spot where [he] stood that day in 1927 when the first talking picture—a Vitaphone—was shown in the city? Perhaps not because at the moment my perch was above the domed, plaster ceiling, that huge oval you looked up at from your seat below and watched the house lights gradually dim as the curtains spread and Al Jolson as Sonny Boy or Buddy Rogers swept through the skies on wings.*[86]

Hiebert's colleague, movie reviewer Bill Diehl, saw the destruction of the Paramount as yet another sign of downtown St. Paul's disturbing decline: "The shuttering of the Paramount removes another lure offered by the Loop, not the most exciting place to dine or seek entertainment even at the present."[87] Diehl expressed hope that someone would eventually build a new single-floor theater in the Paramount's shell. He didn't have to wait long to get his wish. A year after the Paramount closed its doors, a new ultramodern picture house—the Norstar—took its place. In the opinion of reviewer Eleanor Ostman, the Norstar was on "the other end of the design scale" from the old Paramount. Its décor, she wrote, was "rich but simple."[88] Times had indeed changed.

*S*ince older theaters were falling to the wrecking ball and attendance was still lagging far behind its immediate postwar peak, few exhibitors were in the mood to expand their operations. But Ted Mann was not like most exhibitors. He had always believed that the movie business would rebound, especially if the Hollywood studios started producing better motion pictures. The successful opening of the Academy and its long run of *Around the World in 80 Days* had only strengthened his faith in the business's future. "Hollywood has recognized the fact that it must make important pictures," he said, "and it is now in active competition for the amusement dollar, with more talent, stories, and production values."[89]

By the mid-1960s Mann had expanded his holdings to include fifteen movie theaters in the Twin Cities area. No one—not even Maco—could match his dominance. Mann had tightened his grip on the Twin Cities' movie trade in 1960 when he pulled off what the *Minneapolis Star* called "the biggest transaction of its kind in decades." He acquired RKO's three Twin Cities movie houses—the Pan and the Orpheum in Minneapolis and the Orpheum in St. Paul—for a price tag reportedly topping $350,000.[90] He remodeled the Pan, renamed it the Mann (in a self-referential indulgence rarely seen in local movie circles) and staged a gaudy grand opening featuring the Upper Midwest premiere of *Spartacus*. His flair for showmanship was, by this time, becoming legendary. "Ted has never been a stranger to publicity," a reporter for *Greater Amusements* observed, "but the week prior to the opening of the new Mann capped anything that has been seen in this town for some time."[91]

Mann had transformed himself into the Twin Cities' undisputed movie king, and he was not about to rest on his laurels. In 1961 he arranged to bring six Broadway shows to the Minneapolis Orpheum. The city had gone two years without any legitimate stage productions, and Mann was determined to fill the void. "This community should not be deprived of legitimate shows," he said. "I want the people in New York to know that Minneapolis is as great a theater town as any in the country."[92]

Mann also was almost single-handedly responsible for making the Twin Cities a popular test market among Hollywood directors. In the summer of 1961, an audience at the Mann Theater was treated to a sneak preview of *West Side Story*. Director Robert Wise was still putting the finishing touches on the film, and he had come to Minneapolis to gauge audience reaction in a "Midwestern town remote from New York's juvenile gang fights."[93] Wise was so happy with his experience at the Mann that he returned four years later to run a sneak preview of

another movie musical, *The Sound of Music*.[94] Soon, other movie executives were following Wise's lead. Producer Richard Zanuck was among
the first. He tested his new film *The Agony and the Ecstasy* at Mann's
newly acquired St. Louis Park Theater. "You just can't sneak a movie
around Los Angeles anymore," he said. "The audiences are too used to
these previews. They're all critics. We have to get away to find fresh
audiences."[95]

The Hennepin Avenue
theater district during
the Mann Theater's
run of *West Side
Story*, 1961.

Ted Mann had built his little Twin Cities empire by acquiring existing theaters and remaking them as he saw fit. In 1964 he broke from his
well-established pattern and built a new theater—the Southtown—in
Bloomington. The opening of the Southtown was a major event. Not
only was the Southtown Mann's first new theater, it was the first new
non-Cinerama theater to open in the Minneapolis–St. Paul area since
Bill and Sidney Volk debuted the Terrace in 1951. It also was the first
movie theater to be built inside a Twin Cities shopping center.[96] Two
years after the Southtown made its debut, Mann opened another new
theater in Bloomington, the Mann France Avenue Drive-in. He now
owned seventeen theaters in and around Minneapolis and St. Paul—not
counting his interest in Minnesota Entertainment Enterprise's six Twin
Cities–area drive-ins.

Mann had come a long way from his coal-hauling days at the old
Oxford Theater on Selby Avenue. "[His] achievements in the field of
motion picture exhibition loom even larger when it is remembered that

Ted Mann's France Avenue Drive-in opened in 1966 and was still going strong nine years later.

it is only about 15 years ago that he moved into the Minneapolis loop from a small suburban theatre," *Greater Amusements*'s Frank Cooley wrote.[97] But Mann, an entrepreneur of considerable ego and grand ambitions, was not done yet. As the 1960s rumbled to a close, he began making new plans that had little to do with movie exhibition. He put his brother Marvin in charge of the business, moved to California, and started a new career in motion picture production. The first film he financed, *The Illustrated Man*, starring Rod Steiger, was a mind-bending adaptation of a short story collection by futurist Ray Bradbury. It bombed at the box office, but Mann was hooked. He had discovered that he enjoyed playing the Hollywood game. With a determination familiar to anyone who knew him well, he made a business deal that he hoped would vault him into the ranks of big-time Hollywood producers. In the summer of 1970, he sold the leases on his Twin Cities theaters—all twenty-one of them—to General Cinema Corporation, a fast-growing theater chain based in Boston. The price tag was $5.75 million. Now Mann had the money he needed to produce even more films, such as *Buster and Billie* and *Lifeguard*. He eventually would reenter the movie exhibition business, but filmmaking was in his blood now. He had gone Hollywood. Back in the Twin Cities, the Ted Mann era was officially over.

FALL FROM GRACE

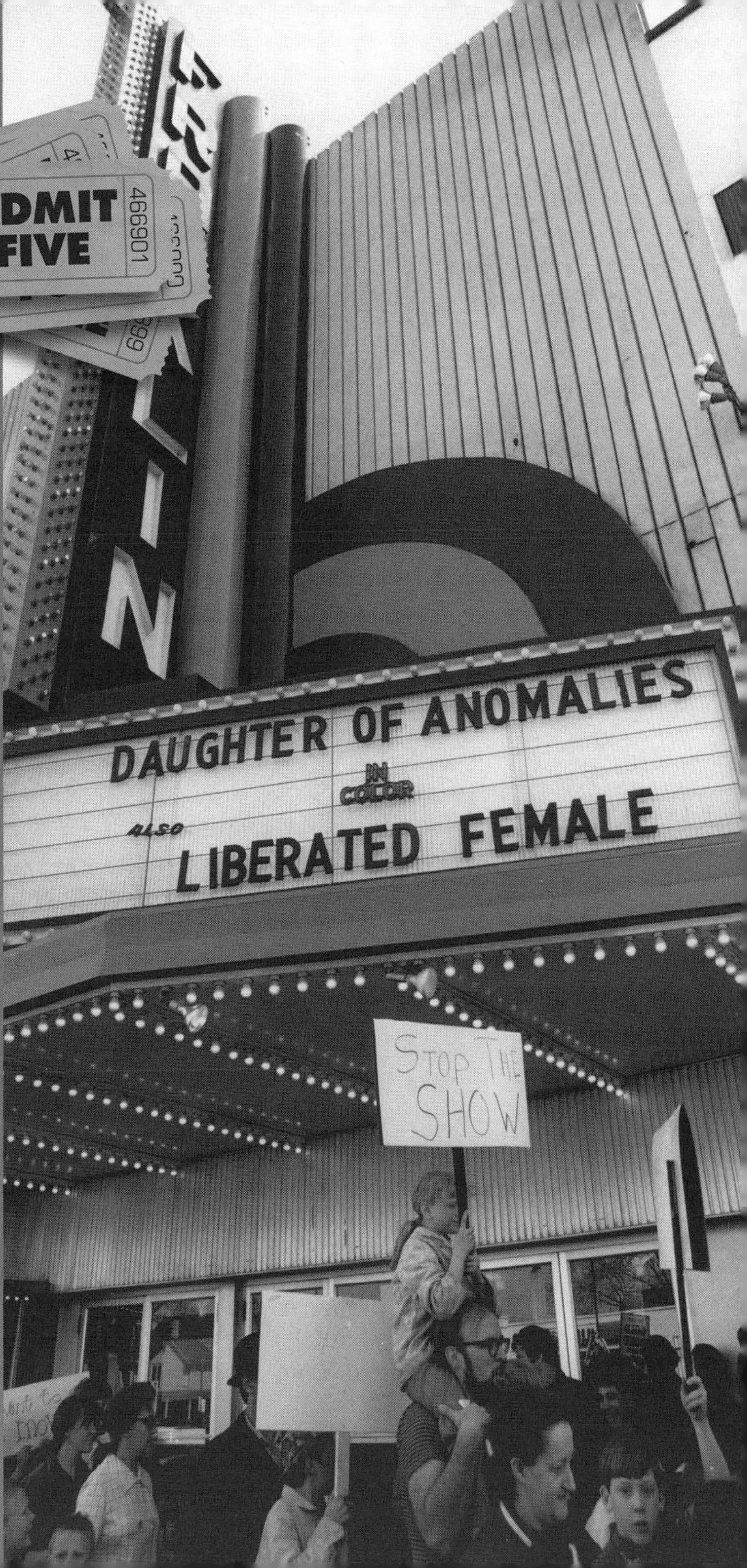

*O*n a pleasant afternoon in the spring of 1971, about twenty people—mostly women and children—gathered at the corner of Tenth and Franklin in South Minneapolis. Some hoisted handmade signs to their shoulders and proceeded to pace the sidewalk. Others stood in place and chanted slogans. The adults explained to anyone who would listen that they were there to save their neighborhood. The target of their protest was the old movie house that had anchored the corner for many years: the Franklin Theater. The Franklin had once been a prototypical neighborhood theater. Kids from blocks around had flocked there to watch serials and westerns and just about any other type of motion picture that Hollywood threw their way—and always at bargain prices. But the previous summer the Franklin had undergone a radical transformation. Kids were no longer welcome there. The Franklin now specialized in "adults-only" movies—in other words, pornography.

The protesters had already tried—without success—to convince the theater's management to switch back to family movies. Now they were hoping to achieve their goal by picketing. "This theater wouldn't exist in other communities because they wouldn't stand for it," one protester complained. "It's here because it's cheap here, and because they thought most of the community would not rise up against it. Well, we're proving them wrong."[1]

It had been more than thirteen years since the nearby Avalon, at Lake Street and Bloomington Avenue, had become the first movie theater in the Twin Cities to adopt an adults-only policy. A smattering of other theaters, including three Minneapolis houses belonging to Ben Berger—the Cedar, the Capri, and the downtown Aster—had experimented with soft-core porn during that time, but they had never provoked much organized opposition. The protest at the Franklin marked a turning point. Many residents in South Minneapolis now feared that pornographers were infesting their neighborhoods, feeding crime and prostitution and lowering property values. What they didn't know was that one man—Ferris Alexander—was largely responsible for the threat that seemed to loom before them.

Ferris Alexander was, in the words of the FBI, "one of the largest smut dealers in the Midwest."[2] He was born in 1918 and had grown up on Minneapolis's northeast side. He and his brothers had helped support their family (Ferris had twelve siblings) during the worst years of the Great Depression by selling newspapers and flowers along East Hennepin Avenue and Central Avenue. Over time he built a small chain of newsstands, including his unofficial headquarters, Hennepin Book

Previous page: Antipornography demonstrators picket outside Ferris Alexander's Franklin Theater, April 10, 1971.

and Magazine, at the corner of East Hennepin and Fourth Street. Hennepin Book was a shabby establishment that sold newspapers, magazines, paperback books, novelties, and cheap jewelry. By the 1950s it also was known as a place where one could purchase—under the counter—"dirty pictures and books." When a series of court rulings during the 1960s eased restrictions on pornography, Alexander brought what had been an illicit commercial enterprise into the open. The market for hard-core pornography proved to be extremely lucrative. Alexander became a rich man.[3]

Ferris Alexander was a stocky man with unkempt white hair and dark, furrowed eyebrows. As a businessman he rarely wasted time on good manners. There was little polish to him. "Ferris is in a class by himself," one former associate said. "He's smart, smart like a fox, but he's like a bull in a china shop. He can be so nice, but he can stand in your apartment and holler and rave and carry on like a maniac from a state mental hospital."[4]

For many years Alexander limited his pornography business to printed merchandise—books, magazines, and photographs. But in the late 1960s he expanded his operations to include movies. At first he was content to equip his bookstores with peep show booths where customers could watch raunchy 8 mm porn films away from prying eyes. But it wasn't long before he began calculating the potential profits to be made by screening the higher-quality 16 mm pornographic features that producers in California were churning out in ever-greater numbers. Realizing that he didn't have the facilities to accommodate the audiences that such movies might attract, he began shopping for theaters. As he soon discovered, no area in the Twin Cities had a larger selection of struggling and available movie houses than the neighborhoods just north of Powderhorn Park in South Minneapolis. In a one-year period beginning in the spring of 1970, Alexander acquired three theaters in the area: the American and the Rialto on Lake Street and the Franklin. In addition, he purchased the Empress in North Minneapolis. Alexander hid his involvement in the deals by forming "partnerships under various names" and placing employees "out front" to act as the theaters' public face.[5] Few people outside of his family realized that he was actually the owner.

By the spring of 1971, when neighborhood groups began picketing the Franklin, advertisements for Alexander's theaters were becoming a familiar sight in the local newspapers. Clumped together under a banner proclaiming "Spectacular Adult Entertainment," the ads warned readers to stay away if they were "offended by total and complete sexual

Once known as one of Minneapolis's top art deco movie houses, the Rialto switched to X-rated double features in the early 1970s.

frankness." Listings for movies such as *Evil Thoughts of Love, Virgin Hostage,* and *The Strange Sex Life of Adolf Hitler* appealed to prurient tastes. Soon Alexander's theaters were attracting patrons from far and wide, including many who "[wore] convention buttons."[6]

Alexander was building a mini-empire of porn houses in neighborhoods that already were losing many longtime residents and established businesses to the suburbs. The conversion of the American, Rialto, Franklin, and Empress into adults-only emporiums just made matters worse. "If you live in a low income area of Minneapolis, you probably have the oldest school buildings, the poorest shopping facilities and the least park space," the *Minneapolis Tribune* observed. "You also are most likely to have no neighborhood theater showing general interest movies."[7] Now that Alexander had taken over most of the remaining theaters near Powderhorn Park, neighborhood children could no longer walk down the street to take in a movie. The old days when Jack Liebenberg's Rialto stood as an art deco monument to the area's vitality were long gone. "We're working night and day to upgrade our neighborhood," one resident said with disgust, "and [now] we have to fight stuff like that coming in."[8] The protesters outside the Franklin expressed confidence that they could convince its owner to abandon porn and switch back to the kind of movies that neighborhood theaters used to show. They didn't know who they were dealing with.

*T*win Cities moviegoers could be forgiven for failing to notice that a pornography merchant was working quietly behind the scenes to acquire some of Minneapolis's most venerable neighborhood movie houses. After all, their minds were elsewhere. Or at least that's the way it seemed during the first three months of 1969. For the first time ever, Hollywood filmmakers had decided to shoot a major motion picture in the Minneapolis–St. Paul area. Starstruck Twin Citians, anticipating a sudden influx of Hollywood glamour, were all atwitter. It didn't matter that the movie's director had chosen their hometown mainly because of its reputation for appallingly nasty winter weather. All they cared about was that Burt Lancaster, Dean Martin, and a bevy of lesser movie stars were on their way and that maybe—just maybe—a few lucky locals would nudge their way into the film as extras. Unlike some movies, which didn't receive titles until late in the production process, there was never any question about what this one would be called. Its title was *Airport*.

The screenplay for *Airport* was based on Arthur Hailey's best-selling novel of the same name. It was a melodramatic web of seemingly unrelated plot lines, all of which intersected during the course of several tense and very snowy hours at a fictional midwestern airport. Lancaster had signed on to play the film's central character, a hard-nosed airport manager. Martin had agreed to take the role of Lancaster's brother-in-law, a playboy pilot. Other stars included Helen Hays as a

Dean Martin arrives in Minneapolis for the filming of *Airport*.

habitual stowaway, Jacqueline Bissett as a love-interest flight attendant, George Kennedy as a crusty airline mechanic, and Van Heflin as a troubled man with an improperly packed briefcase. The Minneapolis–St. Paul International Airport would provide the setting. And as many local movie buffs had hoped, the director needed several hundred would-be actors to serve as poorly paid extras.

The Twin Cities, so long ignored by Hollywood filmmakers, developed a severe case of *Airport* fever. When word leaked out that Burt Lancaster was scheduled to arrive on a late afternoon flight, about one thousand people—most of them women—swarmed the airport in hopes of catching a glimpse of the movie's biggest star. "It was a remarkable scene," *Minneapolis Star* columnist Jim Klobuchar wrote. "The girls were there in regiments, not the vulgarly curious but the legitimately idolatrous. You got the impression they all wanted to try out for the roll in the surf in 'From Here to Eternity.'" But when the flight arrived, Lancaster was not on board. His unexpected absence "left hundreds of housewives demoralized and in a condition of near-riot," but the disappointed crowd eventually dispersed. Lancaster arrived about six hours later to a nearly empty airport.[9]

The following evening, about 850 hand-picked Twin Citians showed up at the airport to begin—and end—their very short careers as movie extras. They had been chosen from a roster of about 7,000 people who applied for the dubious honor. "Never have so many abased themselves so willingly for a mere 15 bucks a night," *St. Paul Dispatch* columnist Carole Nelson wrote. Nelson had herself succeeded in getting called as an extra. But as she and her colleagues soon learned, being an extra in *Airport* amounted mostly to "milling toward each other like members of a sword dance gone berserk."

> *I was very proud of us. Nobody slipped, tripped or fell flat; we just kept milling, returning to "places," remilling and returning and so on and so forth until the herd instinct became ingrained within us.*
>
> *Strong spotlights lined the balcony, casting both light and heat on us winter-clad extras. Crew members equipped with walkie-talkies milled among us and tried to establish some order.*
>
> *Mostly, we stood. And waited 20 minutes for the next five minute milling session.*[10]

Some extras quickly became disillusioned. "This isn't at all what I thought it would be," complained one. "I can hardly see the camera way back there, up on the mezzanine. I'm beginning to wonder if I'll be anything more than a dot on the screen." (She wasn't.) Others remained remarkably upbeat. "Isn't this fun!" exclaimed one particularly cheerful extra. "Just think, I'm actually working with Burt Lancaster!" It didn't seem to matter that Lancaster was nowhere to be seen.[11]

When *Airport* came out the following year, many of the hundreds of extras who had spent that long night at the airport sat through multiple showings of the film at the Cooper Theater in St. Louis Park hoping to pick themselves out of the crowd. Few ever succeeded. The Upper Midwest premiere of the movie, held at the Cooper, was itself something of a disappointment. Local film fans had hoped that Lancaster, Martin, and at least some of the movie's other stars would show up for the event. Instead, they had to make do with Jacqueline Bissett and hometown actress Nancy Nelson, who had a small speaking role. Director George Seaton was there, too, cheerfully fielding questions about the

Feature Presentation

●●●

Har Mar 1 & 2
2100 North Snelling
Avenue, Roseville
Opened 1970

The Har Mar 1 & 2 was the last cinema with high-class pretensions to be built in the Twin Cities before the 1970s' onslaught of unattractive, boxlike movie theaters. It was a two-screen cinema, but both of its auditoriums were capacious and comfortable. With more than 800 gold, rocker-back loungers, the Har Mar 1 was by far the larger of the two auditoriums. Its matching floor-to-ceiling gold wall draperies created an air of elegance. The 500-seat Har Mar 2, with its blue draperies and bright red chairs, achieved what movie critic Bill Diehl called "a more intimate continental feeling."[1] In many ways, the twin theater's lobby was its most memorable feature. Its Venetian glass chandeliers, molded fiber-

Putting finishing touches on the Har Mar 1 & 2.

glass box office, and bubbling window fountains were glitzy touches that few cinema architects would even consider proposing in the years to come. In 1977 the Har Mar 1 was split in half, transforming the duplex into a triplex. Three years later, a retail space behind the theater was converted into eight tiny auditoriums more in keeping

with the bare-bones sensibilities of the multiplex era. With eleven screens, the disjointed Har Mar was, for a time, the largest theater complex in Minnesota. The Har Mar continued to operate until late 2006, when it was made obsolete by a new megaplex less than a mile away at Rosedale Mall.

lousy reviews that New York critics were heaping on his film. (The world premiere had been held at Radio City Music Hall—not in the Twin Cities.) "[*Airport*] is entertainment and I don't see anything wrong with that," Seaton said. "No message. Just entertainment."[12]

*F*or the better part of three decades, the moviegoing landscape in the Twin Cities had remained very stable. If you set aside drive-ins, you could count on one hand the number of new movie theaters built in the metropolitan area since the start of World War II. There was the Cedar, a struggling nabe in Minneapolis's Cedar-Riverside district. There were the Volk brothers' two postwar gems, the Riverview and the Terrace. There was the new home of Cinerama, the Cooper. And there was Ted Mann's Southtown. But that was it. A wartime shortage of building materials and the prolonged box office slump of the 1950s and early 1960s had brought new theater construction to a virtual halt. By the mid-1960s most moviegoers in Minneapolis and St. Paul were patronizing aging theaters from other eras.

But changes were afoot. After years of declining box office, attendance at movie theaters appeared to level off. The first baby boomers were now heading into their prime moviegoing years. Hollywood was producing higher-quality pictures, like *The Sound of Music*, that people actually wanted to see. Suddenly, the movie exhibition business looked a bit less daunting.[13]

On the first day of autumn in 1966, Boston-based General Cinema Corporation opened its first theater in the Twin Cities, the Cinema I & II, adjacent to the Southdale shopping center in Edina. Cinema I & II was something new in the Twin Cities—a theater complex with two screens. Twin cinemas (sometimes known as "multi-theaters," "piggy-back theaters," or "tandem theaters") constituted the newest trend in theater construction. The logic behind them was unassailable. By putting two screens in one building, an exhibitor could run two movies simultaneously with one lobby, one concession stand, and one projectionist. Most twin theaters were located in or adjacent to suburban shopping centers with their sprawling parking lots and hordes of cash-wielding consumers. Cinema I & II's location next to the nation's first fully enclosed, climate-controlled shopping mall seemed to ensure its success. For several years Cinema I & II (later known as the Southdale) remained the Twin Cities' only twin theater. But in 1970 the rush to ring Minneapolis and St. Paul with multiscreen movie houses began in earnest.

The Twin Cities' second twin theater, the Har Mar 1 & 2, was a bit of an anomaly. Unlike most double-screened cinemas before and after, the Har Mar (which perched on one end of the new Har Mar Mall in Rose-ville) had class. Its spacious lobby, with its three Venetian glass chande-liers and bubbling fountains, dazzled. Its two auditoriums, wrapped from floor to ceiling in blue and gold draperies, exuded elegance. Its architect, Benjamin Gingold Jr., was especially proud of the Har Mar's stand-alone, fiberglass box office.

> *It is a sculptural element, standing as a work of art. It is located in the center of the lobby. It doesn't necessarily look like a box office, but its position will indicate to patrons that this is, indeed, its function. The single box office will serve both theaters, its two colors—gold and blue—and flashing lights up the center giving it a duality.*[14]

But as events would soon demonstrate, duality was about the only thing that most multiscreen theaters had in common with the Har Mar. About a year after the Har Mar opened, the new double-screened Jerry Lewis Cinema made its debut in Eagan. It was part of a national chain of unadorned, low-cost franchise theaters designed for automated, push-button operation.[15] Other multiscreen theaters soon followed. They included, among many others, the Skyway I & II in downtown Minneapolis; the Yorktown 2 near Southdale; the area's first quad, the Village 4 in Coon Rapids; and its first six-screener, the Movies at Maplewood. Almost without exception the new multiscreen theaters were glorified boxes with tiny auditoriums and even tinier screens. Stripped of all magic, they had hardly anything in common with recent show houses like the Har Mar, the Southtown, and the Terrace and even less in common with the old picture palaces of the 1920s. Most were owned and operated by large national chains with few connections to the community.

The multiple-screen revolution also claimed two established theaters in the Twin Cities area. In 1971 Harold and Marvin Engler twinned their Hopkins Theater, west of Minneapolis, by turning its balcony into a separate, 300-seat screening room.[16] Two years later, Ted Mann's brother Marvin did virtually the same thing with the old Grand-view Theater in St. Paul.[17] "These were built from scratch on the excel-lent book-keeping theory that you gotta pay rent and heat the joint and hire staff anyway, so why not have two auditoriums under the same roof?" *Minneapolis Star* columnist Don Morrison explained. "For the same basic nut [operating cost], you can offer films to satisfy both the mass audience and the more selective film buff."[18]

The economic benefits of twinning old theaters were hard to refute,

but some exhibitors feared that the trend carried unintended consequences. "A couple of years ago, we couldn't find screens for the product," a local film industry veteran fretted. "Now, we have few pictures—
and more screens than we can keep track of." With the proliferation of
multiscreen theaters, the Twin Cities area was in danger of becoming
overscreened. And theater operators knew that if the supply of screens
outstripped demand, someone was going to lose.[19]

*O*n January 18, 1973, officers with the morals division of the Minneapolis Police Department entered the Rialto Theater on Lake Street
and confiscated a copy of a sixty-one-minute film called *Deep Throat.*
They delivered the film to Hennepin County Municipal Court, where
Judge Eugene Farrell had arranged for a private viewing. After watching
the movie, Farrell declared that *Deep Throat* was hard-core pornography. He ordered the police to retain possession of the film in case pros-
ecutors decided to file criminal obscenity charges against the owners and
operators of the Rialto. But if Farrell—or anyone else for that matter—
thought that a judicial finding would stop the Rialto from showing
Deep Throat, he soon learned otherwise. Two days after the police seized
the film from the Rialto, the theater was back in business with another
print. Police confiscated that one, too. The next day the Rialto opened
with yet another print. That one, too, was confiscated. When the Rialto
opened the following evening with a fourth copy of the film, the police
gave up. They figured that the print was in such poor condition that it
would probably fall apart in a matter of days, anyhow.[20] Ferris Alexander had made his point: he wasn't going to surrender without a fight.

There was no way that Alexander, the undisputed king of the Twin
Cities' porn trade, was going to sit by meekly and watch the police and
the courts try to stop him from showing *Deep Throat.* The movie was a
phenomenon. It was one of the first full-length hard-core porn films
ever released, and it already had racked up incredible grosses in some
of the nation's biggest cities. Alexander wanted a piece of the *Deep
Throat* action, and he did everything he could to ensure that nobody got
in his way. He made sure that the $25,000 deal giving him exclusive
Minnesota screening rights to the movie also included six copies of the
film.[21] As it turned out, the extra prints were the only things that
allowed him to keep showing the movie once the Minneapolis police
started raiding the Rialto.

But Alexander wasn't about to put all his *Deep Throat* eggs in the
Rialto's basket. Even after losing three prints of the movie to the police,

he still had three copies left, and he was determined to make money off of them. He started making plans to show the film at his newest theater, the Capitol on Payne Avenue in St. Paul. Alexander had gone to great trouble to acquire the Capitol. A few months earlier, he and his brother Edward had walked into the theater with a bag full of cash and offered to buy out its owner, longtime Twin Cities exhibitor Martin Lebedoff. Lebedoff didn't bite—at least not initially. "I told them I didn't do business like that and I had an attorney to help me conduct business," he later recalled. But Alexander didn't give up. He eventually purchased the Capitol from Lebedoff, albeit through an intermediary. He paid the intermediary in cash.[22]

Now that he owned the Capitol, he needed a license. In April of 1973, his brother Edward applied for one. The application created an uproar. Hundreds of angry eastsiders packed the St. Paul city council chambers

Feature Presentation

**Jerry Lewis Cinema
Highway 13 and Cedar
Avenue South, Eagan
Opened 1971**

In the early 1970s comedian and movie star Jerry Lewis threw his name behind a shoddy business venture that promised untold riches to anyone willing to invest $55,000 in a new movie theater franchise.[1] Jerry Lewis cinemas were simple, automated facilities that could be operated by one or two people. In 1971 a group of local investors purchased a franchise and opened the Twin Cities' first and only Jerry Lewis Cinema, a nondescript duplex in the parking lot of Eagan's Cedarvale shopping center. It didn't take long for the partners to realize they had made a lousy investment. The theater didn't bring in nearly enough revenue to cover

Opening-day crowd at the short-lived Jerry Lewis Theater in Eagan.

the franchise fee. It was, in the words of the controlling partner, Jack Smith, a "skimming operation" run by "a bunch of promoters in New York." Smith and his partners refused to pay the remaining $25,000 of their franchise fee. About six months

later the company behind the venture went out of business.[2] The theater was renamed the Cedarvale and operated for a few more years before closing for good in 1976.

East side residents pack the St. Paul City Council chambers to oppose Ferris Alexander's plans for the Capitol Theater.

to oppose the granting of the license. A memo submitted by a neighborhood group was damning. "The Alexanders are clearly disreputable pornographic dealers who do not hesitate to violate the law," it concluded. "And if the Alexanders' attempt to turn our Capitol Theater into a pornographic theater is not illegal, it should be."[23] A minister from a nearby Lutheran church predicted that if the council granted the license, "a flood of porno stores, sauna parlors and other theaters" would inundate the neighborhood. In the end the council sided with the opponents and rejected the Alexanders' application. But no one expected the Alexanders to quit. Their attorney, Robert Milavetz, called the council's decision "a futile action."[24] He was right. Less than a month later, a Ramsey County district court judge ordered the city to grant the license, ruling that the council's denial amounted to unconstitutional prior restraint.[25]

The Alexanders were in business. *Deep Throat* began playing at the Capitol during the first week of June. Within days police raided the theater on the grounds that it was in violation of the city's building code. They escorted several hundred patrons out of the theater, but their efforts made little difference. The screenings of *Deep Throat* resumed almost immediately after they left.[26] A few days later, about two dozen people picketed outside the homes of the Alexander brothers and their attorney, Robert Milavetz, but it didn't matter. *Deep Throat* continued to play. The people of St. Paul's east side were learning what the people of South Minneapolis already knew: the Alexanders were hard to budge.[27]

But that didn't mean the Alexanders couldn't be reasoned with—especially if they deemed it to be in their economic interest. About eight weeks after *Deep Throat* began playing at the Capitol, the Alexanders agreed with St. Paul mayor Lawrence Cohen to let another local exhibitor, David Levy, take over booking at the theater. Levy announced that the first show under his management would be the family musical *Oliver!* Neighborhood activists proclaimed victory, but the Alexanders seemed perfectly happy with the outcome. They had made plenty of money off of *Deep Throat* (an FBI informant later claimed that the Alexanders' profit topped $150,000),[28] and besides, business at the Capitol had begun dropping off recently. The Alexanders had squeezed about as much profit as they could out of it. It was time to let someone else worry. If there was one lesson to be learned from the entire episode, it was that the Alexanders knew how to make money from negative publicity. "This type of movie is most successful in areas where there is controversy," Milavetz said. "I think the mayor recognized this in dealing with us."[29]

Minneapolis Star film critic Don Morrison acknowledged at the top of his review that *Harold and Maude* belonged "to a class of movies that I might as well admit I love simply because they are." *Harold and Maude* bore no resemblance to big-budget Hollywood productions like *Airport*. It was a little love story with two unlikely protagonists: a rich young man with a death obsession and a seventy-nine-year-old woman with a zest for life. In his review Morrison seemed almost apologetic for liking a movie that he believed few of his readers would ever bother to see. "It sounds romantically cute," he wrote, "and I guess it is."[30] Few people in the movie business expected *Harold and Maude* to do very well at the box office, and their low expectations seemed justified when the film performed dismally during its nationwide holiday season opening. In Minneapolis its two-week run at the downtown World was typically underwhelming.

Two months after ending its run at the World, *Harold and Maude* returned to the Twin Cities at the 500-seat Westgate Theater at 45th Street and France Avenue. This time the quirky movie that Morrison and many other critics had raved about caught on. Its engagement at the Westgate kept extending week after week. The theater's manager reported that the audience seemed to evolve over time. First there was the "sophisticated older set." Then there was the "university contingent," which was followed—in order—by a "run of senior citizens," "a short hippy phase," and a spike in business from the "high school and college crowd." A year after its opening at the Westgate, the movie was still going strong, and exhibitors around the country were taking notice. Before long *Harold and Maude* was a national box office phenomenon, and its success was due in large measure to its record-setting run at the Westgate. Theater managers nationwide couldn't help but "appreciate the humor of Minneapolis showing New York . . . and the rest of the country how to get it done."[31]

Harold and Maude's septuagenarian star, Ruth Gordon, was the guest of honor when the Westgate celebrated the movie's one-year run. Don Morrison, the film's biggest local booster, was on hand for the event.

> *When the tiny, 5-foot star arrived at the theater, a joyous roar went up from the crowd packed in the lobby despite ushers' efforts to move them into the theater. She and [Douglas] Strand [who had seen the film 104 times] symbolically cut a birthday cake. After the patrons were more or less seated, she walked down the aisle to the stage.*
>
> *I've seen standing ovations in my time and I've heard the rabbit-squeals of teeny-boppers when their latest imaginary sex-object appears. This was different—not just celebrity excitement or pubescent cult cries, but a sweeping great wave of open affection.*[32]

Edina residents, thirsting for movie variety, protest the Westgate Theater's record-setting run of *Harold and Maude*.

Harold and Maude continued to play at the Westgate for another fourteen months. Toward the end of its 114-week run, it even attracted a few protesters. On the anniversary of the movie's second year at the Westgate, a group of local residents picketed the theater in hopes that the management would book another film—almost any film other than *Harold and Maude*.

*C*lyde Cutter was ready to give up. Over the previous two decades, he had successfully operated a string of neighborhood theaters in Minneapolis including the Alhambra, the Broadway, the Paradise, and the Ritz. But now, in the mid-1970s, nearly all of his former movie houses were shut down, and the one that continued to operate—the Paradise (now called the Capri)—was a porn house. Cutter still owned Jack Liebenberg's art deco masterpiece, the Hollywood in North Minneapolis, but these days it caused him nothing but trouble. Audiences were flocking to the new suburban multiscreen theaters. The old downtown houses still got most of the newest movies first. Crowds at the Hollywood were pathetically thin. On a good weeknight 90 percent of the theater's seats were empty. "It's not been very pleasant for us at all," Cutter said. "We're just about ready to fold up because we can't keep going under these circumstances." The Hollywood's previous owner had tried to show porn flicks but gave up under pressure from neighbors. Cutter had hoped that those same neighbors would patronize the Hollywood once he started showing more family-friendly pictures, but they rarely showed up. "I'd sell if I could," he grumbled.[33]

Twin Cities independent theater owners had been struggling for quite a while. Back in 1969 the owner of the Midtown Theater in St. Paul had run an ad that summed up the feelings of many of his colleagues. It ran under the headline "Put up or keep quiet."

> *We are constantly asked why aren't there more pictures for the entire family? The answer is simple—Family pictures don't do business. Recently on 3 successive weeks [we] showed "My Side of the Mountain," "Angel in My Pocket" & "Swiss Family Robinson"—all EXCELLENT FAMILY FILMS—the results were the same—Business terrible. We want to show the best Family Films available—we also want to stay in business. We cannot show family films to empty theaters all the time. If people go to see family pictures they will be produced and shown in our theaters. If they don't, they won't be shown. We ARE showing today 2 of the finest films for the entire family ever to be made [*My Side of the Mountain* and* The Heart is a Lonely Hunter*]. We hope you will attend. If you don't, don't call and tell us you don't like the pictures we're showing.*[34]

The Midway limped along for a few more years before finally suc-cumbing. And it wasn't alone. During the first half of the 1970s, a dis-tressing number of Twin Cities independent neighborhood theaters—including more than a dozen in Minneapolis—either closed or converted into porn houses.[35] Nearly every struggling nabe had its own small legion of defenders, but none inspired the kind of spirited defense reserved for the Parkway Theater in South Minneapolis.

The Parkway, near the corner of Chicago Avenue and 48th Street, was a simple art deco theater designed by one of Jack Liebenberg's early associates, Perry Crosier. (Crosier's other Twin Cities theaters in-cluded the Avalon and Boulevard in Minneapolis, the West Twins in West St. Paul, and the Hopkins.) It had gone through a succession of owners since the 1930s, but for the past ten years or so, it had belonged to a local exhibitor named Mel Lebewitz. Lebewitz had raked in cash during his first few years at the Parkway, thanks largely to lengthy, exclusive second-runs of *The Sound of Music* and *Mary Poppins*. But in recent years business had cooled considerably. In 1975 Lebewitz de-cided it was time to get out. He put the Parkway up for sale.

Lebewitz informed Bill Irvine, the Parkway's young manager, of his decision to sell and told Irvine that he was welcome to make an offer if he was interested. Irvine didn't have to think about it for long. He had grown up in the neighborhood and had worked at the Parkway in var-ious capacities since he was thirteen. He was fond of the old theater, and he wanted to make sure it stayed open. After consulting with his fiancée, Patricia Nikoloff, he went back to Lebewitz with an offer of $70,000—Lebewitz's asking price. Irvine assumed the Parkway would be his. But then someone else made an identical offer, and to Irvine's surprise Lebewitz sold the theater to the other buyer.[36] The Parkway's new owner was a man from Omaha, Nebraska, named Jim Sparks. Sparks already owned a small chain of movie houses in several other states. His theaters showed porn films.

When word got out that the Parkway's new owner was a pornogra-pher, the neighborhood erupted. About 1,400 residents signed a petition asking state regulators to prepare an environment impact statement on the potential effect of a "pornographic theater [on] an extremely frag-ile social, economic and physical urban environment at the leading edge of a blighted and highly segregated sector of the city."[37] When the state declined to get involved, the Minneapolis city council directed its planning and development department to take up the matter. The council's decision sidetracked Sparks's efforts to obtain a license—a

Bill Irvine grills goodies for his Parkway Theater customers, 1985.

process that usually lasted only a few weeks. When the delay stretched from weeks into months, Sparks went to court. In the fall of 1975, a Hennepin County district judge ruled that the city council was unconstitutionally preventing Sparks from showing movies at his theater.[38] A few weeks later, the Parkway reopened with an X-rated double feature: *The Hottest Show in Town* and *Marriage and Other Words.*[39]

The Parkway's neighbors had failed to stop Sparks from turning the theater into a porn house, but they weren't willing to concede defeat. Nearly every day for the next three months, protesters maintained a mostly silent vigil outside the Parkway, handing out flyers and photographing customers. And they were effective. Many would-be patrons, spooked by the protesters' attention, stayed away.[40]

At the same time Sparks faced a more formidable opponent: Ferris Alexander. Alexander considered South Minneapolis his own personal porn theater fiefdom, and he did not want the Parkway to succeed. With his connections to the most powerful distributors in the porn industry, he squeezed Sparks's access to films. The theater at Chicago and 48th was becoming more trouble than it was worth.[41] In February of 1976, Sparks gave up and sold the Parkway to Irvine and Nikoloff.

Sparks's exit from the Twin Cities was, in the words of the *Minneapolis Tribune,* "a happy ending" to a long-running controversy.[42] The people who lived near the Parkway had rid themselves of an unwanted neighbor, and the theater was now in the hands of someone who truly cared for it. But Irvine's experience with the Parkway during the months that followed highlighted one of the main obstacles still facing the owners of independent neighborhood theaters: apathy. After achieving their victory against porn, the Parkway's neighbors went home. Very few of them returned to the theater and bought tickets. Irvine estimated that less than 10 percent of his customers were from the immediate neighborhood. It was frustrating. "Sparks warned me this would happen," Irvine said. "He told me, 'Don't sit there and go broke. You can have some of my X-rated films.'"[43]

Irvine resisted the temptation to take up Sparks on his offer. After several months of screening general interest movies—including Walt Disney films—to smallish audiences, he settled on a new booking policy that turned out to be much more successful. Taking his cue from the college-aged customers who made up a large portion of his audience, he abandoned Walt Disney and began showing art house movies that appealed to film buffs. He even slipped in a mainstream X-rated picture starring Richard Dreyfuss called *Inserts*. By that time, though, few people in the neighborhood seemed to care.[44]

*O*n the screen of the old State Theater in downtown Minneapolis, Roger Daltrey stood silhouetted against a rising sun. The song "Listening to You"—recorded with the new Dolby sound reduction system—blasted through the auditorium. As the final shot of the rock opera *Tommy* faded into red-backgrounded closing credits, the members of the audience—sprinkled lightly among the theater's 2,200 seats—made their ways to the exits. They strolled back through the grand lobby, out the front doors, and onto Hennepin Avenue. It was New Year's Eve 1975, just a few minutes before midnight. As the crowd dispersed, the theater's marquee and the hundreds of light bulbs that surrounded it went dark. The State Theater, the last of the Twin Cities' true picture palaces, had shown its last motion picture.

Downtown Minneapolis had, until that moment, managed to avoid the fate of most other big cities. It had remained a vibrant moviegoing destination, even as the theater business in other downtowns shriveled. But the closing of the State signaled the beginning of a new era. The movies were migrating from the urban core. Now it was just a question of how long the other downtown theaters could last.

The downtown movie business in Minneapolis and St. Paul had been in flux for several years. For one thing, it was becoming increasingly difficult to determine who owned which theaters. An antitrust case initiated by the federal government had forced General Cinema Corporation

(GCC) to divest itself of nine Twin Cities movie houses, including most of the theaters it had acquired from Ted Mann in 1970. But the company that assumed control of the houses that GCC relinquished turned out to be financially crippled. About six months after taking over, it collapsed, and the theaters it had acquired—including the State—reverted back to GCC.[45] Several other downtown theaters, including the Skyway in Minneapolis and the Norstar and Riviera in St. Paul, also experienced some dizzying ownership changes during this period. First, they belonged to the old Paramount subsidiary (Maco).[46] Then, Maco became ABC Theaters. And finally, in 1974, ABC Theaters was purchased by Plitt

Closing night at the State, New Year's Eve, 1975.

Theaters.[47] The constant switching of owners only helped to fuel a growing sense of instability in the downtown movie trade.

But even with all those ownership changes, the downtown theaters in Minneapolis and St. Paul might have continued to thrive if Hollywood had not changed the way it released films. For as long as anyone could remember, the theater business in the Twin Cities and elsewhere had operated in a deceivingly orderly manner. The top movies always opened at the top downtown theaters. When they finished their first runs, they moved on to subsequent-run theaters—usually in the neighborhoods beyond downtown or in the suburbs. The downtown theaters' stranglehold on first-run motion pictures made them the destinations of choice among many moviegoers. Their size and fancy décor only added to their cachet.

Feature Presentation

Skyway 1 & 2
711 Hennepin Avenue,
Minneapolis
Opened 1972

Built on the site of the old Lyric Theater on Hennepin Avenue, the Skyway was downtown Minneapolis's first all-new cinema in nearly four decades. (The last one, the long-forgotten Time Theater, had debuted in 1934.) The Skyway, named after the city's ubiquitous enclosed pedestrian bridges, had two auditoriums—the 976-seat Skyway 1 on the second floor and the 713-seat Skyway 2 on the third floor. It remained a duplex until 1975, when a third screen was added. It got a fourth screen in 1982. Two years later, its original auditoriums were both split down the middle, giving the theater a total of six screens.[1] By that time the Skyway was already on the skids—a grungy, ill-kept multiplex in which pa-

In 1978 the Skyway hosted the world premiere of the Hollywood tearjerker Ice Castles, *complete with a temporary ice rink on Hennepin Avenue.*

trons occasionally feared for their safety. In one disturbing case, two women reported being harassed and groped by a fellow moviegoer in one of the Skyway's notoriously unsupervised auditoriums. An executive with Plitt Theaters downplayed the incident, unhelpfully suggesting that any customers experiencing similar problems should "bang on the [box office] door if you don't see a manager anywhere else."[2] After years of steady decline, the Skyway closed in 1999.

But during the holiday movie season of 1972, the downtown show houses in Minneapolis and St. Paul began losing their grip on first-run motion pictures. It all began with a movie called *Pete 'n' Tillie*, starring Walter Matthau and Carol Burnett. *Pete 'n' Tillie* was the type of holiday release that normally would open only at popular downtown theaters. But to the surprise of almost everyone in the local film trade, Mel Lebewitz—who would later sell his Parkway Theater to pornographer Jim Sparks—acquired exclusive first-run exhibition rights to *Pete 'n' Tillie* for his new multiscreen theater in West St. Paul, the Cina 4. *Pete 'n' Tillie* went on to become just a modest hit, but its run at the Cina 4 was groundbreaking. Mel Lebewitz had demonstrated that the top Hollywood releases did not have to open downtown. Over the next few years a handful of other neighborhood and suburban theaters began successfully bidding for first-run movies.[48]

The threat to the downtown theaters' first-run monopoly became impossible to ignore in the summer of 1975, with the release of *Jaws*. The local bidding for *Jaws* just happened to coincide with General Cinema Corporation's court-ordered sale of nine Twin Cities movie houses. With negotiations under way, neither GCC nor the company that ultimately acquired the theaters was willing or able to commit the cash needed to win the first-run rights to what was expected to be the biggest movie of the summer. In the end *Jaws* opened at two Twin Cities theaters: the Gopher in downtown Minneapolis and the Cina Capri, a small suburban house in White Bear Lake—about ten miles away from St. Paul's theater district. The Gopher and—to the consternation of downtown movie boosters—the Cina Capri both did huge box office with *Jaws*. The first-run movie mold was officially broken.

Since first-run films were now showing as far away as White Bear Lake, the downtown show houses had lost their biggest advantage over the suburban cinemas. Moviegoers from the suburbs now preferred to patronize theaters closer to home, where they could see the same first-run movies that were playing downtown—and where they didn't have to pay for parking. Bookers at the downtown theaters now found it increasingly difficult to secure the films they really wanted, even when they offered to pay a premium. The film companies knew where the money was, and it wasn't downtown. "They'd rather take a smaller bid from an outlying theater because they know the weekly attendance will be there," one booker complained, "and that means a long run for the movie, much more rentals . . . [and] a lot more money in the long haul."[49] It didn't take long for the downtown theaters to begin shutting down.

Downtown St. Paul's theaters buckled in rapid succession. In 1976 Plitt closed the Riviera, promising that the theater would eventually re-open. It never did. The following year, GCC shuttered the World and the Orpheum. (The Orpheum reopened under new ownership a few years later but closed again in a matter of months.) And in the summer of 1978, Plitt boarded up the last remaining movie theater in the St. Paul loop—the Norstar. A Plitt spokesman told *St. Paul Dispatch* columnist Bill Diehl that the company had little choice.

> *We knew the minute [the Orpheum and the World] closed, we were doomed. In some businesses, you're king with a monopoly. But not in this one. We need competition more than anything else. People like the excitement of a lights-on city or area with lots of movement. But there we sat . . . alone.*
>
> *God knows we tried. We thought "King Kong" might really turn things around. It didn't. We went after every type of movie, from schlock to class productions . . . but nothing happened.*[50]

In Minneapolis the demise of the downtown theaters was more of a drawn-out affair. After the State closed at the end of 1975, it took nearly nine years for the rest of the city's old first-run houses to shut down. In 1977 Ben Berger sold the Gopher—along with the neighboring Aster—to none other than Ferris Alexander. In 1983 GCC shuttered the World and the Academy. The following year, it closed the Mann. That left the Skyway (now a four-screen theater) as the only place to see a movie in downtown Minneapolis. For those who had always thought of Henne-pin Avenue as Minneapolis's Great White Way, the news was hard to swallow. The theaters had been essential elements of what the *Minneapolis Star and Tribune* called "the glitter and variety of downtown nightlife."[51] Now they were gone. But then again, no one should have expected that Minneapolis would remain a lively moviegoing destination when so many other big cities had already lost their downtown theaters. "It had to happen," Ben Berger said, referring to Minneapolis's shuttered show houses. "I'm surprised they lasted as long as they have."[52]

*F*riday and Saturday nights took on a decidedly weird aspect in Minneapolis's Uptown district during the summer of 1978. Every week-end at around eleven o'clock, hundreds of people gathered outside the Uptown Theater, dressed in costumes that complemented—for lack of a better term—the old theater's Liebenberg-designed art deco exterior. They wore fishnet stockings, garters, laced bustiers, purple lipstick, party hats, and sunglasses. They carried bags of rice, slices of toasted bread, and loaded squirt guns. Nearly all of them were in a festive mood. The Uptown was the official Twin Cities home of what was turning into one of the biggest cult movies of all time: *The Rocky Horror Picture Show*.

The Rocky Horror Picture Show had performed miserably at the box office when it was released in the fall of 1975. But it had slowly developed a devoted following among young moviegoers who appreciated its campy spin on Hollywood's standard-issue horror and science fiction fare. About a half year after its initial release, *The Rocky Horror Picture Show* began an extended run of midnight showings at the Waverly Theater in New York City. Other theaters around the country

A sparse crowd watches *Easy Rider*, the last movie to show at the St. Paul Orpheum, 1982.

Midnight weirdness at the Uptown, 1978.

began following the Waverly's lead. Soon audience members were dressing up as characters from the film. They talked back to the screen and threw things (toast, for example) around the auditorium at the slightest provocation. They danced in the aisles to the film's signature musical number, "The Time Warp." They turned what had been a major box office flop into the ultimate audience participation film.

The Twin Cities area was a latecomer to the *Rocky Horror* phenomenon. As one reporter pointed out, Minneapolis was "not known as a city that caters much to night people."[53] But it didn't take long for the film to find an audience once the Uptown began its midnight showings in the spring of 1978. The theater's manager, Eric Hollowell, found it difficult to explain the movie's appeal. "I'm not that much of a social scientist," he admitted. "It's a satire on B monster films that also confronts middle-class morality. . . . It seems to interest a particular type of person—somebody who's more creative."[54] As the film's Uptown run continued, more and more *Rocky Horror* aficionados began showing up week after week. Why? "I'm a lunatic," explained one eighteen-year-old fan clad in the gender-bending style of the movie's transsexual antihero, Dr. Frank N Furter. "I like to dress up as one of the characters in the movie. And I'm into rock and roll. It's a fantasy."[55] The fantasy continued at the Uptown for nearly eighteen years.[56]

The five hundred or so moviegoers who congregated at the Southdale on the evening of March 2, 1979, were not sure what they were in for. An ad in the newspaper claimed there would be a sneak preview that night of "what will be one of the most talked about new films of the year." Anyone who sat through the film and came away feeling that it was anything "other than represented" in the ad would get a full refund. Who cared if the movie turned out to be a stinker? It had a money-back guarantee.

It had been nearly two decades since director Robert Wise tested *West Side Story* in Minneapolis. His experience with that film had convinced him and others that the Twin Cities area was a good place to run sneak previews. Now another director was taking a cue from Wise— presumably in hopes of receiving some good, no-nonsense, midwestern feedback. But who was this mysterious director? And what was the movie?

After taking their seats, the audience members were handed blackand-white cards that resolved the mystery. The director was Francis Ford Coppola. The movie was *Apocalypse Now*. The rough cut that flickered up on the screen ran two hours and forty-five minutes. The edits were choppy. The color was messed up. The sound was in and out. But most of the cinematic guinea pigs in the audience were impressed.

As the theater emptied, a small man with a black beard and a worried expression waited outside. A few members of the audience went up to him and introduced themselves. After all, it wasn't often that a person got a chance to meet a world-famous director like Francis Ford Coppola. Freelance writer Syl Jones was among the handful of people who stuck around to talk to the director. He later recounted the conversation.

"What did you think of the audience?" someone asked.

"I don't know," Coppola replied. "I thought it went OK. You know, this is the first time I've seen the whole thing put together like this. It was incredible to me."

When *Apocalypse Now* was released five months later, it was twelve minutes shorter than the rough cut shown to the audience at the South- dale. It was later nominated for eight Academy Awards, including Best Picture and Best Director. (It eventually won two Oscars, for cinema- tography and sound.) Those who had watched the sneak preview had to wonder why Coppola came to the Twin Cities to test his film. What did he think he would learn? "Only Francis knows the answer to that," the local branch manager for United Artists said. "But this area is a good crosscut of American society. It's urban, affluent, has access to rural areas. It's got it all."[57]

$\mathcal{S}$ome things never seemed to change. As the sun slipped behind the trees ringing the 65-Hi Drive-in in Blaine, north of Minneapolis, the scene was reminiscent of the earliest days of outdoor movies in the Twin Cities. Station wagons ferrying mothers, fathers, and pajama- wearing children pulled into the front rows, closest to the screen. Teenagers in souped-up cars staked out their regular spots in the rear. As the countdown clock on the screen ticked off the minutes before the show started, the kids in the back rows—mostly Blainies, from Blaine High School—settled in to watch a steady parade of four- wheeled machinery go by.

There was the shiny yellow Nova with a black top. ("Decent car, man!") There was the green Maverick with a pair of stereo speakers on its roof. There was the eye-catching gold Lincoln convertible. ("Hey! Where's your pink jumpsuit?") And finally there was the scary black and silver Ford van carrying a small cadre of unapproachable outsiders from Irondale High School. ("They'll have a keg. You don't want to mess with them.")[58]

The 65-Hi was among the youngest of the Twin Cities' drive-ins, but it seemed appropriately stuck in time. The 1970s were giving way to the 1980s, but the 65-Hi—like most drive-ins—screamed the 1950s. The theaters' throwback atmosphere was a big part of their appeal. As far as the 65-Hi's projectionist John Schoenhof was concerned, what was true about drive-ins back in the fifties and sixties was true now. "If the film breaks you get a few horns honking," he said, "but most of [the customers] are too busy drinking beer and necking—just the way we used to."[59]

Like many outdoor theaters in the Twin Cities and elsewhere, Medina's Colonial Drive-in had gone to seed by the mid-1980s.

But unfortunately for drive-in movie buffs, times were changing. As the population of the Twin Cities expanded outward, the land on which the theaters were built was becoming more and more valuable. It was no surprise, really. Many drive-in owners had gotten into the business primarily as a real estate proposition. It was not "a permanent kind of situation," said the owner of the 100 Twin, Gerry Herringer. "We really felt that as things developed and the cities grew, we were just holding the land for future development."[60]

The approaching demise of the drive-ins had become obvious as early as 1972, when a Twin Cities real estate developer named Bill Fine bought six outdoor theaters belonging to the industry's local pioneer, Minnesota Entertainment Enterprises. "It's a natural evolution," explained Fine's partner, Robert Kueppers. "It's logical and natural. People in the business have put up screens knowing full well it was an interim use."[61] As land values rose, drive-ins disappeared. The Navarre, near Lake Minnetonka, gave way to a townhouse development. The Minnehaha in Maplewood was absorbed into 3M's corporate campus. The Hilltop, near Columbia Heights, became a Kmart. And the 100 Twin in Fridley was bulldozed to make way for Medtronic's world headquarters.[62]

In the mid-1970s the Twin Cities area had eighteen drive-ins. By the mid-1980s it was down to five: the Cottage View in Cottage Grove, the Flying Cloud in Eden Prairie, the Maple Leaf in Maplewood, the Vali-Hi in Lake Elmo, and Blaine's 65-Hi. None of them was listed in the classified sections of the local newspapers, but all five were—for practical purposes—for sale. And all of them had seen better days. At the end of the season in 1986, a reporter visited the 65-Hi to see how it was faring. He found hundreds of speaker poles tilting at strange angles. The windows of the women's restroom were smashed in. And shards of broken beer bottles glinted "like a field of rhinestones." It was, he wrote, "the only glitter remaining" at one of the Twin Cities' last surviving drive-ins.[63]

$\mathcal{E}$xhibitors didn't talk about theaters anymore. They talked about screens. As more and more single-screen houses in the downtown loops and the neighborhoods went out of business, multiple-screened suburban theaters filled the void—and then some. Between 1981 and 1985, the number of movie screens in the Twin Cities area more than doubled, from 68 to 145. A portion of that increase resulted from a brief boomlet in downtown theater construction. In St. Paul Marvin Mann opened

Feature Presentation

Maplewood I
I-694 and White Bear
Avenue, Maplewood
Opened 1975

Among the earliest and best examples of multiplex-era blandness, the Movies at Maplewood, as the theater was originally known, was the Twin Cities' first six-screen cinema. The standalone structure in the parking lot of Maplewood Mall housed one large auditorium (480 seats), one medium-sized auditorium (280 seats), and four tiny screening spaces not much larger than a classroom. The theater's managers were especially proud of an innovation they called the "light curtain"— a "surrealistic" display of colored lights that oozed across the screen during intermissions, thereby rendering old-fashioned curtains obsolete.[1] The Maplewood I proved so successful that

No-nonsense auditorium at the Movies at Maplewood, a prototypical 1970s multiplex.

in 1981 United Artists opened a virtual clone—the Maplewood II—on the opposite end of the mall's parking lot. With twelve screens, the Maplewood I and II constituted one of the largest movie theater complexes in the nation.[2] The Maplewood complex continued to do brisk business through the 1980s and early 1990s, but the arrival of several next-generation megaplexes in the east metro area spelled its doom. The Maplewood I closed in 2000. The Maplewood II shut down two years later.

the Galtier Plaza Cinema 4 on the third level of a new mixed-use development in the city's Lowertown area. In Minneapolis Harold and Marvin Engler debuted a new five-screen complex at St. Anthony Main, a development of refurbished warehouses across the river from the Hennepin Avenue theater district.[64] But the bulk of the new screens added during the early 1980s were suburban. Roseville in particular was a hub of new theater activity. In 1981 General Cinema expanded the Har Mar (which had already had one of its auditoriums split in two) by carving eight shoebox-like theaters out of an adjacent retail space. Four years later, United Artists opened the five-screen Movies at Pavilion Place about a mile away from the Har Mar.

But additional screens did not necessarily bring additional enjoyment to the people who patronized them. Most of the new multiscreen cinemas conformed to the lackluster, utilitarian sensibilities of the first-generation twin theaters. Architecture critic Bernard Jacob, for one, wondered whether it might not be time to boycott the latest uninspired movie houses "on architectural grounds." As he saw it, the new cinemas embraced the naked pursuit of profit at the expense of movie-going magic.

> More contemporary movie houses have given this "going to the movies" celebration short shrift. It's now a no-nonsense affair: Concrete block walls, tile or concrete floors—and plenty of popcorn. Indeed, in the recently enlarged Har Mar Theaters . . . where some of the theaters could more appropriately be called projection rooms, the main lobby is the reception hall of an entertainment emporium. The refreshment counter is a central command post that is nearly impossible to avoid. For the restless, there is also a room of coin-operated video games off the main lobby.
>
> There is a mercenary aspect to this movie-going that is reminiscent of buying an automobile for which options are much more important than the basic car. The strong-willed, or those on a diet, are particularly put to the test, for even if they resist the refreshment counter, the sound and smell of popcorn and candy for the first half-hour of the movie are bound to drive them crazy.[65]

The combination of small theaters, small staffs, and large volumes of popcorn and other concessions made for messy moviegoing. Soft drinks, with their propensity to slip out of the hands of children and adults alike, were especially problematic. Grumbling about sticky floors became commonplace. *St. Paul Dispatch* columnist Bill Diehl printed a letter from a particularly perturbed reader who fumed about the "filthy conditions, sticky floors, soiled seats, [and] carpeting reeking of

A young moviegoer stocks up on refreshments at the Cottage View Drive-in, 1985.

trash" found at the typical movie complex.[66] A *Minneapolis Star* reader complained that the new theaters, with their untrained staffs, were letting customers bring in their own food. "There is just nothing like a shopping bag full of McDonald's and greasy popcorn and sticky pop to make you wish you had never come," she wrote.[67] But as Diehl pointed out, attendance was "booming," and the number of screens was expanding, despite the aesthetic limitations of the new theaters.[68]

The triumph of the multiscreen movie complex was sealed in the fall of 1988 when the owners of the Twin Cities' last bastion of moviegoing fantasy, the Terrace Theater in Robbinsdale, chopped it up into three separate auditoriums. Jack Liebenberg's atomic age masterwork was by far the largest movie theater still operating in the Minneapolis–St. Paul metropolitan area, and big single-screen theaters were no longer capable of turning an acceptable profit. The Terrace could either go multiscreen or die. Its owners at Midcontinent Theater Company of Minneapolis chose the first option: they kept it alive by partitioning it. In the course of three decades, the Terrace had devolved from one of the nation's most striking movie theaters into a glorified shell housing three ill-fitting auditoriums. Its lovely hilltop view of Crystal Lake had long ago disappeared behind an ugly strip mall.[69] Jack Liebenberg had died three years before the Terrace was carved up. At least he had been spared the sight.[70]

*P*erris Alexander normally avoided public appearances, but he was fed up and his guard was down. He had just rushed over to the Franklin Theater after receiving a panicky phone call from one of his employees. A group of demonstrators, led by Curtis Sliwa and Joe Big Bear of the Guardian Angels, had gathered outside the Franklin to protest pornography and its alleged link to the recent serial killing of three American Indian women. Alexander pushed his way through the crowd, absorbing angry taunts as he went. He tore down leaflets—some of which read "Stop the Nut, Close the Smut"—that the protesters had pasted to the walls. And then, in an uncharacteristic move for such a notorious recluse, he turned to confront his tormentors.

"I bet you're on relief," he shouted at one particularly vehement protester.

"I make an honest living, not a dishonest one like you," the woman replied.

"There's no evidence that people who come here have committed crimes against anyone," Alexander said. "They're not perverts, they're curious. The people who come here are mostly middle-aged or senior citizens. We have a special discount for senior citizens. They're not serial killers, they can barely walk."

The demonstrators jeered at this line of reasoning.

"I'm just surviving here," Alexander continued. He told the crowd that the Franklin attracted only a few dozen customers a day. The crowd continued to heckle him. And then he let slip one of the most revealing public comments he had ever made. "I'm really in the real estate business, if you want to know the truth," he said. This time he really was telling the truth.[71]

Alexander had done well for himself as a pornography merchant, but he had made himself truly wealthy by reinvesting his porn-generated profits in real estate. He had garnered his first big windfall back in 1976 when he and his brother Edward sold the American Theater, near the corner of Lake Street and Nicollet Avenue, to the city of Minneapolis for $325,000. The city later razed the theater to make way for a Kmart.[72] But the money he made off the sale of the American paled in comparison to the profit he cleared a few years later with a savvy investment on Hennepin Avenue. In 1977 he and his brother paid $950,000 to purchase the Gopher and Aster theaters from their longtime owner, Ben Berger. At the time most of the public hand-wringing over the sale concerned the Alexanders' plans to turn the Gopher into yet another porn house. (Berger had been showing soft-core X-rated films at the

Aster for years.)[73] But the Gopher's life as an adults-only theater was a short one. The city was eyeing the Gopher and Aster property for a new development called City Center. Two years after Alexander acquired the theaters, he sold them to the city for $1.5 million. With the money he made from that sale, he then opened a new adult theater and bookstore on the stretch of Hennepin Avenue known as Block E. The city had big plans for that property, too.[74]

Alexander had done just as well, if not better, with St. Paul real estate. In 1983 the city bought five of Alexander's St. Paul properties, including two bookstores and the G&M Bar, "the most notorious bar in the city," for $1.7 million. The purchase of the properties was an integral part of the city's plan to clear space for its top development project—the World Trade Center. Mayor George Latimer hailed the deal as "an extraordinary piece of work." But critics weren't so sure. County assessors estimated the properties were worth only about one-third as much as the city paid for them.[75] Alexander was walking away with much more money than most people believed he deserved. It looked like Alexander got the best of the city. And he even got to keep his only St. Paul theater—the Flick.

The Flick was one of two pornography theaters at the corner of University Avenue and Dale Street, about two miles west of downtown. The other was one of St. Paul's oldest movie houses—the Faust. For nearly ten years the Faust and the Flick had dominated the city's porn film business. (Their only competitor was the Las Vegas Theater [the old Lyceum] downtown.) During that time Alexander and his counterparts at the Faust had fought off the city's every effort to shut them down. In his new deal with the city, Alexander had managed to retain possession of the Flick despite demands that he include it in the purchase package. But he did make one concession. He agreed to sell the Flick to the city for a reasonable $300,000, but only if the Faust went out of business within the next four years. It was a concession that Alexander soon came to regret.

City officials were now on the clock. They had forty-eight months to get rid of the Faust—and by extension, the Flick. Nothing much happened on the Faust-Flick front for the first year and a half after Alexander made his deal with the city. But in 1985 the efforts to rid University and Dale of its two most notorious commercial enterprises gained new momentum. Antipornography activists led by St. Paul city council member Bill Wilson launched an eight-month-long picketing cam-

CONTINUOUS DAILY LIVE ENTERTAINMENT   CONTINUOUS XXX RATED MOVIES

FAUST   NOW SHOWING - "LILITH UNLEASHED" '45' LOVELY DANCERS DAILY COMING SOON, TALES OF CANTERBURY   FAUST

paign outside both theaters. "The neighborhood people in the community are just tired of having their children exposed to this sort of thing,"
Wilson explained. "This activity is not proper or appropriate in a neighborhood." Alexander's attorney, Randall Tigue, dismissed the effort as a
useless waste of time. "After all," he said, "it is bigotry to try to provoke
the community to coerce us out of business because they don't like the
contents of the publications [and films] we provide."[76]

The protests did not succeed in shutting down the Faust and the
Flick, but they did elevate the fight against pornography to a kind of
cause célèbre in St. Paul. Where once the Faust and the Flick had operated largely in the shadows, now they were caught in the public spotlight. City officials, frustrated by their inability to purge the intersection
of its seedy reputation, ramped up their efforts to close down the Faust
before their four-year option to acquire the Flick expired. A provisional
plan to begin condemnation of the property essentially stopped the
clock. Soon representatives of the city's planning department initiated
negotiations with the Faust's Michigan-based owners. After more than
a year of haggling, the two sides reached a deal in early 1989. The city
agreed to buy the Faust for $1.8 million. Having successfully dealt with
the Faust, St. Paul then exercised its option on the Flick.[77] Alexander
went to court in hopes of invalidating his 1983 agreement with the city

Protesters repre-
senting the St. Paul
Pornography Task
Force stake out their
positions in front of
the notorious Faust,
1986.

(the deal he had agreed to didn't look so good now that the owners of the Faust were receiving $1.8 million), but the court ruled against him. He had no choice but to accept the city's $300,000 and walk away.

In three separate real estate deals with the cities of Minneapolis and St. Paul, Alexander had collected about $4 million. Not all of that money was profit, of course, but a substantial portion of it was. Oppo-

Feature Presentation

Galtier Plaza Cinema 4
175 East 5th Street, St. Paul
Opened 1985

Downtown St. Paul had gone seven years without a movie theater (the Orpheum's short comeback attempt in 1982 didn't really count) when the Galtier Plaza Cinema 4 opened in late 1985. Marvin Mann's new four-screen theater was located on the third level of Galtier Plaza, a new downtown development that embodied the urban renewal hopes of many St. Paul boosters. The largest of its four auditoriums seated 310 people; the smallest accommodated just 112. It was a smart little theater that abandoned many of the previous decade's dull, multiplex ways. The auditoriums, for example, featured waterfall-screen curtains and wall draperies reminiscent of earlier dazzlers like the Har Mar 1 & 2.[1] Unfortunately, the Galtier didn't stand a chance. Downtown St. Paul's inability to reinvigorate its service economy ensured the theater's eventual demise. The Galtier showed its last feature film in 1999 and was later converted into a high-tech corporate event and presentation facility.[2]

The Galtier Plaza Cinema 4 gave downtown St. Paul a welcome infusion of glitter, but it failed to attract the crowds it needed to survive.

nents of the deals criticized paying off pornographers as bad public policy. But others were more sympathetic. "It turns our stomachs to imagine owners of the Faust and the Flick Theaters in St. Paul riding off into the sunset with bank accounts fattened by funds of good and decent citizens," the editors of the *St. Paul Pioneer Press Dispatch* wrote, following the city's acquisition of the theaters. "But the benefits of a settlement, for the city as a whole, and for the Dale-University areas especially, justify the buyout."[78] It was possible that, as the *Pioneer Press Dispatch* suggested, Alexander intended to ride off into the sunset after selling his theaters to the same cities that had been trying for years to drive him out of business, but even if that was his plan, it was not to be.

On May 31, 1989—a week after Alexander lost his final appeal in the Flick case—a federal grand jury indicted Alexander and three others on multiple obscenity, tax, and racketeering charges. The indictments were the result of a two-year investigation by the Federal Bureau of Investigation and the Internal Revenue Service. In announcing the indictments, the head of the FBI's Minneapolis office, Jeffrey Jamar, described Alexander as the kingpin of a vast illegal enterprise—one that had "a tremendous [negative] impact on the community." The government not only hoped to send Alexander to prison but planned to use federal racketeering laws to seize Alexander's assets. "The idea is to end the conduct, not let [him] serve five years and walk away with millions of dollars," Jamar said.[79]

It took nine months for the case to go to trial. In his testimony Alexander claimed that he was a simple businessman who catered to his customers' wishes. He said he was unschooled in many of the intricacies of running a business and trusted others to handle his legal and financial affairs. When the prosecutor asked Alexander why he often used aliases in his business dealings, he explained that he had no choice: when people heard his name, they wanted nothing to do with him. "I don't know why," he said. "I'm not a bad guy."[80]

In the end the jury decided that he was a bad guy. Alexander was convicted on twenty-five counts of obscenity, tax fraud, and racketeering.[81] He was sentenced to six years in prison. The government confiscated nearly $9 million worth of books, videotapes, and other inventory from his many properties.[82] Alexander appealed the seizure of his assets, claiming that the government had violated his constitutional rights, but the U.S. Supreme Court disagreed. In a five-to-four decision the justices ruled that the government had acted properly in confiscating assets resulting from Alexander's "prior racketeering offenses."[83] Alexander's

Ferris Alexander confronts reporters after his conviction on obscenity, tax fraud, and racketeering charges.

© 2007 STAR TRIBUNE/Minneapolis–St. Paul

luck had run out. The man who had turned some of the Twin Cities' proudest neighborhood theaters into murky dens of pornography headed off to prison. In the epilogue to their coverage of the original trial, the editors of the *Star Tribune* rejoiced that Alexander would no longer be able to bring neighborhoods "down to his own grimy level." But they also acknowledged that he had, in one respect, won the battle.

> *Ironically. One reason Alexander's kind of enterprise appears on the way out is that the business of selling sex has gone legit. The same stuff Alexander has been selling behind painted over windows is now available in splashy video stores and otherwise mainstream newsstands. There thus appears to be little danger that the verdicts against him will seriously infringe on anyone's right to read or view sexually explicit material.*
>
> *[They] should, however, help keep many urban neighborhoods and business districts clean, decent and safe. [They] may even give some a chance to recover from the rot that Alexander brought with him. The reign of the porn king is over. May his like not be seen again.*[84]

RENAISSANCE

*F*or three-quarters of a century, thousands upon thousands of Twin Cities moviegoers had trekked to the downtown loops to catch the latest Hollywood attractions. In Minneapolis they packed a string of movie theaters stretching down Hennepin Avenue. In St. Paul they congregated at a cluster of cinemas within a few blocks of the corner of Seventh and Wabasha. Inside the theaters patrons lost themselves for an hour or two in make-believe worlds populated by glamorous film stars. Outside they blended into electric cityscapes of assertive marquees and flashing signs with stacked letters (O-R-P-H-E-U-M; L-Y-R-I-C; S-T-A-T-E) that extended high into the urban night. Hennepin Avenue in Minneapolis and Seventh Street in St. Paul shimmered with Hollywood-generated excitement. They were alive with movies. But by the mid-1980s the movies had all but abandoned downtown.

In Minneapolis the Orpheum, Mann, Academy, and World were slowly deteriorating behind boarded windows and padlocks. The Gopher and Aster were mere memories, having been replaced several years earlier by the new City Center development. And the State was limping along not as a movie theater but as the spiritual home of the Jesus People Church. The Skyway was still operating, but whatever appeal it once had had vanished after being carved into a six-screen multiplex. Besides the Skyway, the only place to see a movie on Hennepin Avenue was Ferris Alexander's makeshift Adonis Theater, and the Adonis catered primarily to gay men.

The situation was no better in St. Paul. The city's only remaining downtown movie theater, the Galtier 4, was struggling. The Strand was gone, as were the Riviera and the Lyceum. What remained of the old theater district along Seventh Street bore little resemblance to its former self. The city had turned the block between Wabasha and St. Peter into a pedestrian plaza in the name of downtown revitalization. But Seventh Place, as the plaza was known, had devolved into a bleak corridor lined with empty storefronts. The retired Norstar Theater came to life occasionally for performances of the Actors Theatre stage company. Across the plaza the Orpheum—dark since 1982—served as the temporary home of Garrison Keillor's live public radio program *A Prairie Home Companion*. But between shows the area displayed little of the urban exuberance for which it once was known.

The Twin Cities' surviving downtown theaters—the ones that for years had played movies—were now in limbo. They had endured through the knock-down-build-up urban renewal era of the 1960s and 1970s, but they remained endangered. Classic theaters were vanishing

St. Paul's restored
World Theater looked
much as it did in 1910,
when it debuted as
the Shubert.

from cities throughout the nation. Moviegoers no longer came downtown to see a show. They stayed in the suburbs. If the Twin Cities' old
downtown theaters were going to survive, they would have to adapt.
They would have to leave the movies behind.

The movement to find new uses for old movie houses began in St.
Paul, a couple blocks north of Seventh and Wabasha, at the World Theater. The World was St. Paul's oldest surviving show house. It had
debuted as the Sam S. Shubert Theater in August of 1910 (its fraternal
twin, the Minneapolis Shubert, opened almost simultaneously) and
had hobbled along for twenty years as a moderately successful legitimate theater and vaudeville house. In 1933 Al Steffes acquired the Shubert, gave it an art deco makeover, and renamed it the World. From that
moment on, stage shows were out; movies were in. Over the years the
World went through a series of incarnations—first as a venue for art

films, then as a first-run ace house, and finally as the city's slightly seedy home of second-run movies and double features. By the 1970s the World had severed nearly every outward link to its live theater past. Its lobby was clad in shabby wood and vinyl wall coverings. Vertical wooden battens covered curved boxes that had once offered intimate views of the stage. And a false ceiling concealed a second balcony that had not been used since the days of the Great Depression.[1] John Elzey, a student of early theater in St. Paul, was one of the few people to catch a glimpse of what was hidden above the ceiling tiles.

> *Finding a flashlight and a portion of an old-style doorknob, the manager walked to an ancient blue, wood paneled door. He inserted the doorknob spindle, opened the door, and led the way up a narrow stairway. When he reached the top, the manager screwed a light bulb into the socket of a wall sconce, and in the musty dimness one could make out the old balcony. Paper was peeling, plaster had fallen away, and the dust of ages was everywhere. It was strange looking down on top of the false ceiling, hanging suspended from its many wires. From beneath came the garish sounds of a James Bond movie.[2]*

When General Cinema finally abandoned the World in the fall of 1977, it appeared that the old theater would probably be demolished to make way for yet another parking lot. But as it happened, Minnesota Public Radio (MPR) was looking for a new home for its increasingly popular live entertainment program, *A Prairie Home Companion*. It leased the World, tore away the false ceiling, and reclaimed the theater's long-neglected stage. For six years, host Garrison Keillor and his band of radio performers broadcast their weekly program live from the World. But in early 1984 the ceiling—the real one—of the old theater began crumbling. Flakes and chunks of plaster showered down on the audience. Keillor and his crew escaped to the vacant Orpheum. Now the question was what to do about the World.

The executives at MPR could have settled for ceiling repairs and left it at that. But after considering all their options, they decided to do something that had never been done at any of the Twin Cities' great show houses: they set out to restore the World to something approaching its original glory. Hardly a square inch of the theater went untouched. Workers installed new plumbing, new electrical wiring, new stage rigging, and a new marquee. The façade regained its dignified presence. The interior, resplendent with intricate plasterwork, polished wood, and gold leaf, rediscovered its long-lost grandeur. The $3.5 million restoration took two years and was nearly complete (the restrooms were in a state of minimal usefulness) when *A Prairie Home Companion* returned to the World in January of 1986. In his opening monologue Keillor reminded listeners that the program was "coming to you live for the first time in a long time from our old home in the World Theater... at the crossroads of downtown St. Paul."[3] Minnesota Public Radio had proven that old downtown theaters were worth reviving—not as movie houses but as live performance spaces. It was a lesson that Minneapolis had yet to learn.

*I*n the fall of 1985, as workers across the river rushed to finish the refurbishing of the World, the two thousand members of the Jesus People Church—the congregation that had been worshiping for six years at the State Theater on Hennepin Avenue—packed up their Bibles and baptismal font and headed for the suburbs. Once they were gone, it became clear that they had left the State in curious condition. Over the years the members of the congregation had spent more than a million dollars on upkeep, but in doing so, they had altered the theater's flamboyant interior. Modesty, for example, had compelled them to cover up the unclothed plaster cherubs that populated the auditorium.[4] Structurally, the State was in remarkable shape for its age (it was sixty-four years old), but it still felt obsolete. It was a theater with no obvious purpose. The Jesus People Church didn't want it anymore. Exhibitors

The State Theater might have succumbed to the push for urban renewal had it not found temporary life as the spiritual home of the Jesus People Church.

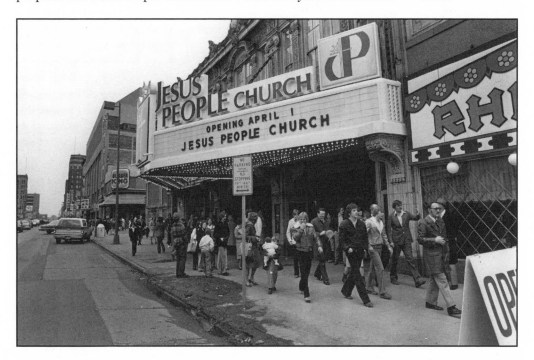

had long since abandoned hope that picture palaces could turn a profit. No one had put forward a serious proposal to convert the theater into a live performance venue, as MPR had done with the World. By default the State now appeared to be doomed.

Less then two weeks after the Jesus People Church held its last service at the State, the Minneapolis city council began considering the theater's fate. The building's owners wanted the council to let them tear it down to make way for a new $130 million retail and office complex. There was no way, they insisted, to preserve the State intact within the scope of the project. But preservationists, emboldened by the successful restoration of the World, rose up to oppose the plan. "It's the last remaining theater from the 1920s," said Charlene Roise, president of the Preservation Alliance of Minnesota. "It has unquestioned historical and architectural significance. We owe it to ourselves to keep it around."[5] Russell Fridley, the director of the Minnesota Historical Society, agreed. "We think it's an important historic site of statewide significance," he explained. "It's a unique example and the finest example of a theater of that era in the entire state."[6]

The council was split. Most members shared a desire to burnish Hennepin Avenue's tarnished image, but some were reluctant to sacrifice any more of the city's architectural heritage. "I'd like to see some real interest on the part of the developer to do something innovative," said council member Sharon Sayles-Belton. "They have a record for historic preservation in other cities. I'd like to see it demonstrated here." Sayles-Belton and her allies advocated designating the State as a historic structure—an action that would prohibit the developers from altering the building's exterior without city approval. Supporters of the developers' plan were skeptical. "I would like to see [the State] saved if feasible, but there are a tremendous number of theaters in Minneapolis," council member Barbara Carlson argued. "No one [else] has come in with a proposal. I'm afraid we'll have to say goodbye to the developer if the theater is designated for historic preservation."[7]

The debate dragged on for months. At one point the developers offered to save a few pieces of the theater and incorporate them into the project, but preservationists dismissed the idea as unworkable. "It's like cutting out the Mona Lisa's eyes, lips and nose and putting [them] into an 8-by-10 chrome and glass frame," said Robert Roscoe of the city's Heritage Preservation Commission. "For sure you wouldn't have the smile anymore."[8] Finally, in the fall of 1986, the standoff ended. The developers agreed to incorporate the entire theater—not just pieces of it—into their plans. The council responded favorably. It approved the project and authorized $29 million in tax increment bonds to finance the development. Under the agreement the city pledged to cover all costs related to the restoration of the State and to assume ownership of the revamped theater as it neared completion.[9] The city of Minneapolis was officially in the theater business.

Legal snags slowed the process, but the dusty work of rehabilitating the State finally got under way in 1990. Scaffolding went up. Decaying plaster came down. Layers of acoustical tiles were removed, revealing long-forgotten murals. Immodest plaster cherubs reappeared after years of church-imposed exile. New chandeliers, dripping with crystal and cobalt blue glass grapes, were lowered over the auditorium. Dutch metal—more affordable than gold leaf—swathed the walls and statuary. The old stage house, which was too shallow to accommodate modern Broadway touring shows, was lopped off to create a much roomier space. The State was returning to its grandiose roots. "I agree with Liberace," said restoration specialist Ray Shepardson. "Too much of a good thing is wonderful."[10] As work progressed, the city's investment in the

Feature Presentation

Willow Creek Cinema
9500 Shelard Parkway,
Plymouth
Opened 1989

Cineplex Odeon, which led the movement to inject more glamour into the multiplex, put its concepts to work for the first time in the Twin Cities at the eight-screen, 2,000-seat Willow Creek Cinema in Plymouth. Willow Creek was unlike previous multiplexes in the metro area. With its marble floors, "striking interior design," comfortable seats, and wide screens, it encouraged patrons to demand more from their moviegoing experience than they had come to expect during the dull old days of the 1970s and early

The opening of Cineplex Odeon's Willow Creek Cinema in 1989 ushered in the new luxury multiplex trend in the Twin Cities.

1980s. Like most of Cineplex Odeon's new theaters, Willow Creek put a high priority on popcorn, candy, and pop. Its large concession stand, located in the center of the lobby, featured the latest equipment, designed to simplify serving and allow the hiring of inexperienced and inexpensive workers.[1]

The renovated State.

restoration project—originally set at $5.8 million—rose quickly to $8.8 million.[11] Critics complained about the escalating costs, but nearly everyone who witnessed the theater's transformation insisted the results were worth the investment. "This area has a lot of theaters, but there aren't going to be many like this one," said Fred Krohn, the president of the group that had been hired to manage the State. "You're going to walk in there and know you're in a theater."[12]

On October 27, 1991, ninety-five-year-old musician Andre Basque sat down at a grand piano on the stage of the newly restored State Theater and began playing a vaguely familiar but exotic tune. As he played, a dancer draped in red struck poses that conjured images of ancient Egypt. Sixty-eight years earlier, in 1923, Basque and another dancer—Olga Ziceva—had performed the same number on the same stage during a vaudeville-style prelude to the showing of the Norma Talmadge film *Within the Law*. Now he was repeating the performance at the State's grand reopening. He was one of the Twin Cities' last living links to the days of silent movies and Finkelstein and Ruben. The spotlight seemed to agree with him. "It's such a wonderful place," he said of the refurbished State. "It's a real theater again." As was the case in 1923, Basque's performance was the opening act for what was actually the main attraction. The following week, the State debuted its first big show, the Minnesota Opera's staging of *Carousel*. Its days as a picture palace were over, but its new life as a stage for live performances was just beginning. Critics suspected that the State ultimately would prove to be a money pit, but others remained optimistic. "The State has been saved," wrote the editors of the *Star Tribune*. "The dreamers were right."[13]

$\mathcal{I}$t had been years since a mainstream Hollywood film had sparked the kind of moral outrage that had once inspired those Twin Citians who were easily offended to boycott local movie theaters. (The porn films favored by Ferris Alexander's customers fell into a separate category.) Audiences were becoming increasingly desensitized to on-screen nudity and violence. It was hard to imagine, for example, that anyone had ever believed Jane Russell's cleavage posed a threat to public morality. Even so, Hollywood still was capable of producing movies that offended the sensibilities of some Twin Cities moviegoers. And some subjects automatically invited scrutiny—religion, for instance.

On the evening of August 12, 1988, nearly four hundred people gathered outside the Cooper Theater in St. Louis Park to express their outrage over a new movie called *The Last Temptation of Christ*. The film, directed by Martin Scorsese, depicted Jesus Christ as a man who doubted his own divinity. In one scene that particularly angered many Christians, the title character dreamed that he married and made love to the prostitute Mary Magdalene. The day before in California, an estimated 25,000 demonstrators had packed the streets outside Universal Studios to protest the movie's world premiere. The rally outside

A prayer vigil outside the Cooper Theater during the local premiere of *The Last Temptation of Christ*, 1988.

the Cooper was one of nine follow-up demonstrations held in cities across the United States.[14]

Roman Catholic archbishop John Roach of St. Paul had stoked opposition to the movie by declaring that it "distorts the Jesus people know from the Gospels and is sure to be highly offensive to many."[15] None of the protesters who showed up at the Cooper had seen the film, but most agreed with Roach's assessment. "It's a movie straight from hell," proclaimed a demonstrator from St. Agnes Catholic Church in St. Paul. "People have a duty to stand up against evils in our community."[16] The protesters carried placards denouncing the movie, handed out leaflets, sang hymns, and prayed. At one point one of them asked a woman entering the theater why she was "going to see something that degrades the Lord?" The woman replied that she had the right to go wherever she wanted and that she didn't "need some religious person who hasn't seen the movie telling me otherwise."[17]

Anyone familiar with the history of protests against movies in the Twin Cities could have predicted the results of the demonstrations outside the Cooper. If anything, the public haranguing of *The Last Temptation of Christ* only boosted the Cooper's box office take—and this for a movie that many reviewers had already panned as boring. "I just wanted to see what the big deal was all about," explained one moviegoer from New Hope. "The hype attracted my curiosity about the film." The 7:00 PM showing at the Cooper was just a few seats short of a sellout.[18]

*T*he stretch of Hennepin Avenue between Sixth Street North and Seventh Street North—widely known as Block E—was a civic embarrassment. Its best-known bar, Moby Dick's, was, in the words of at least one police officer, a "literal den of thieves." A few doors down, Brady's Pub had a similar reputation. Dubious characters of various descriptions flopped at the Rand Hotel. Pinballers with twitchy fingers fed quarters into willing machines at Pete's Sport Center. At Ferris Alexander's American Empress customers perused stacks of magazines, many of which could not be found down the way at Shinder's newsstand. Alexander's Adonis Theater showed movies that definitely were not made for family audiences. Drug dealers, pimps, and thugs prowled the sidewalk. Police records showed that the block accounted for about a quarter of all the crimes reported downtown. It was, said Minneapolis city council president Alice Rainville, "a place to find vice at a price."[19]

But Block E also was home to two of the city's oldest theaters: the Academy and the World. The Academy had opened in 1910 as the Shubert Theater. The World, which debuted five years later, was originally known as the Garden. Both theaters fronted Seventh Street—not Hennepin—but their status as defunct movie houses added to the perception that the entire block had descended into a state of perpetual decay. In 1988 city planners decided that the time had come to rid downtown of its most notorious eyesore. Block E was condemned. Every building—even the Academy and the World—was slated for demolition.

Few people, if any, shed tears for the World. It was an architectural nonentity. The Academy was a different matter. When the Minneapolis Community Development Agency recommended that the theater not be saved, preservationists mobilized. They began referring to the old theater by its original name—the Shubert—in an effort to emphasize its historical significance. They also played up the superior characteristics of its interior. The Shubert's broad and shallow auditorium had what real estate developer Charles Leer would later call "the unique ability to bring audience and performer together." Skeptics pointed out that Ted Mann had scrubbed the theater of much of its charm when he turned it into a motion picture house back in the 1950s. Leer and other preservationists countered that the skeptics had it all wrong.

> In public discussions of the preservation of the Shubert, too much has been made of the deterioration or removal of the original decorative elements, such as the ornamental ceiling, boxes and plaster work, and the excessive cost of restoring them. Restoration of the architectural details misses the point. The surface appearance is secondary to the interior configuration and function.[20]

In the end the old theater won a reprieve. The city went ahead with the demolition of most of Block E—including the World—but left the Shubert standing. Minneapolis's oldest surviving show house would remain where it was until a plan for the rebirth of the entire block was in place. Maybe the Shubert would be incorporated into the new development, whatever it turned out to be. Maybe it wouldn't. But at least it would survive to see another day.[21] The Shubert had made history as the home of Buzz Bainbridge's stage company, as the first Minneapolis theater to show *The Birth of a Nation*, as a burlesque house, as a church, and as Ted Mann's classiest downtown cinema. It deserved one last chance to live.

*C*orporatized, cookie-cutter multiplexes now dominated the movie exhibition landscape—both nationally and locally. By the late 1980s three national chains—United Artists, General Cinema, and Cineplex

Odeon (the successor to the old Plitt theater circuit)—controlled more than half of all the screens in the Minneapolis–St. Paul metropolitan area. Most of the big circuits' theaters were nondescript 1970s-vintage multiscreen cinemas like UA's Maplewood I and II and General Cinema's four-screen Southdale in Edina. Many were located inside or adjacent to shopping malls. Nearly all of them contained between three and seven screens. The only exceptions were a trio of eight-screeners: UA's Brookdale Square and General Cinema's Burnhaven and Har Mar annex. (The original three-screen Har Mar was—by location and design—a separate theater.) Of the scores of single-screen theaters that had once peppered the Twin Cities area, only six were still in business: the Suburban World, Uptown, Parkway, Riverview, and Campus in Minneapolis and the Heights in Columbia Heights. And most of them were struggling to get by.

Over the years the Twin Cities' movie trade had produced a succession of local theater chain operators who reveled in competing head-to-head with the national circuits. Moses Finkelstein, Isaac Ruben, Louis Rubenstein, Abe Kaplan, Al Steffes, Ben Berger, Bill Volk, Sidney Volk, Ted Mann—they all had done their part to maintain a good dose of local control over the movie business in Minneapolis and St. Paul. But by the late 1980s the national chains had achieved almost total hegemony. The Engler family, which had operated theaters in the Twin Cities for nearly sixty years, had sold out a few years earlier. Only one local exhibitor was capable of competing directly with the nationals. And he had a familiar name.

Steve Mann was a second-generation exhibitor with an impressive pedigree. His father, Marvin Mann, and his uncle, Ted Mann, had dominated the Twin Cities' movie business for many years. Now he was trying to build a regional theater chain of his own. His company, Cinemaland (later, Mann Theaters), operated ten theaters in the Twin Cities area, including venerable movie houses like the Grandview, Highland, and Suburban World and aging multiscreen complexes like the Village 4 in Coon Rapids and the Apache 6 in Columbia Heights. Steve Mann had grown up among some of the Twin Cities' most successful movie exhibitors and had seen how the business had changed over the past two decades. As the 1980s came to a close, he was plotting an expansion strategy based in part on the proposition that the movie exhibition business had strayed too far from its roots. Mann and many of his competitors were convinced that their customers were growing weary of no-frills theaters with tiny screens, poor sight lines, and sticky floors. They

Steve Mann, left, and
brother Benji Mann
with a lobby display
for the movie *Congo*,
1994.

believed it was time to reintroduce a little magic into the moviegoing experience. "There's definitely a trend around the country toward making movie theaters more luxurious," he said.[22]

The move to lavish luxury upon the moviegoing public had begun several years earlier with the rise of Cineplex Odeon. The Canadian-based company had grown exponentially during the 1980s, thanks largely to its rethinking of the multiplex concept. Cineplex Odeon's new theaters were, when compared with earlier multiplexes, bigger (with at least eight screens), fancier (with inlaid marble floors and custom-designed carpets), and more convenient (with massive, well-staffed concession stands). Whereas the auditoriums in the old bare-bones shoebox theaters were long, narrow, and low-ceilinged, Cineplex Odeon's auditoriums were short, wide, and lofty. The new configuration allowed for bigger screens and created the impression of spaciousness. The main objective, according to the company's corporate literature, was to create an atmosphere "reminiscent of the movie palaces of the 1920s."[23]

Cineplex Odeon opened its first new Twin Cities theater, the Willow Creek Cinemas, in the Minneapolis suburb of Plymouth in the spring of 1989. Willow Creek was an eight-screen, 2,000-seat complex done up in art deco style. Audience members glided through the lobby on polished marble floors. They settled into plush seats set off from each other to provide unobstructed views of the oversized screen. And they

Feature Presentation

Mall of America 14
I-494 and 24th Avenue
South, Bloomington
Opened 1992

General Cinema's fourteen-screen multiplex in the new Mall of America shopping center once ranked as the largest in Minnesota. The seating capacities of its auditoriums ranged from 136 to 453.[1] In all, it could accommodate about four thousand moviegoers at one time. The Mall of America 14 was similar in design to another recently completed GCC complex, Centennial Lakes 8 in Edina. The color scheme was heavy on red. The auditoriums were short and broad, with high ceilings and wide screens. Its layout was Y-shaped, with seven auditoriums on each arm. The lobby featured a large central concession stand, while both of the auditorium wings had their own smaller concession areas. The Mall of America 14 also was among the first cinemas in Minnesota to make special accommodations for patrons in wheelchairs. The back rows of most of the auditoriums included open areas for full access. The larger auditoriums included wheelchair seating areas located in plateaus about halfway down the aisles.[2]

General Cinema's Mall of America 14 was just one of many attractions at Bloomington's new megamall.

munched popcorn drizzled with real butter—not the yellowish, butter-like substitute that had become a multiplex staple in the 1970s. The renaissance of the Twin Cities movie theater was underway.

The following year brought the debuts of two more eight-screeners, both of which followed the pattern established by Cineplex Odeon. General Cinema opened the Centennial Lakes 8 a few blocks south of Edina's Southdale shopping center. Centennial Lakes 8 replaced the old Southdale theater, which had opened as the Cinema I & II—the Twin Cities' first two-screen theater—back in 1964. Also that year, Steve Mann introduced his first eight-plex, the Mann Maple Grove, in hopes of drawing audiences from Minneapolis's fast-growing northwestern suburbs. Both theaters offered customers a moviegoing experience far superior to the kind they had endured at the old multiplexes. "The whole idea of presentation has become very important to the exhibitors," explained General Cinema's Robert Miller after overseeing the successful opening at Centennial Lakes. "We're seeing a lot more old-fashioned amenities, like waterfall curtains, that add to the presentation of a movie."[24]

Two years later, General Cinema upped the ante even further with the opening of a fourteen-screen theater at the new Mall of America in Bloomington. Like the Centennial Lakes 8, the Mall of America 14 had all the extras that moviegoers were coming to expect, including wide screens, state-of-the-art sound systems, and comfortable seats with ample leg room and (this was new) drink holders built into the armrests. But the addition of such a large theater complex in the southwest metro area created a sticky problem. General Cinema already operated three theaters in the vicinity: Southtown, Burnhaven, and Centennial Lakes. It seemed inevitable that those cinemas would now lose business to the new complex at the megamall. But Mike Skradski, the manager of the Mall of America 14, insisted he wasn't worried. "It's better to have our hand in our pocket than to have someone else's," he said.[25] Even so, the cannibalizing of older theaters by the big chains remained a real menace.

*O*n the evening of January 31, 1991, the credits for the film *Dances with Wolves* finished rolling across the huge screen at the Cooper Theater in St. Louis Park, and the curtain closed. It was a tribute of sorts. The curtain was ripped. It had been more than a year since it had been used to open or close a show. But the employees at the Cooper decided that the time was right to give the massive swath of torn fabric a final bow. The Cooper—the longtime home of Cinerama in the Twin Cities—had finished its twenty-nine-year run.[26]

Some people speculated that the Cooper had been done in by the construction of Interstate 394 just beyond its parking lot. Others mentioned the heavy costs of renovation, made prohibitive by the recent discovery of asbestos insulation within the theater's walls. But in the end the Cooper fell victim to the whims of a changing marketplace. It was, in effect, killed by a corporate sibling.

Cineplex Odeon had acquired the Cooper along with a portfolio of other Twin Cities cinemas when it bought Plitt Theaters in 1985. In the years since then, it had failed to invest in the Cooper's upkeep. The seats were tattered. The carpets were worn. The walls were smudged. The air conditioning system broke down at inopportune times. Moviegoers who recalled coming to the Cooper to watch big-screen spectacles like *This Is Cinerama* and *It's a Mad, Mad, Mad, Mad World* were dismayed to discover how far the old, round theater had fallen.[27]

Closing night at the Cooper.

© 2007 STAR TRIBUNE/Minneapolis–St. Paul

But to those familiar with the workings of the modern movie industry, the Cooper's passing came as no surprise. Cineplex Odeon's first newly constructed theater in the Twin Cities, Willow Creek, was just three miles away. The company had little interest in operating two theaters so close to each other. If one had to go, the Cooper was the obvious choice. When a deal to sell the Cooper to General Mills fell through (General Mills had proposed tearing down the theater and replacing it with an Olive Garden restaurant), executives at Cineplex Odeon made it clear that they would not transfer ownership to anyone who wanted to continue running it as a cinema. It didn't matter to them that many Twin Cities moviegoers harbored fond memories of the Cooper. Cineplex Odeon wanted to make sure it didn't open the door to a potential competitor.[28]

After the curtain closed on *Dances with Wolves*, several members of the audience lingered to offer eulogies. "I canceled everything to be here tonight," said a thirty-three-year-old man who remembered coming to the Cooper to see *How the West Was Won* twenty-six years earlier. "My wife understands," he added. Another man, who had come to the Cooper that night unaware that it was about to close, seemed genuinely crestfallen after hearing the news. "There's another piece of my childhood," he said. "If you grew up in St. Louis Park in the sixties, you grew up at the Cooper."[29] A year later, the Cooper was gone.

One by one, a procession of semitrailers backed up to the loading docks behind the Orpheum Theater on Hennepin Avenue. With military-like efficiency road crews unloaded the trucks' contents: 375 costumes, tons of lighting equipment, and a mind-boggling assortment of set pieces, including an 8,000-pound helicopter and a 600-pound statue of Vietnamese leader Ho Chi Minh.[30] The touring production of the hit Broadway musical *Miss Saigon* was set to open at the Orpheum in a matter of days—on January 11, 1994. Anticipation was high. A few years earlier, it would have been hard to imagine that any Broadway show—let alone one as big as *Miss Saigon*—would play at this particular venue.

The Orpheum, like every other theater on Hennepin Avenue, had fallen on hard times. Originally designed for vaudeville, it had spent most of its life as a motion picture house. Ted Mann had turned it back into a venue for live stage performances in the early 1960s, and for a while it did very well. But it wasn't long before the crowds started to dwindle. Mann sold out. By the mid-1970s the Orpheum had fallen into the hands of a group of investors led by singer Bob Dylan. But by that time the Hennepin Avenue theater district had lost its luster. The Orpheum went dark for long stretches. It fell into disrepair. Flaps of peeling paint hung from its ornate ceiling. Vagrants climbed fire escapes to sleep on its roof.[31] In 1988 Dylan put the troubled theater on the market. The question was, who would want to buy it? As it turned out, the city did.

Minneapolis had acquired the State Theater, just a block down Hennepin, about a year and a half earlier. Now the city had an opportunity to add another historic show house to its portfolio. Supporters of the idea imagined a reinvigorated entertainment district anchored by two resurrected theaters. Opponents argued that the city should avoid sinking money into such a financially dubious enterprise. In the end, though, the supporters won. The city of Minneapolis was now the proud owner of two decrepit theaters.

For several years the Orpheum remained something of an after-thought as the city focused on the State. But once the State reopened, attention turned to its neglected neighbor. The 2,700-seat Orpheum was larger than the State and could—with work—accommodate even the biggest Broadway megaproductions. In 1992 the city council approved a $10 million renovation of the theater, to be funded primarily by a one-dollar-per-ticket surcharge. Work on the theater soon got under way. The stagehouse was extended thirty feet out toward Tenth Street. New loading docks were added. Dressing rooms, restrooms, and mechanical systems were upgraded. The interior décor was restored.[32] By the time the trucks carrying sets, costumes, and props for *Miss Saigon* arrived in Minneapolis, the Orpheum had rejoined the ranks of the nation's great theaters. A few corners had been cut along the way. The carpeting, for example, had been cleaned rather than replaced. But considering where the old theater had been, and how far it had come, it was hard to complain. "The overall effect is magnificent," the editors of the *Star Tribune* exclaimed, "not only in improving what the audience will see but also in promising to make theater-going at the Orpheum a more comfortable, convenient and satisfying experience than ever before. Bravo!"[33]

*T*he threat of overscreening had been a periodic worry among Twin Cities exhibitors almost from the time movies first became popular during the early years of the century. Now, with the arrival of high-quality multiplexes like Willow Creek, the Centennial Lakes 8, and the Mall of America 14, the threat posed by too many screens was back, and none of the major players in the local movie business seemed anxious to call a truce in what was shaping up to be a theater-building arms race. In late 1993 United Artists opened its largest Twin Cities cinema complex, the Woodbury 10, east of St. Paul. Now all the Twin Cities' biggest exhibitors were in the expansion game. It was getting increasingly difficult to find any place in the metro area that didn't already have more than enough movie screens to serve its population. But that didn't stop theater operators from looking. In Eagan, for example.

The story of how Eagan—a booming suburb south of St. Paul—got its first big theater complex was a tale of dots prevailing over stickpins. For several years Steve Mann had used a map marked with colored dots to trace the development of movie theaters in the Twin Cities area. After a quick glance at this low-tech tracking device, it was obvious that Eagan was one of the few communities in the area that could still accommodate a large multiplex. Mann began entertaining entreaties from a local developer who wanted him to build a theater near Eagan's Town Center shopping mall. "When a theater goes in . . . restaurants follow," Mann explained.[34] Mann considered the idea but did not act immediately.

In the meantime another local exhibitor, Mike Muller, was looking over his own map of the Twin Cities area. Muller was the owner of Muller Family Theatres, a company that operated a chain of cinemas on the outer fringes of the metropolitan area—places like Monticello, Delano, and Waconia. Like Steve Mann, Muller came from a family of theater owners. His grandfather Alfred Muller had endeared himself to his fellow independent exhibitors back in the 1930s by going to court and successfully challenging the standard contract that the big motion pictures studios required film bookers to sign. (The case went all the way to the U.S. Supreme Court.) Now Mike Muller was looking to expand the family theater chain into suburbs closer to Minneapolis and St. Paul. His five-county map, studded with color-coded stickpins— not dots—led him to conclude, as Mann did, that Eagan was ripe for a new movie theater complex. After a quick check of the city's zoning map, he identified what appeared to be the perfect property.

> Found the piece of land. Called the guy. And he said, "Well, what do you want to put up?" And I said, "It's entertainment." "Bowling alley?" "No." We went on and on. He asked me different things. "Roller rink?" He never touched on a theater. He says, "Well, tell me what it is." I say, "Well, we're in the motion picture business." He says, "I got somebody that's already asked." And I say, "Can you tell me who?" "Well I can't at this time," he says, "but give me two weeks and call me back. They come to the table—I have to deal with them. If they don't, we can talk about it."[35]

When Muller called back two weeks later, he discovered that he was too late. Steve Mann had decided to pull the trigger on the Eagan deal and had purchased the same property that Muller had pinpointed. Mann's new nine-screen theater opened in Eagan in November of 1994.

The fact that two local exhibitors had homed in on a single piece of property south of St. Paul demonstrated that the competition to build new theaters in the Twin Cities was intensifying. Shut out of Eagan, Muller set his sights on a less obvious locale—the northeastern metro area. In the summer of 1995, he opened a fourteen-screen complex in White Bear Township. His competitors questioned his judgment. "Fourteen screens?" an incredulous Steve Mann asked. "In White Bear? Whatever turns you on, I guess."[36] It was too early to tell whether

Muller's gamble in White Bear would pay off, but one thing was certain: the rush to build new theaters was far from over. Even bigger cinema complexes were on the way.

*M*ost of the moviegoers who packed the Uptown Theater during the first few weeks of 1993 came to be entertained—and surprised. The word of mouth on the theater's latest offering had been phenomenal. It wasn't what people were saying; it was what they *weren't* saying. The movie contained a plot twist that was almost impossible to predict. Its distributor, Miramax, had begged reviewers not to reveal the secret, and the reviewers had obliged. Now people from around the Twin Cities were streaming into the Uptown to find out what all the buzz was about. At each showing, when the surprise twist was revealed, the audience's reaction was almost always the same. No gasps. No giggles. Just an occasional murmur or whisper. "The only thing you hear," said the film's producer after observing audiences in several cities, "is the whir of people's brains, taking it all in."[37]

The Crying Game was a revelation in more ways than one. Not only did its plot contain a mind-bending turn of events, but its success at the box office helped reconfigure the moviegoing landscape across the United States—and in the Twin Cities. *The Crying Game* was the kind of small-budget independent film that Hollywood typically shunned. Its plot was convoluted. Its stars were not even close to household names. And its main character was an Irish terrorist. But despite its presumed drawbacks, it made a lot of money. At the Uptown, for example, *The Crying Game* brought in $81,000 during its second week—an all-time record for the theater.[38]

For years independent films like *The Crying Game* had been difficult to find in the Twin Cities. The Uptown showed them. So did Bill Irvine at the Parkway. And Al Milgrom at the University Film Society had been toiling diligently since 1962 to bring underappreciated motion pictures by little-known directors to discriminating film buffs. Otherwise, the pickings of independent films were slim at best. But now *The Crying Game* had proved that independent films could draw big audiences in the Twin Cities. Soon films that, in the past, would have gone virtually unnoticed—films like *Howards End, Like Water for Chocolate,* and *Strictly Ballroom*—began showing up in multiplexes. "The malls are wising up," Milgrom observed. "They have seen some gold in those art-film hills."[39]

In 1995 Landmark Theatres, the national chain that owned the Uptown, opened a five-screen sister theater just down the street. The Lagoon Cinema, as it was called, would specialize in independent films, foreign-language cinema, and documentaries. With six screens in the Hennepin-Lake neighborhood, Landmark could now open a film at the Uptown and move it over to the Lagoon if it proved successful. In the past it often had been forced to give up money-making films earlier than it would have liked because of prior commitments at the Uptown.[40]

The big national circuits had already tightened their grip on the mainstream movie theater market in the Twin Cities. Now another chain—Landmark—was moving in to control a niche market. Granted, there weren't many exhibitors in Minneapolis and St. Paul who were trying to make a living out of showing independent films, but those who were knew they would have to adapt. "There are distributors who are

Feature Presentation

Lagoon Cinema
1320 Lagoon Avenue,
Minneapolis
Opened 1995

Located in Minneapolis's hip Uptown district, the Lagoon was the first Twin Cities theater built specifically for showings of independent, foreign-language, and art films that previously had been relegated to old single-screeners like the Parkway and the Campus. The Lagoon's five auditoriums could seat from 124 to 300 people. Its screens were taller than those found in most similarly sized theaters so that every patron had a clear view of the subtitles found on many foreign films. Whimsical touches, including tree-shaped lobby lights and moon-shaped wall sconces, played to the quirky tastes of the theater's unconventional clientele. The conces-

The whimsical appeal of Landmark's Lagoon Cinema.

sion stand, with its selection of fragrant cappuccinos, mochas, and teas, appealed to customers unimpressed by thirty-two-ounce Cokes. The Lagoon was, in many ways, the sister theater

of the much older—and much larger—Uptown Theater, just a block away. New releases often played for a week or two at the Uptown and then moved to the Lagoon for extended runs.[1]

stringing us along because they want to see if they can get into the Lagoon," Al Milgrom said, "but the Lagoon can put on only so many titles. There are many films of quality out there to show." The Parkway's Bill Irvine admitted feeling some trepidation, but he insisted his theater would survive. "Everybody said when the Mall of America came in [with its fourteen screens], we'd be out of business. Well, we're still here," he said. "I'm going to have to play it by ear. I don't know myself how things are going to work out. But it's going to force me to sharpen things up."[41]

*T*he crowd that came to the Mall of America to see the new Jodie Foster film *Contact* wasn't sure what to make of the two goateed gentlemen standing in front of the screen in their slick designer suits. But then the men introduced themselves, and it all began to make sense. They represented one of the big Hollywood studios, and they were looking for discerning moviegoers to attend a sneak preview of the yet-to-be-released film *Great Expectations,* starring Robert De Niro and Gwyneth Paltrow. Or at least that's what they claimed. They passed out a synopsis of the film along with a cast list. They asked some questions about the audience's movie preferences. And then they began the selection process. Invitees had to be between the ages of seventeen and forty-nine and could not be affiliated with the entertainment industry. Those who qualified received passes and were instructed to arrive at Edina's Centennial Lakes multiplex at 5:30 PM the following Monday. The men departed. The audience sat back and enjoyed *Contact.*

The scene outside the Centennial Lakes 8 on July 14, 1997, resembled a Hollywood premiere. The invitees had been told to dress up for the occasion, and more than a few of them had arrived in tuxedos and evening gowns. As they waited in line to get into the theater, they noticed about a dozen fidgety people milling about, separate from the crowd. "There were a lot of Hollywood types there," one of the audience members later recalled. "[They were] dressed a little flashier than we do in Minnesota, moving real fast, looking real nervous." When the doors finally opened, the would-be previewers sifted through a cordon of uniformed guards who were checking to make sure no one sneaked in a camera. At the concession stand pass holders jostled with pushy studio reps who, according to one observer, seemed to think they deserved "their own special, 'I'm from Hollywood, you know,' popcorn."

When all the audience members had taken their seats, a man stood up and made several announcements. Anyone who wanted to go to the restroom would have to carry a special red ticket. No one would be allowed to leave the theater without completing a survey form. The movie ran more than three hours, so those who didn't think they could last that long should leave now while they had the chance. The man also mentioned that the movie featured many special effects—a detail that didn't seem to make sense, given that the film was supposed to be based on a Charles Dickens novel. The man took his seat, as did several other people, some trying to hide their faces behind tubs of popcorn. The lights dimmed. The screen came alive with the image of a colossal passenger ship and the movie's title: *Titanic.*

Most of the people in the audience realized immediately that they had been hoodwinked, but few, if any, were tempted to complain about it. *Titanic* was—unlike *Great Expectations*—a potential blockbuster. Newspapers, magazines, television, and the Internet were bursting with stories about *Titanic:* its whopping $200-million-plus budget; its dreamy stars, Leonardo DiCaprio and Kate Winslet; its allegedly monomaniacal director, James Cameron. For the five hundred or so local film fans who had come to Centennial Lakes to watch *Great Expectations,* this was a stunning turn of events. They were about to become the first people besides Cameron to see the most expensive movie ever made.

The studio executives whose careers hinged on *Titanic'*s box office performance could have screened the sneak preview anywhere, but like Robert Wise and Francis Ford Coppola before them, they had chosen the Twin Cities. "For a movie to be really big, it [has to work] from the middle of the country out," explained Tom Sherak, chairman of 20th Century Fox's domestic film division. "And Minneapolis, to me, represents what the middle is like."

When the movie was over, the members of the audience filled out their surveys and filed out of the theater. A few of them were pulled aside to participate in a twenty-minute focus group discussion attended by James Cameron. Others unwittingly shared their opinions with eavesdroppers strategically deployed in the theater's restrooms. Most of the screeners were impressed with the film. ("The special effects were awesome.") Only a few expressed any major reservations. ("It sank in a big, big way.") One audience member reported that, when Cameron left the theater, he had a huge smile on his face. In an interview later with *Star Tribune* movie critic Colin Covert, Tom Sherak claimed the reaction of the Centennial Lakes crowd convinced the studio that it had a major hit on its hands. "What the screening said to us was that we had an epic that could do very, very well," he said. "[It's] the 1990s version, in our minds, of *Dr. Zhivago*, one of those love stories that could last forever." *Titanic* went on to become the highest-grossing motion picture of all time. It won eleven Academy Awards, including Best Picture.[42]

*G*eneral Cinema's fourteen-screen theater complex at the Mall of America had reigned for five years as the king of the Twin Cities' multiplexes. But usurpers were approaching the gates—and they were coming in numbers that were difficult to fathom. In December of 1997, Illinois-based Kerasotes Theatres opened a sixteen-screen complex in Coon Rapids. The following month, two more multiplexes—Mike Muller's ten-screener in Lakeville (eventually an eighteen- and then twenty-one-screener) and Steve Mann's twelve-screener in Plymouth—debuted in the Twin Cities. And that was just the beginning. Over the next four years ten theater complexes—all of them with at least fifteen screens—opened in the metro area. Apple Valley, Inver Grove Heights, Eagan, Mounds View, Brooklyn Center, Maple Grove, Edina, and Eden Prairie each got one. Oakdale got two. The megaplexes, as they quickly became known, were big and held a common advantage over their predecessors: stadium seating.

Stadium, or tiered, seating actually was nothing new. Several of the Twin Cities' older theaters, including the Suburban World and the Riverview, had been constructed with rows of seats rising at steep angles. But over the years theater architects had abandoned what was once known as bleacher seating in favor of cheaper designs featuring gently sloping floors. With the introduction of the megaplex concept in the mid-1990s (AMC's Grand 24 in Dallas, Texas, was widely considered the first true megaplex), stadium seating quickly established itself as the new industry standard. In traditional theaters the slope between rows never topped four inches. In the new megaplexes, with their stepped floors, each row was at least fourteen inches higher than the one in front of it. "It's all about sightlines," Mike Muller explained. "Unless you have Kevin McHale sitting in front of you, you're guaranteed an unobstructed view."[43]

The megaplexes were nothing more than beefed-up versions of the spiffy Cineplex Odeon–style multiplexes that had begun showing up in the Twin Cities in the late 1980s. But their size (megaplexes could play the most popular movies at staggered times on multiple screens) and amenities (especially stadium seating) gave them significant advantages over theater complexes that a few years earlier had been considered state of the art. As the megaplexes multiplied, their predecessors dropped away. Mike Muller's Lakeville megaplex forced the demise of three older multiplexes in Burnsville: General Cinema's eight-screen Burnhaven and a pair of United Artists four-screeners at the Burnsville Center shopping mall. In the east metro area the addition of two megaplexes in Oakdale triggered the closings of UA's first-generation multiscreeners at Maplewood Mall and its much newer ten-screen complex in Woodbury. In 2001 Megastar's Southdale 16 in Edina put the eleven-year-old Centennial Lakes 8 out of business. A few years later, Steve Mann shut down his multiscreen theaters in Eagan and Maple Grove after national chains opened megaplexes nearby.

The Twin Cities' movie business had always operated as a kind of fraternity. Theater operators like Theo Hays, Al Steffes, George Granstrom, Ben Berger, and Ted Mann had competed with each other—and with the big national circuits like Paramount and RKO—but most of them had considered themselves friends and had adhered to an unwritten code of conduct: exhibitors did not encroach on each other's territory. It just wasn't done. But times had changed. The out-of-state corporations that dominated the megaplex era of movie exhibition did not concern themselves with local traditions. "They build on top [of us]," Steve Mann said. "They don't care what they do. The respect there is gone."[44] Exhibitors were now engaged in a cutthroat game in which each player scrambled to identify the next big megaplex opportunity. The problem was, the Twin

The massive Rosedale AMC almost immediately put two nearby theaters, the Har Mar and Pavilion Place, out of business.

Cities area was nearing the saturation point. Ten years after the arrival of the first megaplex, nearly every theater zone in the area had its own cinema complex with stadium seating. Even downtown Minneapolis.

*A*s the new millennium approached, the prospects for a movie-going renaissance in downtown Minneapolis and downtown St. Paul had never looked bleaker. In a two-week period in April of 1999, the Twin Cities' last surviving downtown theaters—the Skyway in Minneapolis and Steve Mann's Galtier Cinema 4 in St. Paul—went dark. "It's the same old story," Mann said of the vanishing downtown theaters. "You need something to get people downtown or they'll just go to the local suburban theater where it's not a hassle to park."[45] For the first time in nearly a century, there was no place to see a movie in either of the two downtowns. And it didn't look like the situation would change anytime soon. Plans to open a new theater complex in St. Paul's World Trade Center had fallen through. In Minneapolis the only legitimate hopes for the return of downtown movies hinged on the long-stalled redevelopment of the bulldozed stretch of Hennepin Avenue known as Block E. The latest plans for Block E still faced plenty of hurdles, but there now was at least one new reason for optimism: the Shubert Theater was no longer in the way.

The Shubert had been sitting by itself near the southwest corner of the block since 1988, when the city council voted to spare it from the mass demolition that erased most of its neighbors from the downtown cityscape. While its continued presence reassured preservationists, it annoyed would-be developers. None of the redevelopment proposals presented to the city included plans to refurbish the Shubert. As far as developers were concerned, the old theater was just getting in the way. "It just takes away so much rentable area," explained developer Harold Brandt.[46] With the city council desperate to make something out of the gaping emptiness that was Block E, it appeared the Shubert's time had run out. But then the old theater won another reprieve—and just in time.

In the summer of 1998, city council members approved a plan to move the Shubert—all six million pounds of it—to a new address about one and a half blocks down Hennepin Avenue. The following winter, the eighty-eight-year-old show house, perched carefully on seventy hydraulic dollies, set off on a slow motion journey to its new home. It took twelve days for the Shubert to reach its destination, but the snail-like move soon set additional wheels in motion.[47] The theater's new owner, a nonprofit agency called Artspace, began making plans to turn the theater into one of the region's premier dance venues. Over on Block E, developers moved forward with plans to build a huge retail and entertainment complex—including a multiscreen cinema—on what was now a completely vacant chunk of downtown real estate.

When the new Block E development opened in 2002, its main attractions included a fifteen-screen megaplex operated by Crown Theatres, a family-run chain based in Connecticut. Block E's developers had approached several exhibitors about operating the new cinema, but Crown was the only one willing to sign a lease. Crown officials insisted that Minneapolis's population figures—nearly 30,000 people lived downtown and nearly 450,000 were within a five-mile radius—ensured that the Block E megaplex would succeed.[48] Others remained skeptical. Steve Mann, for one, was convinced that the Block E theater would face the same predicament he had encountered with the Galtier Cinema 4 in downtown St. Paul. "Why would you go to a theater in downtown Minneapolis?" he asked. "What reason would you go? You've got to deal

Feature Presentation

**Lakeville 21 Theatre
20653 Keokuk Avenue,
Lakeville
Opened 1998**

Muller Family Theatres' sprawling Lakeville complex, on the southern fringes of the metropolitan area, opened in January of 1998 with ten screens. One month later, it added eight more, making it, in the words of the *Minneapolis Star Tribune*, "the most mega of megaplexes in Minnesota to date."[1] (It eventually expanded to twenty-one screens.) Like most of the megaplexes that debuted in the Twin Cities area near the turn of the millennium, Lakeville offered its patrons stadium seating with rocking chairs and cupholder armrests, high-tech sound systems with Dolby and digital

Mike Muller's Lakeville theater opened with ten screens but was built to accommodate twenty-one.

stereo, a choice of restrooms, and a large lobby with multiple concession stands. Its largest auditorium seated 475 people and boasted a twenty-two-by-fifty-foot screen.

with the element. Downtown's had some problems—muggings and shootings and so on and so forth. You're going to pay for parking. Why would you do it?"[49]

After their first few years operating the Block E 15, representatives of Crown Theatres remained publicly upbeat about the movie business in downtown Minneapolis. But their competitors suspected all was not well on Hennepin Avenue. "It's a nice theater," Steve Mann said of the megaplex on Block E. "It's stadium seating. It's a beautiful complex. I'm just glad it's not mine."[50]

*I*n the fall of 2000, as work proceeded on the new Block E complex, the Minneapolis City Council voted to spend $22 million on three old Hennepin Avenue theaters. A portion of the money was earmarked for further improvements at the previously refurbished State and Orpheum. But the bulk of the sum was set aside to pay for the renovation of the latest addition to the city's theater portfolio: the Mann. The city had acquired the old vaudeville house from Ted Mann the previous year, and now the council members hoped to turn it into a restored live performance venue, along the lines of the State and the Orpheum.[51]

Expectations for the Mann Theater renovation were considerably lower than they were for the State and Orpheum projects. In the words of *Star Tribune* architecture critic Linda Mack, the Mann was "Hennepin Avenue's ugly duckling"—an old playhouse with a plain façade, "buried" inside an unattractive building. "Everyone expected a quick and dirty job," Mack wrote.[52]

But then workers began stripping away the modern décor that had transformed the old RKO Pan into the Mann back in 1961. Behind heavy draperies and sodden wallboard, they found tantalizing hints of the building's past: "ghostly outlines" of long-lost decorations and, in a few cases, intact plaster ornaments that had survived the 1961 makeover. One day, while clearing out the attic, the renovators discovered a collection of boxes. Inside, they found original drawings of the old vaudeville house's interior—its plasterwork, its pilasters and columns. The discovery marked a turning point in the project. "Instead of imagining what the auditorium looked like," Mack wrote, "the designers could see it."

> There was no turning back. The architects redesigned some areas, and the City Council raised the budget. The plaster workers . . . the construction crew . . . the painters . . . and everyone involved gave it their all to create what you see today: a lovely cream-and-gold auditorium punctuated with a touch of blue.

Stripped of the dark gray paint and restored by stained-glass artist Travis Stevens, the [art glass ceiling] monitor is a beauty. The canvas murals that surrounded it weren't restored, but the lovely pumpkin-gold paint on the dome sets off the Kokomo glass. The auditorium's subtle paint scheme, devised by Tony Heinsbergen, son of the original painter, creates a more elegant feel than the State or the Orpheum. Four chandeliers stored in the Orpheum's basement add the perfect touch.[53]

The reborn Pantages.

When the newly restored theater opened in late 2002, the name above its marquee was the same one that had appeared when it originally opened in 1916: Pantages. Forty-one years earlier, Ted Mann had purchased the old show house, modernized it, and given it his own name. If he hadn't done so, it might never have survived the urban renewal purges of the 1960s and 1970s. But now his name was gone from the bright lights of Hennepin Avenue. And given the fact that he had planned to demolish the old Pantages before finally selling it to the city, the retiring of his name should have come as no surprise. Ted Mann did not live to witness the rebirth of his eponymous Minneapolis theater. He died in Los Angeles in 2001.[54]

*T*he Heights Theater in Columbia Heights had never ranked among the Twin Cities' top show houses. Opened in 1926 as a Prohibition-era real estate investment by local brewer Arthur Gluek, the Heights was one of Minneapolis's most far-flung neighborhood theaters. For much of its life, it had played second-, third-, and fourth-run movies to working-class audiences. Like many other neighborhood houses, it had limped along from week to week, making just enough money to keep its

Tom Letness's refurbished Heights Theater was a glittering example of how old neighborhood theaters could be coaxed back to life.

marquee lit. But unlike many similar theaters, it was a survivor. It had endured at least three fires, a close call with a tornado, and three major renovations of questionable merit. It had continued showing films through the tough years of the 1950s and 1960s and had retained its original auditorium while many other single-screen theaters were either being twinned or run out of business by multiplexes. Sometimes it seemed that nothing could kill the Heights. But by the late 1990s, the Heights was reeling.

The old theater on Central Avenue may have been a survivor, but it had not aged particularly well. Its original brick and tile façade was hidden behind steel panels painted an incongruous aqua blue. The auditorium was a stylistic disgrace of shiny turquoise. The windows on the second floor were broken, and snow was blowing in. The plumbing, electrical, heating, and cooling systems were antiquated. When Tom Letness, a potential buyer from South Dakota, took his first tour of the place in the summer of 1998, he couldn't get out fast enough. "I was in this building for five minutes and I was just like, I can't wait to get out of here," he recalled. "I don't like it. It's got the creeps. And I don't want anything to do with it."[55] But Letness's partner, Dave Holmgren, detected promise in the Heights where Letness saw mainly pitfalls. After talking over the upsides and downsides, the two men purchased the aging building and began the long process of restoring the theater.

Despite obvious flaws, the Heights had its buried charms. The auditorium still had its stage, orchestra pit, and dressing rooms—all remnants of the days when management brought in vaudeville acts to supplement the picture shows. Much of the theater's original ornamental plaster was preserved behind featureless World War II–era walls. Inspired by every little treasure they unearthed, Letness and Holmgren slowly restored the Heights' long-obscured charisma. They installed a motorized grand drape of rich scarlet to curtain the proscenium. From the ceiling they suspended antique lead crystal chandeliers. They added a new screen, new projectors, and a new sound system. And in an act of faith that bolstered their reputations as restorers of the first order, they acquired a Wurlitzer organ and mounted its console on an elevating platform in the old orchestra pit. As the audience members settled into their seats before each show, the theater filled with the bellowing sounds of another era as the organist, seated at the console, levitated magically in front of the screen. It had been more than half a century since talking pictures put movie theater organists like Eddie Dunstedter out of work. Now, thanks to Letness and Holmgren, the old music was back.

Letness and Holmgren's lovingly restored Heights was a rarity in the Twin Cities. Only four other single-screen theaters—the Uptown, Parkway, Riverview, and Oak Street (the old Campus)—continued to operate as movie houses into the new millennium, but none of them could match the Heights' meticulously refurbished magnetism. The Uptown still had its couple-friendly balcony and art deco accoutrements. The Parkway still sold bargain-priced popcorn and candy. The Riverview still oozed with space-aged optimism. And the Oak Street still felt Liebenbergish and Kaplanesque. But all four suffered from various levels of benign neglect. They continued to draw moviegoers, but not enough of them to justify the kind of major restoration that Letness and Holmgren had undertaken at the Heights.

The only other old neighborhood theaters that continued to show movies in the Twin Cities were Steve Mann's Grandview and Highland in St. Paul. Both had switched from one-screen to two-screen configurations during the 1970s, and both continued to do respectable business. But as the last remaining movie theaters within St. Paul's city limits, they teetered on the edge of viability. In 2002 Mann signed an agreement to sell the Highland to Steppingstone Theatre, a St. Paul–based children's theater organization. But when news of the deal became public, local residents, fearing the loss of one of the Twin Cities' last surviving neighborhood movie houses, rose up in protest. Local politicians got involved. The Steppingstone plan fizzled. In 2004 the city council agreed to loan Mann $213,000 and to place a moratorium on new theater construction if he would keep running the projectors at the Highland and Grandview through 2013. "We're not talking about a grocery store here," explained council member Pat Harris. "The Highland and Grandview are neighborhood identifiers. It says something about the city to have viable, historic theaters." Mann agreed to the city's terms. St. Paul's oldest movie theaters would survive to see another decade.[56]

While the Highland, Grandview, Heights, Uptown, Parkway, Riverview, and Oak Street continued to show movies, other old Twin Cities theaters lived on as venues for different forms of entertainment. The Southern (Minneapolis's oldest surviving neighborhood theater) and the Ritz in Northeast Minneapolis both hosted dance companies. The Suburban World and the Varsity booked private events and live open-to-the-public music performances. The Avalon (Minneapolis's first full-time porn house) was reborn as the home of the In the Heart of the Beast Puppet and Mask Theatre. The Franklin (the only Minneapolis theater to survive Ferris Alexander's ownership) reemerged as a visual

The Ritz Theater in Northeast Minneapolis finds new life as a dance space, 2006.

and performing arts center. The Loring, rechristened the Music Box, served as the semipermanent home of a three-man comedy show called *Triple Espresso*. The Cedar, near the University of Minnesota's West Bank campus, presented music and dance by performers representing a variety of cultures. In St. Paul the Mounds, east of downtown, reopened as a community arts center. And the show house formerly known as the Norstar—on the site of the old picture palace the Capitol—continued to attract crowds as the home stage of the Park Square Theater.

Local film buffs could take some satisfaction in knowing that a few of the Twin Cities' oldest motion picture houses were still standing at

Eight years after showing its last movie, the Jack Liebenberg–designed Terrace was still awaiting its fate.

the turn of the twenty-first century. But only a handful of the old cinemas were still showing movies. Who knew how long the projectors would continue to run?

In the summer of 2006, Bill Irvine sold his Parkway Theater to the owner of the Mexican restaurant next door. Plans for the old theater on Chicago Avenue were nebulous, but the new owner envisioned a kind of cinema and live performance hybrid.[57] It had been thirty years since Irvine rescued the Parkway from porn house oblivion. Now he was walking away from the one business he really knew. He no longer had it in him to operate an independent single-screen theater in a chain-dominated multiplex world where new films were released on DVD at about the same time they appeared in subrun houses like the Parkway. "I guess it's like an athlete," he said. "You just get to a point where you know it's time to go."[58]

Feature Presentation

Block E 15
600 Hennepin Avenue,
Minneapolis
Opened 2002

Many people in and out of the film exhibition business considered Crown Theatres' fifteen-screen megaplex a monumental gamble. Located on the third level of Minneapolis's newest commercial development, Block E 15 filled the downtown cinema void created by the Skyway Theater's closing in 1999. But many of the same problems that doomed the Skyway—a small downtown population base, high crime rates, and a dearth of free parking—confronted Block E 15 as well. Recognizing the challenges it faced, Crown Theatres stuffed its new megaplex with amenities aimed at keeping and luring moviegoers downtown. Block E 15's audito-

Crown Theatre's fifteen-screen megaplex, on the third floor of downtown Minneapolis's Block E development.

riums featured stadium seating with high-back rockers and THX high-fidelity sound systems. Employees patrolled the auditoriums at fifteen-minute intervals to discourage rowdy behavior. And in an effort to attract suburban commuters, Crown of-

fered vouchers for three hours of free (and later, reduced-price) parking.[1] Company officials reported that Block E 15 was "living up to expectations" during its first four years of operation, with an average annual attendance of about 700,000.[2]

*B*y lunchtime the thirty or so people who were milling outside St. Paul's Fitzgerald Theater (formerly the Shubert and the World) were beginning to lose interest. They had come to Exchange Street hoping to catch a glimpse of a movie star or two, and most of them were still waiting. A few—the ones who had shown up early—had spotted the paparazzi's latest Hollywood obsession, actress Lindsay Lohan, slipping into the theater, hidden behind a pair of large, black sunglasses. But that was about as exciting as the stargazing got. At the senior apartment complex next door, several residents monitored the goings-on from perches just off the sidewalk. They were, without exception, unimpressed. "It's just us old buggers sitting out here getting some air," said one. "It's pretty much just another day for us."[59]

Inside the Fitzgerald the scene was considerably more chaotic. The celebrated director Robert Altman had just started shooting his last film, *A Prairie Home Companion.* The movie was a behind-the-scenes reimagining of Garrison Keillor's long-running and identically named radio variety show, which had been broadcasting from the Fitzgerald (or the World) for twenty-five years. Now the old theater, which had spent much of its life as a movie house, was serving as the setting of a major motion picture. Keillor had written the screenplay. He also was playing a major role in the movie. His costars included Meryl Streep, Kevin Kline, Virginia Madsen, Woody Harrelson, Lily Tomlin, and the paparazzi-dodging Lindsay Lohan.

For the next four weeks starstruck Twin Citians devoured every *Prairie Home Companion*–related tidbit that leaked out from the Fitzgerald—and elsewhere. Local gossip columnists hyperventilated over reports that Lohan had been seen crying while talking on a cell phone outside the theater. Film critics, granted access to the set, gushed over the collegial atmosphere that Altman cultivated among his actors. Dozens of extras, hired as fake audience members, showed up in carefully calibrated attire ("no red," "no all-black," "pretend its autumn"), sat quietly in the Fitzgerald's auditorium, and clapped when directed to do so.[60]

Not since 1970, when Burt Lancaster and Dean Martin came to town to shoot *Airport,* had the Twin Cities witnessed such Hollywood star power. Minneapolis and St. Paul had experienced a modest filmmaking boom in the 1990s, serving as the locations for such films as *Drop Dead Fred* (1991), *The Mighty Ducks* (1993), *Grumpy Old Men* (1994), and *Fargo* (1996), but none of those films had the cachet of *A Prairie Home Companion.* It was a big movie with a big director and

A Prairie Home Companion star Lindsay Lohan takes a photograph of some of the fans lined up across the street from the Fitzgerald Theater.

big stars. Like the radio program on which it was based, it reflected a mythical Minnesota sensibility that appealed to many Twin Citians. And it didn't hurt that it took place in a real Twin Cities theater.

Over the years Hollywood producers had mostly ignored Minneapolis and St. Paul when choosing places to hold their world premieres— even when their movies were shot in the Twin Cities. (The Arnold Schwarzenegger comedy *Jingle All the Way,* released in 1996, was a rare exception.) And although *A Prairie Home Companion* seemed a logical choice for a St. Paul world premiere, it ultimately debuted elsewhere— in Berlin, Germany. Nonetheless, its Midwest premiere, held on May 3, 2006, at the Fitzgerald, was a major event for St. Paul. As the stars of the movie made their six-block trek from Rice Park to the Fitzgerald in horse-drawn carriages, the city briefly basked in their glow.[61]

On the way to the Fitzgerald, the parade of movie stars turned onto Wabasha and crossed the intersection of what had once been Seventh Street. It was only appropriate. There had been a time, not so long ago, when people could stand at the corner of Seventh and Wabasha and imagine that they had landed on a Hollywood set bustling with excitement and glowing with neon. Back then the movies were everywhere. A half block down Seventh, the Paramount and Orpheum seemed to stare at each other like prizefighters awaiting the bell. Looking up Wabasha, you could see the Riviera (the Riv) on your left and the Tower and the Strand on your right. Farther up the street there was the slightly seedy Lyceum (the Lice) and, finally, the World. But the movies were gone now. Granted, the Fitzgerald, as the World was now known, was hosting the regional premiere of *A Prairie Home Companion,* but it was a one-time proposition. The movie would debut at the Fitzgerald and then go on to open the following month at hundreds of theaters around the country—most of them multiplexes, and only one of them (Crown's Block E 15) in downtown St. Paul or downtown Minneapolis.

Nearly one hundred years earlier, Moses Finkelstein and Isaac Ruben had opened their first movie theater, the Princess, about a half block east of the corner of Seventh and Wabasha. Now a shiny retail and office complex sat on the site where the Princess once stood. Over in Minneapolis the downtown lot where Theo Hays's Bijou Theater had once operated was now a car dealership. A few of Jack Liebenberg's greatest creations, including the Suburban World and the Uptown, continued to plug along, but two others—the Hollywood and the Terrace— faced possible annihilation. Ted Mann had prolonged the lives of some of Hennepin Avenue's grandest theaters, making their later restoration possible, but none of them showed movies anymore. Even the porn houses were gone. The corner of University and Dale in St. Paul, home of the notorious Faust and Ferris Alexander's Flick, was finally showing signs of recovery with the construction of a new library.

Meryl Streep meets her fans during St. Paul's star-studded premiere of *A Prairie Home Companion.*

But in some ways moviegoers in Minneapolis and St. Paul had never had it so good. The Twin Cities area was bursting with movie screens—

most of them ensconced in modern megaplexes designed for maximum comfort and convenience. The sound quality in the new theaters was superior. The screens themselves were bigger. (Mike Muller had his Monster Screen, Marcus Theaters had its Ultracinema, and other exhibitors were planning to introduce Imax—another large-screen format previously confined to a venue at the Minnesota Zoo.)[62] Sight lines had improved immensely thanks to stadium seating. And the plethora of screens made it unlikely that anyone showing up to see the most popular new movies would ever have to wait more than an hour or so for a seat. For those who preferred old movie houses, there was always the restored charm of the Heights, the postwar sleekness of the Riverview, and the evocative (albeit twinned) ambience of the Grandview and the Highland. There were even two drive-ins—the Cottage View and the Vali-Hi—where nostalgic film fans could convince themselves that perhaps times had not changed that much after all. And perhaps they hadn't.

Back in 1911 an early motion picture devotee asserted in the *St. Paul Pioneer Press* that "the moving picture show, like the automobile, is here to stay." He was correct. And as far as many other Twin Citians—both past and present—were concerned, he was right on one other count as well. "I maintain that as a whole these [movie theaters] are interesting," he wrote, "and I know of no better place to spend a little leisure time than at a moving picture show."[63]

Appendix

MINNEAPOLIS-AREA MOVIE THEATERS

Theater	Address	Years of Operation	Other Names
Academy	20 N 7th St	1957–1983	Shubert, Alvin
Adke	1721 Franklin Ave E	1908–1909	
Agate	2215 Franklin Ave E	1911–1920	
Air Dome	13 N 10th St	1914–1917	
Alcazar	1307 Franklin Ave E	1914–1916	Franklin, Zenith
Alhambra	3211 Penn Ave N	1915–1957	
Alvin	20 N 7th St	1937–1953	Shubert, Academy
American	16 E Lake St	1911–1982	
Apache	37th Ave NE and Stinson Blvd, Columbia Heights	1979–2003	Chief
Apple Valley	7200 147th Ave SW, Apple Valley	1989–2003	
Arbor Lakes	12575 Elm Creek Blvd, Maple Grove	2001–	
Arion	2510 Central Ave	1911–1957	Echo
Aster	605 Hennepin Ave	1911–1979	
Auditorium	11th St and Nicollet Ave	1905–1925	Lyceum
Avalon	1506 E Lake St	1937–1984	Seventh Ward, Reno, Rosebud, Royal
Bell	1527 Franklin Ave E	1915–1917	Olympic
Bijou	18 Washington Ave N	1941–1960	
Block E	600 Hennepin Ave	2002–	
Blue Mouse	711 Hennepin Ave	1920–1923	Lyric, Skyway
Boulevard	5315 Lyndale Ave S	1933–1998	
Brandt	3954 Minnehaha Ave	1916–1919	Ha Ha, Falls, Minnehaha
Broadway	1006 W Broadway Ave	1921–1967	
Brookdale	1108 Brookdale, Brooklyn Center	1969–1985	
Brookdale	5801 John Martin Dr, Brooklyn Center	1994–1999	Brookdale East
Brookdale Discount	5810 Shingle Creek Pkwy, Brooklyn Center	2000–2006	Brookdale Square

Theater	Address	Years of Operation	Other Names
Brookdale East	5801 John Martin Dr, Brooklyn Center	1972–1993	Brookdale
Brookdale Square	5810 Shingle Creek Pkwy, Brooklyn Center	1981–2000	Brookdale Discount
Brooklyn Center	Hwy 252 at I-94 and I-694, Brooklyn Center	2000–	
Brynwood	1410 Glenwood Ave	1936–1956	
Bungalow	1305 W Lake St	1914–1915	Melba
Burnhaven	14551 Burnhaven Dr, Burnsville	1986–1998	
Burnsville I	I-35W and Co Rd 42, Burnsville	1977–2000	
Burnsville II	I-35W and Co Rd 42, Burnsville	1983–2001	
Calhoun	1300 W Lake St	1915–1921	
Camden	4217 Webber Pkwy	1910–1982	
Campus	300 Oak St	1935–1990	Oak, Oak Street
Capri	W Broadway Ave and N Oliver Ave	1966–1975	Logan, Paradise
Carmike	15630 Cedar Ave S, Apple Valley	1998–	
Casino	257 Plymouth Ave	1926–1928	Plymouth
Cedar	713 Cedar Ave	1916–1925	
Cedar	416 Cedar Ave	1949–1985	
Cedarvale	Hwy 13 and Cedar Ave S, Eagan	1974–1976	Jerry Lewis
Centennial Lakes	7311 France Ave S, Edina	1990–2005	
Central	2007 Central Ave	1910–1919	
Century	38 S 7th St	1929–1964	Miles, Garrick
Champlin	Hwy 169 and 117th Ave N, Champlin	2002–	
Chanhassen	Hwy 5 and Market Blvd, Chanhassen	1998–	
Chateau	1906 4th Ave S	1934–1957	
Chief	37th Ave NE and Stinson Blvd, Columbia Heights	1969–1978	Apache
Cinema I & II	W 69th St near France Ave, Edina	1967–1974	Southdale
Colonial	1923 4th Ave S	1920–1921	Crown, Jewel

Theater	Address	Years of Operation	Other Names
Coon Rapids Showplace	Hwy 10 and Foley Blvd, Coon Rapids	1997–	
Cooper	5755 Wayzata Blvd, St. Louis Park	1962–1991	
Cort	808 E Lake St	1911–1916	
Cosy	2221 Crystal Lake Ave	1912–1920	
Cozy	307 Central Ave	1910–1911	
Cozy	405 Plymouth Ave	1919–1934	Roxy
Crown	1923 4th Ave S	1911–1919	Jewel, Colonial
Crystal	305 Hennepin Ave	1910–1942	
Cyril	114 Hennepin Ave	1910–1919	Rose
Dewey	203 Washington Ave N	c. 1905–1929	
Diamond	802 6th Ave	1911–1915	Home
Dreamland	319 Plymouth Ave	1909–1914	
Eagan	1225 Town Centre Dr, Eagan	1994–2005	
Eagan	2055 Cliff Rd, Eagan	1999–	
Eagle	1417 SE 4th	1913–1915	
East Lake	1537 E Lake St	1913–1964	
Eden Prairie	8251 Flying Cloud Dr, Eden Prairie	2002–	
Eden Prairie East	8251 Flying Cloud Dr, Eden Prairie	1989–1999	
Eden Prairie West	8251 Flying Cloud Dr, Eden Prairie	1976–2002	
Edina	3911 W 50th St, Edina	1936–	
El Lago	3506 E Lake St	1926–1965	
Electric	23 Washington Ave N	1909–1911	
Elite	2934 Lyndale Ave S	1911–1915	
Elite	2517 27th Ave S	1912–1929	
Elk	2707 E Lake St	1911–1917	
Emerson	2605 Emerson Ave N	1915–1927	
Empress	412 W Broadway Ave	1920–1982	
Esquire	729 Hennepin Ave	1938–1941	Time, Newsreel, Pix
Excelsior	26 Water St, Excelsior	1971–1974	Tonka, Excelsior Dock
Excelsior Dock	26 Water St, Excelsior	1975–	Tonka, Excelsior
Fairview	2900 Washington Ave N	1912–1924	Hawthorn

Theater	Address	Years of Operation	Other Names
Falls	3954 Minnehaha Ave	1933–1948	Brandt, Ha Ha, Minnehaha
Forest Park	40th Ave NE and 7th St	1908–1917	
Franklin	1307 Franklin Ave E	1914–1990	Alcazar, Franklin
Garden	622 Hennepin Ave and 16 N 7th St	1915–1926	Milo, World
Garrick	2541 Nicollet Ave	1913–1917	La Salle
Garrick	40 S 7th St	1915–1929	Miles, Century
Gateway	111 Nicollet Ave	1915–1917	
Gayety	103 Washington Ave N	1910–1942	
Gem	212 Hennepin Ave	1905–1912; 1914–1919	Rex
Gem	1330 Marshall St	1912–1917	
Glen Lake	2201 6th Ave N	1917–1918	Penn
Glenwood	1222 Western Ave	1913–1915	
Glenwood Palace	1229 Glenwood Ave	1915–1930	
Golden Valley	7731 4th Ave N, Golden Valley	1950–1951	
Gopher	1706 4th Ave S	1913–1928	
Gopher	619 Hennepin Ave	1938–1979	Grand
Granada	3020 Hennepin Ave	1928–1949	Suburban World
Grand	242 Hennepin Ave	1938–1950	
Grand	623 Hennepin Ave	1911–1936	Gopher
Grandview	406 Cedar Ave	1911–1918	
Ha Ha	3954 Minnehaha Ave	1921–1926	Brandt, Falls, Minnehaha
Harriet	4312 Uptown Ave S	1911–1916	
Hawthorn	2900 Washington Ave N	1911–1912	Fairview
Heights	3951 Central Ave NE, Columbia Heights	1926–	
Hennepin	910 Hennepin Ave	1921–1922	Orpheum
Hollywood	2815 Johnson Ave	1936–1987	
Home	4215 Washington Ave N	1915–1917	
Homewood	1919 Plymouth Ave	1924–1963	
Hopkins	5th St and Excelsior Ave W, Hopkins	1942–1985	
Hopkins	1118 Main St, Hopkins	1996–	
Idle Hour	1706 E Lake St	1912–1915	

Theater	Address	Years of Operation	Other Names
IDS Center	IDS Center	1973–1976	
Iola	1418 Franklin Ave E	1910–1912	
Ione	309 Cedar Ave	1911–1919	
Iris	2533 Bloomington Ave	1911–1923	
Isis	30 S 6th St	1908–1915	
Jerry Lewis	Hwy 13 and Cedar Ave S, Eagan	1971–1972	Cedarvale
Jewel	1923 4th Ave S	1918–1919	Crown, Colonial
Joy	38 Washington Ave S	1911–1915	Novelty
Knollwood	8337 Hwy 7, St. Louis Park	1981–2000	
Kome-On	1015 6th Ave N	1914–1915	
Lagoon	2962 Hennepin Ave	1913–1928	Uptown
Lagoon	1320 Lagoon Ave	1995–	
Lake	15 W Lake St	1910–1912	
Lake	2719 E Lake St	1916–1961	
Lakeville	I-35 and Co Rd 70, Lakeville	1998–	
La Salle	2541 Nicollet Ave	1917–1950	Garrick
Leola	4944 34th Ave N	1927–1967	
Liberty	1013 6th Ave N	1913–1930	
Logan	2029 W Broadway Ave	1925–1928	Paradise, Capri
Loring	1405 Nicollet Ave	1921–1956	
Lyceum	718 Hennepin Ave	1887–1909	Lyric
Lyceum	11th and Nicollet Ave	1924–1951	Auditorium
Lyndale	624 20th Ave N	1910–1913	
Lyndale	2932 Lyndale Ave S	1915–1952	
Lyra	16 Washington Ave N	1927–1930	
Lyric	718 Hennepin Ave	1909–1961	Lyceum
Lyric	711 Hennepin Ave	1923–1971	Blue Mouse, Skyway
Main	1029 NE Main St	1911–1926	
Majestic	1326 Washington Ave S	1906–1923	
Mall of America	I-494 and 24th Ave S, Bloomington	1992–	
Mann	708 Hennepin Ave	1961–1984	Pantages, Pan
Maple Grove	13644 80th Circle N, Maple Grove	1991–	

Theater	Address	Years of Operation	Other Names
Mazda	246 Hennepin Ave	1910–1923	Savoy
Melba	1305 W Lake St	1913–1914	Bungalow
Metro	2519 27th Ave S	1931–1952	
Metropolitan	320 1st Ave S	c. 1898–1937	
Miles	46 S 7th St	1909–1915	Garrick, Century
Milo	626 Hennepin Ave	1908–1917	Garden, World
Minnehaha	3954 Minnehaha Ave	1926–1928	Brandt, Ha Ha, Falls
Minnesota	36 S 9th St	1928–1941	Radio City
Moon	228 Central Ave	1911–1914	
National	44 S 3rd St	1916–1919	
New Lake	31 Lake St	1913–1939	Vogue, Stage 7
Newsreel	729 Hennepin Ave	1941–1946	Time, Esquire, Pix
Nicollet	1347 Nicollet Ave	1911–1920	
Nile	3736 23rd Ave S	1931–1982	
Nokomis	3749 Chicago Ave	1916–1951	
Northern	404 20th Ave N	1911–1926	
Northtown	2605 Emerson Ave N	1933–1952	
Northtown	113 Northtown Dr, Blaine	1973–1997	
Novelty	38 Washington Ave S	1908–1912	Joy
Oak	309 Oak St	1916–1923	Campus, Oak Street
Oak Park	1607 Plymouth Ave	1914–1924	
Oak Street	309 Oak St	1995–	Oak, Campus
Olympic	1527 Franklin Ave E	1911–1914	Bell
Orient	44 S 3rd St	1911–1921	
Orpheum	910 Hennepin Ave	1922–1979	Hennepin
Orpheum	25 S 7th St	1904–1922	Seventh Street
Owl	Coon Rapids Blvd and Crooked Lake Blvd, Coon Rapids	1974–1976	
Oxboro	97th St and Lyndale Ave S, Bloomington	1951–1967	Studio 97
Palace	412 Hennepin Ave	1916–1953	
Pan	708 Hennepin Ave	1946–1960	Pantages, Mann
Pantages	708 Hennepin Ave	1916–1946	Pan, Mann
Paradise	2027 W Broadway Ave	1931–1963	Logan, Capri
Park	2424 Riverside Ave	1911–1957	

Theater	Address	Years of Operation	Other Names
Park	725 S 10th	1911–1930	
Parkway	4814 Chicago Ave	1932–	
Pearl	2100 20th Ave N	1915–1916	
Penn	2201 6th Ave N	1915–1917	Glen Lake
Penn	2224 W Broadway Ave	1920–1925	
Pix	729 Hennepin Ave	1948–1952	Time, Esquire, Newsreel
Plaza	2533 Bloomington Ave	1916–1917	
Plymouth	257 Plymouth Ave	1910–1919	Casino
Plymouth	3400 Vicksburg Ln, Plymouth	1998–	
Princess	12 NE 4th St	1909–1942	
Radio City	3640 S 9th St	1944–1958	Minnesota
Regent	602 Hennepin Ave	1914–1916	
Reno	1506 E Lake St	1928–1930	Seventh Ward, Avalon, Rosebud, Royal
Rex	212 Hennepin Ave	1912–1914	Gem
Rialto	735 E Lake St	1916–1990	
Richfield	65th St and Nicollet Ave, Richfield	1948–1965	
Ridge Square	Plymouth Rd and Hwy 12, Minnetonka	1982–1997	
Ritz	347 13th Ave NE	1928–1971	
Riverview	3800 42nd Ave S	1948–	
Robin	4707 42nd Ave N, Robbinsdale	1938–1949	
Rose	114 Hennepin Ave	1919–1925	Cyril
Rosebud	1506 E Lake St	1923–1928	Seventh Ward, Avalon, Reno, Royal
Roxy	405 Plymouth Ave	1934–1951	Cozy
Royal	1506 E Lake St	1909–1923	Seventh Ward, Avalon, Reno, Rosebud
Royal	Excelsior Ave and Hwy 7, Hopkins	1936–1949	Star
St. Anthony Main	115 SE Main St	1986–	
St. Louis Park	4835 W Lake St, St. Louis Park	1939–1980	
St. Louis Park	5400 Excelsior Blvd, St. Louis Park	1995–	
Savoy	242 Hennepin Ave	c. 1910–1930	Mazda
Scenic	253 Hennepin Ave	1908–1912	

Theater	Address	Years of Operation	Other Names
Seventh Street	21 S 7th St	1922–1940	Orpheum
Seventh Ward	1504 E Lake St	1913–1914	Avalon, Rosebud, Royal, Reno
Seville	413 Hennepin Ave	1910–1915	
Shakopee Town	1116 Shakopee Town Rd	1990–	
Shelard Park	Hwy 12 and Co Rd 18, St. Louis Park	1976–2000	
Shubert	22 N 7th St	1910–1936	Alvin, Academy
Skyway	711 Hennepin Ave	1972–1999	Blue Mouse, Lyric
Southern	1420 Washington Ave S	1910–1934	
Southdale	W 69th St, Edina	1975–1990	Cinema I & II
Southdale	69th St and France Ave, Edina	2001–	
Southtown	I-494 and Penn Ave S, Bloomington	1964–1995	
Springbrook	141 N 85th Ave NE, Blaine	1990–2000	
Stage 7	31 W Lake St	1968–1975	New Lake, Vogue
Standish Miles	3736 23rd Ave S	1926–1930	
Star	121 Washington Ave S	1914–1922	
Star	905 20th Ave N	1910–1917	
Star	Excelsior Ave and Hwy 7, Hopkins	1950–1953	Royal
State	809 Hennepin Ave	1921–1975	
Stockholm	103 Washington Ave S	1919–1939	
Strand	37 S 7th St	1915–1929	
Studio 97	97th St and Lyndale Ave S	1968–1986	Oxboro
Suburban World	3022 Hennepin Ave	1954–1994	Granada, Suburban World Cinema Grill
Suburban World Cinema Grill	3022 Hennepin Ave	2000–2002	Granada, Suburban World
Terrace	W Broadway Ave at 36th Ave N, Robbinsdale	1951–1999	
Third Ward	729 Plymouth Ave	1911–1923	
Time	729 Hennepin Ave	1934–1938	Esquire, Newsreel, Pix
Tonka	26 Water St, Excelsior	1941–1971	Excelsior, Excelsior Dock
Trail 4	Cliff Rd and Hwy 13, Burnsville	1972–1977	
Unique	520 Hennepin Ave	1904–1931	

Theater	Address	Years of Operation	Other Names
University	1310 SE 4th St	1915–1939	Varsity
Uptown	2962 Hennepin Ave	1929–	Lagoon
Valley West	France Ave and Old Shakopee Rd, Bloomington	1971–1980	
Varsity	1308 SE 4th St	1938–1988	University
Village 4	2040 Northdale Blvd NW	1971–1998	
Vista	1403 Franklin Ave E	1911–1928	
Vogue	31 W Lake St	1940–1967	New Lake, Stage 7
Wayzata	619 Lake St E, Wayzata	1932–1985	
Westgate	45th St and France Ave	1937–1977	
Westwind	Hwys 7 and 101, Minnetonka	1989–2001	
Willow Creek	9500 Shelard Pkwy, Plymouth	1989–	
Wonderland	27 Washington Ave S	1908–1930	
World	16 N 7th St	1933–1983	Milo, Garden
Yorktown	Yorktown Center, Edina	1973–1997	Yorktown Cinema Grill
Yorktown Cinema Grill	Yorktown Center, Edina	2000–2005	Yorktown
Zenith	1307 Franklin Ave E	1910–1911	Alcazar, Franklin
Zone	1300 6th Ave S	1911–1916	

ST. PAUL-AREA MOVIE THEATERS

Theater	Address	Years of Operation	Other Names
Acme	435 W 7th St	1913–1914	
Airdome	Wabasha St and College Ave	1914	
Alhambra	16 E 7th St	1911–1932	Penny Parlor, Cameo
Arcade	947 Arcade St	1918–1978	
Astor	449 Wabasha St	1920–1928	Gaiety, Cort, OK, Riviera
Astor	108 Concord St	1929–1976	Palace, Concord
Avalon	619 4th St, White Bear Lake	1928–1973	White Bear Cinema
Beaux Arts	391 Selby Ave	1934–1959	Elk, Rialto, Summit
Bijou	463 N Snelling Ave	1910–1915	
Bluebird	902 Rice St	1915–1948	Eagle, Royal
Blue Mouse	20 E 7th St	1914–1922	
Cameo	16 E 7th St	1933–1936	Penny Parlor, Alhambra
Capital	490 Rice St	1910–1911	
Capitol	22 W 7th St	1920–1929	Paramount
Capitol	1077 Payne Ave	1930–1977	Venus
Centre	1978 University Ave	1940–1965	
Cina 4	1361 S Robert St	1972–1998	
Cine Capri	521 3rd St, White Bear Lake	1968–1976	White Bear
Colonial	380 Wabasha St	1913–1914	
Colonial	446 Wabasha St	1911–1912	Crystal, Rex, Starland, Strand
Comet	176 E 7th St	1920–1921	Star, Northern, Hippodrome, Lyric, State
Como	536 University Ave	1914–1932	
Concord	108 Concord St	1926–1928	Palace, Astor
Cort	449 Wabasha St	1916–1917	Gaiety, OK, Astor, Riviera
Cottage Grove	Hwy 61 and 80th St, Cottage Grove	1975–1987	
Cozy	389 W 7th St	1915–1928	Tuxedo, Gem
Crystal	446 Wabasha St	1906–1910	Rex, Colonial, Starland, Strand
Dale	633 Selby Ave	1915–1959	
Dayton	894 E 7th St	1916–1923	

Theater	Address	Years of Operation	Other Names
Deluxe	287 Maria Ave	1915–1953	
Dewey	166 S Wabasha St	1912–1913	Ivy
Eagle	900 Rice St	1914–1915	Bluebird, Royal
Eastside	311 Ramsey St	1964–1970	Little
Elk	391 Selby Ave	1913–1916	Rialto, Summit, Beaux Arts
Elvy	966 Payne Ave	1915–1917	Lyceum
Empire	Wabasha St and 3rd St	1902–1907	
Empress	479 Wabasha St	1911–1916; 1923–1925	Hippodrome, Liberty, Lyceum, Las Vegas
Family	927 W 7th St	1959–1960	Grand, Garden
Faust	626 University Ave	1912–1989	
Fitzgerald	494 Wabasha St	1994–	Shubert, World
Forest	924 E 7th St	1916–1933	Roxy
Frances	209 E 7th St	1919–1920	
Gaiety	447 Wabasha St	1911–1916	Astor, Cort, OK, Riviera
Galtier Plaza	175 E 5th St	1985–1999	
Garden	927 W 7th St	1917–1949; 1956	Grand, Family
Garrick	34 W 6th St	1917–1949	Grand Opera, Strand
Gem	178 Concord St	1907–1908	
Gem	18 E 7th St	1909–1923	
Gem	389 W 7th St	1933–1959	Cozy, Tuxedo
Grand	927 W 7th St	1950–1951	Garden, Family
Grand Opera House	34 W 6th St	1891–1914	Strand, Garrick
Grandview	1830 Grand Ave	1933–	
Hamline	1541 University Ave	1916–1963	
Har Mar	2100 N Snelling Ave, Roseville	1970–2006	
Highland	760 Cleveland Ave S	1940–	
Hillside	Concord St and Grand Ave, South St. Paul	1966–1972	
Hippodrome	176 E 7th St	1912–1913	Star, Northern, Comet, Lyric, State
Hippodrome	479 Wabasha St	1916–1917	Empress, Liberty, Lyceum, Las Vegas
Ideal	215 Grand Ave, South St. Paul	1915–1925	
Inver Grove Showplace	Hwy 52 at Upper 55th St, Inver Grove Heights	1998–	

Theater	Address	Years of Operation	Other Names
Ivy	166 S Wabasha St	1916–1917	Dewey
Las Vegas	479 Wabasha St	1972–1976	Empress, Hippodrome, Liberty, Lyceum
Leona	183 E Fairfield Ave	1915–1917	New Ray
Liberty	135 Eaton Ave	1914–1916	Friedman(?), Red Mill(?)
Liberty	479 Wabasha St	1918–1921	Empress, Hippodrome, Lyceum, Las Vegas
Little	311 Ramsey St	1919–1920	Eastside
Little	302 University Ave	1930–1931	Verdi
Lyceum	966 Payne Ave	1908–1914	Elvy
Lyceum	479 Wabasha St	1926–1972	Empress, Liberty, Las Vegas
Lyric	149 E 7th St	1907–1911	
Majestic	37 E 7th St	1911–1921	
Majestic	441 Cedar St	1907–1911	Orpheum Music Hall
Maplewood I	I-694 and White Bear Ave, Maplewood	1975–2000	
Maplewood II	Beam Ave and Southlawn Ave, Maplewood	1981–2002	
Metropolitan Opera House	100 E 6th St	1890–1936	
Midtown	1533 W Como Ave	1935–1974	
Mohawk	631 S Smith Ave	1922–1953	
Mounds	1029 Hudson Rd	1926–1967	
Mozart Hall	406 N Franklin Ave	1896–1919	
New Ray	183 E Fairfield Ave	1918–1954	Leona
Norstar	22 W 7th St	1966–1978	Capitol, Paramount
Northern	176 E 7th St	1906–1907	Star, Hippodrome, Comet, Lyric, State
O.K.	447 Wabasha St	1918–1919	Gaiety, Cort, Astor, Riviera
Oakdale	Exit 57 off I-694, Oakdale	2002–	
Oakdale North	5677 Hadley Ave N, Oakdale	2000–	
Odeon	501 Mississippi St	1921–1922	Rex
Ohio	510 Ohio St	1915–1922	
Olympic	176 E 7th St	1900–1901	Star, Northern, Hippodrome, Comet, State
Orpheum Music Hall	441 Cedar St	1904–1906	Majestic

Theater	Address	Years of Operation	Other Names
Orpheum	365 St. Peter St	1906–1925	President
Orpheum	19–21 W 7th St	1931–1982	Palace, Palace Orpheum
Oxford	1053 Grand Ave	1922–1928	Uptown
Oxford	989 Selby Ave	1937–1951	Selby
Palace	108 Concord St	1914–1925	Concord, Astor
Palace	19–21 W 7th St	1917–1922	Palace Orpheum, Orpheum
Palace Orpheum	19–21 W 7th St	1923–1930	Palace, Orpheum
Palm	999 Payne Ave	1910–1916	
Paramount	22 W 7th St	1929–1965	Capitol
Park	1595 Selby Ave	1914–1953	
Pavilion Place	1655 W Co Rd B2	1985–2007	
Penny Parlor	16 E 7th St	1909–1910	Alhambra, Cameo
Plaza	White Bear Ave and Larpenteur Ave	1967–	
President	365 St. Peter St	1926–1938	Orpheum
Princess	21 E 7th St	1910–1931	
Radio	1195 E 7th St	1923–1932	
Randolph	1326 Randolph Ave	1937–1956	
Ray	976 Bush Fauquier	1914–1916	
Red Mill	127 Eaton Ave	1929–1932	Liberty
Regent	434 Wabasha St	1919–1928	
Rex	446 Wabasha St	1910–1911	Crystal, Colonial, Starland, Strand
Rex	501 Mississippi St	1915–1919; 1922–1923	Odeon
Rialto	393 Selby Ave	1917–1918	Elk, Summit, Beaux Arts
Riviera	449 Wabasha St	1929–1976	Gaiety, Cort, OK, Astor
Rosedale	850 Rosedale Center, Roseville	2006–	
Roseville	1211 W Larpenteur Ave, Roseville	1975–	
Roxy	924 E 7th St	1934–1958	Forest
Royal	945 W 7th St	1910–1916	
Royal	900 Rice St	1949–1954	Eagle, Bluebird
St. Clair	1560 St. Clair Ave	1925–1977	
Savoy	118 Eaton St	1911–1913	
Selby	989 Selby Ave	1913–1936	Oxford

Theater	Address	Years of Operation	Other Names
Shubert	494 Wabasha St	1910–1933	World, Fitzgerald
Signal Hills	S Robert St and W Butler Ave, West St Paul	1982–1998	
South 1 & 2	333 Concord St	1973–1976	
Star	176 E 7th St	1901–1911; 1915–1919	Olympic, Comet, State
Starland	448 Wabasha St	1912–1921	Crystal, Rex, Colonial, Strand
State	176 E 7th St	1925–1953	Star, Northern, Hippodrome, Comet, Lyric
Strand	34 W 6th St	1915–1916	Grand Opera, Garrick
Strand	448 Wabasha St	1922–1976	Crystal, Rex, Colonial, Starland
Summit	393 Selby Ave	1918–1933	Elk, Rialto, Beaux Arts
Topic	399 Prior Ave	1915–1916	
Tower	438 Wabasha St	1921–1959	
Tryst	2511 University Ave	1914–1922	
Tuxedo	389 W 7th St	1929–1932	Cozy, Gem
Unique	163 E 7th St	1907–1919	
Unique	240 E 7th St	1920–1922	
Uptown	1053 Grand Ave	1929–1976	Oxford
Venus	1077 Payne Ave	1915–1929	Capitol
Verdi	302 University Ave	1914–1929	Little
Victoria	825 University Ave	1916–1924	
West Twins	924 S Robert St	1939–1969	
White Bear	521 3rd St, White Bear Lake	1939–1968	Cine Capri
White Bear Cinema	619 4th St, White Bear Lake	1973–1979	Avalon
White Bear Township	I-35E and Co Rd J, White Bear Township	1995–	
Woodbury	1470 Queens Dr, Woodbury	1993–	
World	494 Wabasha St	1933–1994	Shubert, Fitzgerald
Wynnsong	2430 Hwy 10, Mounds View	1999–	

TWIN CITIES-AREA DRIVE-IN THEATERS

Name	Location	Years of Operation
Bloomington	E 78th St and 12th Ave S, Bloomington	1947–1975
Rose	Snelling Ave and Co Rd C, Roseville	1948–1979
Corral	S Robert St and Mendota Rd, West St. Paul	1949–1972
Starlite	Hwys 52 and 152, Robbinsdale	1949–1981
Hilltop	47th St and Central Ave NE, Hilltop	1949–1971
100 Twin	I-694 and Central Ave, Fridley	1949–1985
7-Hi	Hwys 7 and 101, Minnetonka	1950–1971
Navarre	Co Rd 15 between Spring Park and Minnetonka Beach	1953–1979
Lucky Twin	Hwy 13 east of I-35W, Burnsville	1955–1980
Flying Cloud	Hwys 169 and 212, Eden Prairie	1958–1988
Coon Rapids	US 10 and E River Rd, Coon Rapids	1958–1985
Maple Leaf	Hwys 36 and 61, Maplewood	1959–1994
Minnehaha	Minnehaha Ave and E McKnight Rd, Maplewood	1962–1972
65 Hi	101st St and Central Ave NE, Blaine	1965–2001
France Avenue	I-494 and France Ave, Bloomington	1966–1984
Cottage View	9338 S Point Douglas Rd, Cottage Grove	1966–
Colonial	Hwys 55 and 101, Medina	1966–1983
Vali Hi	11260 Hudson Blvd N, Lake Elmo	1968–

Notes

Chapter 1

1. *Minneapolis Tribune,* August 4, 1896.

2. *Minneapolis Journal,* May 2, 1915.

3. *Minneapolis Tribune,* November 20, 1896.

4. *St. Paul Pioneer Press,* April 16, 1916.

5. Lucile M. Kane and John A. Dougherty, "Movie Debut: Films in the Twin Cities, 1894–1909," *Minnesota History,* Winter 1995, 346.

6. James Gray, "Metropolitan Books Finest Attractions of Recent Years—Casey Players Return," *St. Paul Magazine,* Fall 1929.

7. Paul Stanley Newman, "Careers in Contrast: The Managerial Practices of L. N. Scott and Theo Hays and Their Influence on Twin Cities Entertainment, 1890–1929" (Ph.D. diss., University of Minnesota, 1991), 163.

8. 1880 Minneapolis City Directory.

9. Paul S. Newman, "Theodore L. Hays: Theatrical Good Neighbor at the Turn of the Century," *Minnesota History,* Summer 1993, 239.

10. *Minneapolis Tribune,* July 1, 1893.

11. *Penny Press* (Minneapolis), June 29, 1895.

12. *Minneapolis Journal,* October 15, 1904.

13. Quoted in Lawrence James Hill, "A History of Variety-Vaudeville in Minneapolis, Minnesota, from Its Beginning to 1900" (Ph.D. diss., University of Minnesota, 1979), 282.

14. *Minneapolis Journal,* October 24, 1904.

15. Newman, "Careers in Contrast," 185.

16. Douglas Gomery, *Shared Pleasures: A History of Movie Presentation in the United States* (Madison: University of Wisconsin Press, 1992), 14–15.

17. *Minneapolis Journal,* October 24, 1904.

18. *Minneapolis Tribune,* December 29, 1908.

19. Quoted in Kane and Dougherty, "Movie Debut," 349.

20. *Minneapolis Tribune,* October 7, 1911.

21. Merritt Crawford, "The March of the Years," *Moving Picture World,* March 26, 1927, 284.

22. *Minneapolis Tribune,* December 1, 1907.

23. Ibid., October 7, 1911.

24. *St. Paul Dispatch,* February 17, 1964.

25. Kane and Dougherty, "Movie Debut," 350.

26. Theodore Hays to A. W. Dingwall, March 20, 1908, Theodore Hays Papers, roll 4, frame 1178, Minnesota Historical Society collections, St. Paul, MN [hereafter MHS collections].

27. Kane and Dougherty, "Movie Debut," 355–56.

28. Dean S. Potter, "Hiawatha: A Poem, a Legend, and Minnesota's First Movie," *Sun Country,* July-August 1986, 14–17; *Minneapolis Journal,* August 9, 1909; June 2, 1925.

29. *Moving Picture World,* October 23, 1909, 563.

30. Kane and Dougherty, "Movie Debut," 356.

31. *Minneapolis Journal,* September 3, 1911.

32. *Minneapolis Tribune,* October 7, 1911.

33. *Minneapolis Journal,* September 3, 1911.

34. *Minneapolis Tribune,* October 7, 1911.

35. *St. Paul Pioneer Press,* October 21, 1911.

36. *Minneapolis Journal,* September 3, 1911.

37. *Minneapolis Tribune,* October 28, 1911.

38. *Minneapolis Journal,* November 11, 1915.

39. Audley Mitchell Grossman, "The Professional Legitimate Theater in Minneapolis from 1890 to 1901" (Ph.D. diss., University of Minnesota, 1957), 98–103.

40. *Minneapolis Tribune,* October 7, 1911.

41. Ibid.

42. Ibid., October 14, 1911.

43. *Minneapolis Journal,* October 22, 1911.

44. *Minneapolis Tribune,* January 24, 1913.

45. *Minneapolis Journal,* September 7, 1913.

46. *St. Paul Pioneer Press,* August 24, 1913.

47. "Western Financier Criticises Films," *Motion Picture World,* October 9, 1915, 302.

48. James S. McQuade, "The Belasco of Motion Picture Presentations," *Moving Picture World,* December 9, 1911, 797.

49. *Minneapolis Journal,* September 10, 1911.

50. Ross Melnick, "Rethinking Rothafel: Roxy's Forgotten Legacy," *The Moving Image* 3 (Fall 2003): 64–65.

51. Samuel Rothapfel, "Dignity of the Exhibitor's Profession," *Moving Picture World,* February 26, 1910, 289 (quoted in Melnick, "Rethinking Rothafel," 65).

52. Melnick, "Rethinking Rothafel," 65.

53. *St. Paul Pioneer Press,* September 2, 1911; *St. Paul Daily News,* September 13, 1911.

54. McQuade, "The Belasco of Motion Picture Presentations," 796.

55. *Moving Picture World,* September 7, 1912, 994.

56. *Minneapolis Journal,* August 20, 1913.

57. Samuel Rothapfel, "Putting Your House in Proper Order," *Moving Picture World,* July 3, 1920, 67.

58. Newman, "Careers in Contrast," 158.

59. Ibid., 159.

60. *Minneapolis Journal,* August 19, 1913.

61. *St. Paul Pioneer Press,* November 1, 1914.

62. Ibid., May 31, 1914.

63. Ibid., May 24, 1914.

64. Crawford, "The March of the Years," 285.

65. Eric Niderost, "'The Birth of a Nation': When Hollywood Glorified the KKK," www.historynet.com.

66. *Twin City Star* (Minneapolis), May 1, 1915.

67. Ibid., October 16, 1915.

68. *St. Paul Daily News,* October 20, 1915.

69. Ibid., October 26, 1915.

70. Ibid., October 27, 1915.

71. Ibid., October 28, 1915.

72. *Minneapolis Journal,* October 17, 1915.

73. Ibid., November 15, 1915.

74. Ibid., November 19, 1915.

75. Ibid., November 20, 1915.

76. Ibid., November 24, 1915.

77. *The Appeal* (St. Paul and Minneapolis), November 30, 1915.

78. *St. Paul Dispatch,* July 24, 1917.

79. *St. Paul Pioneer Press,* July 30, 1917.

80. Ibid., August 12, 1917.

81. *Moving Picture World,* September 1, 1917, 1417.

Feature Presentations

p. 9, note 1. *Minneapolis Journal,* December 6, 1908.

p. 9, note 2. *Moving Picture World,* November 18, 1916.

p. 12, note 1. *Minneapolis Journal,* August 29, 1909.

p. 21, note 1. *St. Paul Pioneer Press,* August 27, 1910.

p. 24, note 1. Southern Theater, National Register of Historic Places Inventory—Nomination Form, 1980.

Chapter 2

1. *Minneapolis Journal,* May 23, 1926.

2. Ibid.

3. *St. Paul Union Advocate,* June 8, 1906.

4. *Minneapolis Journal,* September 21, 1913; May 23, 1926.

5. *St. Paul Dispatch,* April 7, 1910.

6. *St. Paul Pioneer Press,* July 13, 1910.

7. *Minneapolis Journal,* May 23, 1926.

8. *Twin City Reporter* (Minneapolis), September 24, 1915.

9. Kirk J. Besse, *Show Houses Twin Cities Style* (Minneapolis: Victoria Publications, 1997), 86.

10. *Minneapolis Journal,* September 21, 1913.

11. *Minnesota Union Advocate* (St. Paul), December 12, 1913.

12. *Minneapolis Journal,* August 30, 1914.

13. *Moving Picture World,* May 27, 1916.

14. *Minneapolis Journal,* November 23, 1914; *St. Paul Daily News,* December 24, 1915.

15. *Moving Picture World,* December 16, 1916.

16. *Minneapolis Journal,* September 6, 1914.

17. *Minneapolis Labor Review,* March 8, 1918.

18. *Moving Picture World,* June 8, 1918.

19. Ibid., May 5, 1917.

20. *St. Paul Pioneer Press,* May 17, 1918.

21. Hyman Berman and Linda Mack Schloff, *Jews in Minnesota* (St. Paul: Minnesota Historical Society Press, 2002), 12, 16–17.

22. Martin Lebedoff interview by Rhoda G. Lewin, May 6, 1987, transcript, Upper Midwest Jewish Archives.

23. *Greater Amusements,* June 14, 1940.

24. "Official Annual Year Book," *Labor Review* (Minneapolis), August 31, 1917; *Moving Picture World,* September 22, 1917.

25. Martin Lebedoff interview by Rhoda G. Lewin, May 6, 1987.

26. *Minneapolis Journal,* July 9, 1915.

27. Ibid., July 1, 1915.

28. *St. Paul Pioneer Press,* September 9, 1920.

29. Charlotte Herzog, "The Movie Palace and the Theatrical Sources of Its Architectural Style," in Ina Rae Hark, ed., *Exhibition: The Film Reader* (New York: Routledge, 2002), 51.

30. *St. Paul Daily News,* April 15, 1919.

31. *St. Paul Pioneer Press,* September 9, 1920.

32. Ibid., September 12, 1920.

33. *Minneapolis Journal,* February 14, 1921.

34. *St. Paul Dispatch,* August 15, 1918.

35. *Minneapolis Tribune,* February 6, 1921.

36. *St. Paul Pioneer Press,* April 23, 1921.

37. *New York Times,* July 24, 1916.

38. *St. Paul Pioneer Press,* November 26, 1916.

39. Leigh Ann Wheeler, *Against Obscenity: Reform and the Politics of Womanhood in America, 1873–1935* (Baltimore, MD: Johns Hopkins University Press, 2004), 32–39.

40. *St. Paul Pioneer Press,* October 8, 1916.

41. *Moving Picture World,* February 19, 1916; June 3, 1916.

42. *Minneapolis Journal,* December 14, 1920.

43. *Moving Picture World,* January 29, 1921.

44. *Minneapolis Journal,* February 18, 1921.

45. Wheeler, *Against Obscenity,* 61.

46. *Minneapolis Journal,* February 9, 1921.

47. Clipping from unknown source, February 10, 1921.

48. *St. Paul Daily News,* February 20, 1921.

49. Gilman to Hays, March 12, 1921; Gilman to Meyers, March 12, 1921, Robbins Gilman and Family Papers, MHS collections.

50. *Minneapolis Journal,* October 2, 1922; Wheeler, *Against Obscenity,* 68.

51. Gilman to Hays, September 17, 1924, Robbins Gilman and Family Papers, MHS collections.

52. Hays to Gilman, September 19, 1924, Robbins Gilman and Family Papers, MHS collections.

53. *Minneapolis Journal,* July 12, 1927.

54. *Exhibitors Herald and Moving Picture World,* February 4, 1928.

55. *Minneapolis Journal,* February 21, 1929.

56. *Moving Picture World,* December 4, 1915.

57. *Minneapolis Journal,* June 3, 1916.

58. Ibid., February 8, 1921; *Minneapolis Tribune,* February 10, 1921.

59. *St. Paul Pioneer Press,* January 26, 1921.

60. *Minneapolis Tribune,* February 10, 1921.

61. *Minneapolis Journal,* February 14, 1921.

62. *Minneapolis Tribune,* April 3, 1921.

63. *Moving Picture World,* November 19, 1921.

64. *St. Paul Dispatch,* November 4, 1921.

65. *Minnesota Union Advocate* (St. Paul), January 29, 1925.

66. *Moving Picture World,* July 10, 1926.

67. Gomery, *Shared Pleasures,* 53.

68. *Minneapolis Journal,* June 11, 1922.

69. *Moving Picture World,* October 20, 1923.

70. Gomery, *Shared Pleasures,* 54.

71. *Moving Picture World,* October 20, 1923.

72. St. Paul Society for the Prevention of Cruelty, minutes, February 6, 1923, MHS collections.

73. *St. Paul Echo,* November 27, 1926.

74. Ibid., December 18, 1926.

75. *Twin City Star* (Minneapolis), December 23, 1916.

76. *St. Paul Echo,* November 27, 1926.

77. Ibid., August 21, 1926.

78. Ibid., August 28, 1926.

79. *Capitol Theatre Magazine,* June 14, 1924.

80. *Minneapolis Journal,* November 4, 1928.

81. *Twin City Herald* (Minneapolis), September 16, 1933.

82. *Minneapolis Journal,* November 4, 1928.

83. *St. Paul Dispatch,* March 1, 1927.

84. Ibid., July 12, 1922; *St. Paul Pioneer Press,* July 30, 1922.

85. *Moving Picture World,* May 14, 1927.

86. *St. Paul Pioneer Press,* March 27, 1927; October 21, 1951; *St. Paul Dispatch,* April 6, 1927.

87. *St. Paul Dispatch,* April 6, 1927; undated *St. Paul Pioneer Press* clipping.

88. *Minneapolis Journal,* June 9, 1927; June 27, 1927; Dave Wood, "In Search of an Historic Area Movie," *Lake Area,* February 1982, 1, 18.

89. *Minneapolis Journal,* June 27, 1927.

90. Ibid., February 24, 1927.

91. Ross Melnick and Andreas Fuchs, *Cinema Treasures: A New Look at Classic Movie Theaters* (St. Paul, MN: MBI Publishing, 2004), 43.

92. Ibid.; Gomery, *Shared Pleasures,* 60–61.

93. *Minneapolis Journal,* June 10, 1925; December 27, 1925.

94. Ibid., September 18, 1927; *St. Paul Pioneer Press,* September 17, 1927.

95. Larry Millett, *Lost Twin Cities* (St. Paul: Minnesota Historical Society Press, 1992), 298–99.

96. *Exhibitors Herald and Moving Picture World,* February 11, 1928; *Minneapolis Journal,* March 30, 1928.

97. *Exhibitors Herald and Moving Picture World,* March 31, 1928.

98. *St. Paul Daily News,* July 15, 1929.

99. *Exhibitors Herald-World,* July 20, 1929.

Feature Presentations

p. 40, note 1. *Minneapolis Journal,* February 3, 1916.

p. 40, note 2. *Minneapolis Journal,* October 29, 1916.

p. 47, note 1. Kirk J. Besse, *Show Houses Twin Cities Style* (Minneapolis: Victoria Publications, 1997), 20–22.

p. 47, note 2. *St. Paul Pioneer Press,* April 22, 1923.

p. 47, note 3. Thomas Johnson and David Fantle, "George Burns Recalls the Old St. Paul Orpheum," *Mpls.St.Paul,* July 1980, 70.

p. 52, note 1. Stephen L. Adams, "St. Paul's Capitol Theatre: A True Cathedral of Motion Pictures," *Theatre Organ,* May/June 1991, 18; Larry Millett, *Lost Twin Cities* (St. Paul: Minnesota Historical Society Press, 1992), 296–97.

p. 56, note 1. State Theater, National Register of Historic Places Inventory—Nomination Form, 1985.

p. 62, note 1. *Moving Picture World,* February 14, 1920.

p. 62, note 2. *Minneapolis Journal,* July 27, 1922.

p. 66, note 1. Millett, *Lost Twin Cities,* 298–99.

Chapter 3

1. *Moving Picture World,* April 2, 1927.

2. *St. Paul Pioneer Press,* March 23, 1927.

3. *St. Paul Dispatch,* March 25, 1927.

4. Lisa Schrenk, "Birth of the Movies," *Architecture Minnesota,* November-December 1984, 46.

5. *Gopher* (University of Minnesota), 1912 (vol. 29), 599.

6. *City Pages,* June 10, 1998.

7. Herbert Scherer, *Marquee on Main Street: Jack Liebenberg's Movie Theaters, 1928–1941* (Minneapolis: University Gallery, University of Minnesota, 1982), 25.

8. Herbert Scherer, "Tickets to Fantasy: The Little Theater around the Corner," *Hennepin County History,* Fall 1987, 12–13.

9. "Granada Grand Opening Program," scrapbooks, Liebenberg and Kaplan Papers, Northwest Architectural Archives, University of Minnesota [hereafter NWAA].

10. *Minnesota Union Advocate* (St. Paul), February 21, 1929.

11. *Exhibitors Herald-World,* March 16, 1929.

12. *Variety,* May 22, 1929.

13. *Minnesota Union Advocate* (St. Paul), February 21, 1929.

14. *Greater Amusements*, August 1, 1931.

15. Ibid., April 9, 1932.

16. Ibid., July 11, 1931.

17. Ibid., April 23, 1932.

18. Ibid., May 7, 1932.

19. *Variety*, August 13, 1930.

20. Ibid., May 24, 1932.

21. Ibid., March 21, 1933.

22. *St. Paul Dispatch*, January 26, 1931.

23. Gilman to Winter, April 23, 1931, Robbins Gilman and Family Papers, MHS collections.

24. Ibid.

25. *St. Paul Pioneer Press*, November 30, 1931.

26. *Northwest Monitor* (Minneapolis and St. Paul), December 30, 1930.

27. *Greater Amusements*, January 10, 1931; January 17, 1931.

28. Ibid., February 14, 1931.

29. Ibid., April 30, 1932.

30. Ibid., May 28, 1932.

31. *Variety*, December 13, 1932.

32. *Minneapolis Tribune*, January 31, 1933.

33. *Greater Amusements*, March 18, 1933.

34. Ibid., May 7, 1932; *St. Paul Pioneer Press*, March 19, 1933.

35. World opening night program, October 14, 1933, MHS collections.

36. *Greater Amusements*, July 16, 1932.

37. For a concise description of the art deco movement and its influence on theater design, see Scherer, *Marquee on Main Street*, 19–23.

38. "St. Paul Heritage Preservation Site Nomination: Grandview Theater," 1990, Lucile Kane and John Dougherty Movie Theater files, MHS collections.

39. *St. Paul Pioneer Press*, October 15, 1933.

40. Ibid., September 23, 1934.

41. Ibid., March 19, 1933.

42. *Greater Amusements*, April 24, 1936.

43. For an intriguing reconsideration of movie theater receipts and attendance during the 1930s, see Lary May, *The Big Tomorrow: Hollywood and the Politics of the American Way* (Chicago: University of Chicago Press, 2000), 121–22.

44. Martin Lebedoff, interview by Rhoda G. Lewin, transcript, May 6, 1987, Jewish Historical Society of the Upper Midwest.

45. Evelyn Fairbanks, *The Days of Rondo* (St. Paul: Minnesota Historical Society Press, 1990), 140.

46. *Greater Amusements*, October 31, 1934.

47. Ibid., July 26, 1935.

48. Ibid., October 25, 1935.

49. Scherer, *Marquee on Main Street*, 44.

50. Ibid., 22, 32; Scherer, "Tickets to Fantasy," 14.

51. Liebenberg to Hays, August 13, 1935, Liebenberg and Kaplan Work Files: Bijou Theater, NWAA.

52. *Greater Amusements*, June 10, 1938.

53. *Minneapolis Times*, July 18, 1940.

54. *St. Paul Pioneer Press*, February n.d., 1939.

55. *St. Paul Dispatch*, June 8, 1933.

56. *Minneapolis Tribune*, September 1, 1934.

57. Ibid.

58. Anonymous to L. N. Scott, November 18, 1934, Louis N. Scott Papers, MHS collections.

59. *Greater Amusements*, June 14, 1935.

60. "The New Pictures," *Time*, April 4, 1938.

61. *Variety*, March 2, 1938.

62. *St. Paul Dispatch*, March 24, 1938.

63. "The New Pictures," *Time*, April 4, 1938.

64. Margarita Landazuri, "Strange Cargo," www.tcm.com.

65. *Variety*, June 12, 1940.

66. *Greater Amusements*, July 1, 1938.

67. Ibid.

68. *Variety*, December 7, 1938.

69. Ibid., March 26, 1941.

70. Ibid., June 14, 1939.

71. Ibid., October 9, 1940.

72. Gomery, *Shared Pleasures*, 80.

73. *Greater Amusements,* May 17, 1940.

74. Gomery, *Shared Pleasures,* 80–81.

75. *Greater Amusements,* February 4, 1938.

76. *Variety,* December 27, 1939.

77. Besse, *Show Houses Twin Cities Style,* 55.

78. Dave Kenney, *Minnesota Goes to War: The Home Front during World War II* (St. Paul: Minnesota Historical Society Press, 2005), 5–6.

79. *Greater Amusements,* December 19, 1941.

80. *Variety,* May 1, 1942.

81. *Greater Amusements,* April 9, 1943.

82. Melnick and Fuchs, *Cinema Treasures,* 101.

83. *Greater Amusements,* June 26, 1942; *St. Paul Pioneer Press,* September 27, 1943; July 14, 1944.

84. "When Stars 'Fell' on Minnesota," *Minnesota History,* Fall 1974, 109.

85. *Greater Amusements,* August 17, 1945.

86. Ibid., May 11, 1945.

87. Liebenberg and Kaplan to Schmid, February 23, 1943, Liebenberg and Kaplan Papers, NWAA.

88. *Greater Amusements,* June 1, 1945.

89. Ibid., September 7, 1945.

90. Ibid., March 29, 1946.

Feature Presentations

p. 75, note 1. *Minneapolis Journal,* September 16, 1928.

p. 80, note 1. St. Paul Heritage Preservation Site Nomination: Grandview Theater, 1990; *St. Paul Dispatch,* December 14, 1973.

p. 86, note 1. Scherer, *Marquee on Main Street,* 44; Scherer, "Tickets to Fantasy," 13; Crier (Edina), April 1934; Besse, *Show Places Twin Cities Style,* 102.

p. 86, note 2. *Star Tribune,* January 12, 1989.

p. 93, note 1. Scherer, *Marquee on Main Street,* 33; Scherer, "Tickets to Fantasy," 14.

p. 96, note 1. "A Look at the New Uptown Theatre," *Northwest Architect,* March-April 1940, 9–10.

p. 104, note 1. *St. Paul Dispatch,* September 12, 1939; *Highland Villager,* May 11, 1977.

Chapter 4

1. *Hill Herald,* November 20, 1924.

2. Esther Bergman, interview with the author, September 15, 2006.

3. *Greater Amusements,* October 15, 1943; October 5, 1945.

4. Ibid., October 26, 1945.

5. Ibid., August 9, 1946.

6. Ibid., January 3, 1947; January 10, 1947.

7. Ibid., January 10, 1947.

8. *Minneapolis Star,* December 24, 1952.

9. *Greater Amusements,* April 11, 1947; April 18, 1947.

10. *Minneapolis Tribune,* April 23, 1947.

11. Ibid., April 24, 1947.

12. *Greater Amusements,* April 25, 1947.

13. Ibid., April 23, 1948.

14. *Minneapolis Tribune,* August 30, 1947; *Greater Amusements,* September 5, 1947.

15. *Greater Amusements,* August 22, 1947.

16. *Minneapolis Star,* August 30, 1947.

17. *Greater Amusements,* March 15, 1946; March 7, 1947; March 21, 1947.

18. Ibid., August 22, 1947.

19. Ibid., October 17, 1947.

20. Ibid., May 21, 1948.

21. Bill Sears to Ted Mann, February 17, 1948, Liebenberg and Kaplan Papers, NWAA.

22. *Greater Amusements,* October 23, 1942.

23. Ibid., July 22, 1938.

24. Ibid., December 24, 1948.

25. Ibid., January 27, 1950; August 11, 1950.

26. Ibid., December 30, 1949.

27. Dorothy Saltzman and Zelda Baker, interview with the author, July 9, 2006.

28. *Greater Amusements,* July 12, 1940.

29. Ibid., August 9, 1946.

30. "Quality and Service: An Answer to the Movie Slump?" *Business Week,* September 15, 1951, 125.

31. *Minneapolis Journal,* undated, Liebenberg and Kaplan Papers, NWAA.

32. "Quality and Service," 125.

33. For an excellent summary of the motion picture industry's prolonged postwar slump, see Barak Y. Orbach, "Antitrust and Pricing in the Motion Picture Industry," University of Michigan Law School, John M. Olin Center for Law & Economics Working Paper Series, 26–30.

34. *Greater Amusements,* November 7, 1952.

35. Ibid., December 21, 1951.

36. Gomery, *Shared Pleasures,* 83–88; "Quality and Service," 118–21.

37. *Greater Amusements,* December 31, 1948.

38. Ibid., December 21, 1951.

39. Gomery, *Shared Pleasures,* 83–88; "Quality and Service," 118–21.

40. *Greater Amusements,* November 17, 1950.

41. Ibid., April 13, 1951.

42. Ibid., March 11, 1949.

43. Ibid., August 10, 1951.

44. Ibid., February 27, 1953.

45. Gomery, *Shared Pleasures,* 239–41.

46. *Greater Amusements,* October 23, 1953.

47. Ibid., July 29, 1955.

48. Ibid., October 9, 1953.

49. Ibid., December 18, 1953.

50. Ibid., September 24, 1954.

51. Ibid., November 30, 1956.

52. Ibid., June 29, 1956.

53. Ibid., August 24, 1956.

54. Ibid., November 30, 1956.

55. Ibid.

56. *East Minneapolis Argus,* August 15, 1957.

57. Gerry Herringer, interview with the author, July 12, 2006.

58. Barbara Flanagan, interview with the author, August 15, 2006.

59. *Minneapolis Tribune,* July 13, 1957.

60. *Greater Amusements,* March 17, 1950.

61. Ibid., June 4, 1954; July 2, 1954.

62. Gerry Herringer, interview with the author, July 12, 2006.

63. "Limit on Movie Censorship," *Business Week,* May 31, 1952, 33.

64. *St. Paul Dispatch,* January 18, 1951.

65. *Greater Amusements,* August 24, 1956; October 5, 1956; November 30, 1956.

66. Ibid., November 16, 1956.

67. *Time,* December 24, 1956.

68. *Minneapolis Tribune,* December 26, 1956.

69. Ibid., January 1, 1957.

70. Ibid., January 3, 1957.

71. Ibid., January 5, 1957.

72. *Greater Amusements,* January 11, 1957.

73. *Minneapolis Star,* January 4, 1957.

74. *Minneapolis Tribune,* March 2, 1958.

75. Harold and Marvin Engler, interview by the author, August 1, 2006.

76. *Greater Amusements,* June 7, 1963.

77. Ibid., February 8, 1957.

78. Ibid.

79. Michael Downing, *Spring Forward: The Annual Madness of Daylight Saving Time* (Washington, DC: Shoemaker & Hoard, 2005), 127.

80. Millett, *Lost Twin Cities,* 261–62.

81. Dave Kenney, *Twin Cities Album: A Visual History* (St. Paul: Minnesota Historical Society Press, 2005), 193.

82. *St. Paul Pioneer Press,* August 27, 1958; *Greater Amusements,* September 5, 1958; *Minneapolis Tribune,* February 8, 1959.

83. *Minneapolis Tribune,* September 8, 1960.

84. *Greater Amusements,* September 25, 1964; January 19, 1962.

85. Ibid., December 11, 1964.

86. *St. Paul Dispatch,* September 16, 1965.

87. *St. Paul Dispatch and Pioneer Press,* May 9, 1965.

88. *St. Paul Pioneer Press,* November 3, 1966.

89. *Minneapolis Star,* November 4, 1960.

90. Ibid., November 4, 1960; *Greater Amusements,* March 31, 1961.

91. *Greater Amusements,* March 31, 1961.

92. *Minneapolis Tribune,* May 28, 1961.

93. Ibid., July 31, 1961.

94. *Greater Amusements*, February 26, 1965.

95. *Minneapolis Tribune*, March 29, 1965.

96. *Greater Amusements*, August 7, 1964.

97. Ibid.

Feature Presentations

p. 112, note 1. *Greater Amusements*, June 18, 1948; Sol Fisher to Jack Liebenberg, May 30, 1948, Liebenberg and Kaplan Papers, NWAA.

p. 117, note 1. *Minneapolis Star*, July 3, 1951.

p. 117, note 2. *St. Paul Pioneer Press*, November 11, 1988.

p. 121, note 1. Riverview Theater, lobby display.

p. 132, note 1. *Minneapolis Star*, March 21, 1962.

p. 132, note 2. Besse, *Show Houses Twin Cities Style*, 130.

p. 138, note 1. *Minneapolis Star*, August 7, 1964; Besse, *Show Houses Twin Cities Style*, 138.

Chapter 5

1. *Minneapolis Star*, May 8, 1971.

2. Federal Bureau of Investigation, internal memorandum, Minneapolis to Director and New York, February 9, 1969.

3. *Minneapolis Star*, November 17, 1975.

4. Ibid.

5. Federal Bureau of Investigation, internal memorandum, January 29, 1973.

6. *Minneapolis Star*, May 8, 1971.

7. *Minneapolis Tribune*, March 17, 1971.

8. *Minneapolis Star*, May 8, 1971.

9. Ibid., February 17, 1969.

10. *St. Paul Dispatch*, February 18, 1969.

11. Ibid.

12. *Minneapolis Star*, March 19, 1970.

13. *Greater Amusements*, July 1965.

14. *St. Paul Pioneer Press*, September 13, 1970.

15. *St. Paul Dispatch*, September 13, 1971.

16. *Minneapolis Tribune*, August 5, 1971.

17. *St. Paul Dispatch*, December 14, 1973.

18. *Minneapolis Star*, October 14, 1971.

19. *St. Paul Dispatch*, November 1, 1972.

20. Ibid., March 13, 1973; Federal Bureau of Investigation, internal memorandum, January 29, 1973.

21. Federal Bureau of Investigation, internal memorandum, January 29, 1973.

22. *Minneapolis Star*, November 17, 1975.

23. Minnesota Civil Liberties Union Records, Alexander v. City of St. Paul, undated memorandum, MHS collections.

24. *St. Paul Dispatch*, May 4, 1973.

25. Ibid., May 31, 1973.

26. *St. Paul Pioneer Press*, June 3, 1973.

27. Ibid., June 12, 1973.

28. Federal Bureau of Investigation, internal memo, February 27, 1974.

29. *St. Paul Dispatch*, July 27, 1973.

30. *Minneapolis Star*, December 29, 1971.

31. Ibid., October 2, 1972.

32. Ibid., March 23, 1973.

33. Ibid., March 11, 1974.

34. *St. Paul Dispatch*, May 3, 1969.

35. *Minneapolis Star*, March 11, 1974.

36. Bill Irvine, interview by the author, July 19, 2006.

37. *Minneapolis Star*, October 22, 1975.

38. *Minneapolis Tribune*, September 25, 1975.

39. Ibid., November 6, 1975.

40. *Minneapolis Star*, November 10, 1976; Bill Irvine, interview by the author, July 19, 2006.

41. Bill Irvine, interview by the author, July 19, 2006.

42. *Minneapolis Tribune*, February 20, 1976.

43. Ibid., May 26, 1976.

44. Ibid., April 22, 1977.

45. *St. Paul Dispatch*, October 8, 1975.

46. Ibid., October 26, 1973.

47. *St. Paul Pioneer Press*, May 26, 1974.

48. Bill Irvine, interview by the author, July 19, 2006.

49. *St. Paul Dispatch*, July 24, 1978.

50. Ibid.

51. *Minneapolis Star and Tribune*, January 21, 1984.

52. Ibid.

53. *Minneapolis Tribune*, September 29, 1978.

54. *Minneapolis Star*, August 8, 1978.

55. Ibid.

56. *Star Tribune*, March 2, 1996.

57. *St. Paul Dispatch*, March 15, 1979.

58. *Minneapolis Tribune*, July 28, 1978.

59. *Minneapolis Star*, June 27, 1975.

60. Gerry Herringer, interview by the author, July 12, 2006.

61. *St. Paul Pioneer Press Dispatch*, June 10, 1985.

62. *Minneapolis Star and Tribune*, October 26, 1986.

63. Ibid.

64. *St. Paul Pioneer Press Dispatch*, December 16, 1985.

65. *Minneapolis Star and Tribune*, June 5, 1982.

66. *St. Paul Dispatch*, November 30, 1983.

67. *Minneapolis Star*, March 9, 1981.

68. *St. Paul Dispatch*, November 30, 1983.

69. *St. Paul Pioneer Press Dispatch*, November 11, 1988.

70. *Minneapolis Star and Tribune*, March 25, 1985.

71. *Star Tribune*, May 5, 1987.

72. *Minneapolis Tribune*, August 10, 1976.

73. Ibid., June 14, 1977.

74. *City Pages*, September 3, 1986.

75. *St. Paul Dispatch*, October 7, 1983.

76. *St. Paul Pioneer Press Dispatch*, July 12, 1986.

77. Ibid., February 16, 1989.

78. Ibid., February 4, 1989.

79. *Star Tribune*, June 1, 1989.

80. Ibid., April 18, 1990.

81. Ibid., May 24, 1990.

82. Ibid., August 7, 1990.

83. Ibid., June 29, 1993.

84. Ibid., May 30, 1990.

Feature Presentations

p. 149, note 1. *St. Paul Pioneer Press,* September 13, 1970.

p. 153, note 1. Melnick and Fuchs, *Cinema Treasures,* 156.

p. 153, note 2. Jack Smith, interview by the author, June 29, 2006.

p. 162, note 1. Besse, *Show Houses Twin Cities Style,* 91–92.

p. 162, note 2. *Minneapolis Tribune,* July 28, 1979.

p. 170, note 1. *St. Paul Dispatch,* December 16, 1974.

p. 170, note 2. *St. Paul Pioneer Press,* December 7, 1980.

p. 176, note 1. *St. Paul Dispatch,* December 5, 1985.

p. 176, note 2. *St. Paul Pioneer Press,* March 12, 2002.

Chapter 6

1. *St. Paul Pioneer Press Dispatch,* April 28, 1986.

2. John Myles Elzey, "Professional Legitimate Theatre in St. Paul, Minnesota, 1890–1918" (Ph.D. diss., University of Minnesota, 1972), 170–71.

3. *Minneapolis Star and Tribune,* January 12, 1986.

4. *City Pages,* December 4, 1985; *St. Paul Pioneer Press,* August 29, 1991.

5. *Minneapolis Star and Tribune,* December 15, 1985.

6. Ibid., July 19, 1986.

7. *City Pages,* December 4, 1985.

8. *Preservation News,* July 1986.

9. *Minneapolis Star and Tribune,* October 25, 1986.

10. *Star Tribune,* October 26, 1991.

11. Ibid., June 30, 1990.

12. *St. Paul Pioneer Press,* August 29, 1991.

13. *Star Tribune,* October 26, 1991.

14. *St. Paul Pioneer Press Dispatch,* August 13, 1988.

15. Ibid., August 12, 1988.

16. *Star Tribune,* August 13, 1988.

17. *St. Paul Pioneer Press Dispatch*, August 13, 1988.

18. Ibid.

19. *Minneapolis Star and Tribune*, September 18, 1986; *Star Tribune*, October 3, 1988; October 18, 1988.

20. *Star Tribune*, April 21, 1990.

21. Ibid., 1988.

22. *St. Paul Pioneer Press Dispatch*, November 11, 1988.

23. Annual Report, Cineplex Odeon Corporation, 1985, 13 (quoted in Gomery, *Shared Pleasures*, 109).

24. *Star Tribune*, September 7, 1990.

25. *St. Paul Pioneer Press*, August 14, 1992.

26. *Star Tribune*, February 3, 1991.

27. *Twin Cities Reader*, August 29, 1990.

28. *St. Paul Pioneer Press*, March 17, 1991.

29. *Star Tribune*, February 1, 1991.

30. Ibid., January 14, 1994.

31. Ibid., January 10, 1988.

32. Ibid., January 29, 1993.

33. Ibid., November 21, 1993.

34. Steve Mann, interview by the author, July 26, 2006.

35. Mike Muller, interview by the author, July 13, 2006.

36. *St. Paul Pioneer Press*, June 1, 1995.

37. Mark Harris, "The Little Movie That Could," *Entertainment Weekly*, February 12, 1993.

38. Ibid.

39. *Star Tribune*, October 24, 1993.

40. Ibid., February 9, 1995.

41. Ibid.

42. *Star Tribune*, November 2, 1997.

43. Ibid., December 21, 1997.

44. Steve Mann, interview by the author, July 26, 2006.

45. *Star Tribune*, April 14, 1999.

46. Ibid., December 12, 1997.

47. Ibid., February 19, 1999; *St. Paul Pioneer Press*, February 24, 2006.

48. *Star Tribune*, November 2, 2002.

49. Steve Mann, interview by the author, July 26, 2006.

50. Ibid.

51. *Star Tribune*, September 28, 2000.

52. Ibid., November 24, 2002.

53. Ibid.

54. Ibid., January 17, 2001.

55. Tom Letness, interview by the author, July 5, 2006.

56. *Star Tribune*, February 10, 2004.

57. Ibid., November 24, 2006.

58. Bill Irvine, interview by the author, July 19, 2006.

59. *St. Paul Pioneer Press*, June 30, 2005.

60. Ibid., July 20, 2005.

61. Ibid., May 4, 2006; *Star Tribune*, May 4, 2006.

62. *Star Tribune*, April 12, 2006.

63. *St. Paul Pioneer Press*, October 21, 1991.

Feature Presentations

p. 185, note 1. *St. Paul Pioneer Press*, November 11, 1988; *Star Tribune*, May 5, 1989.

p. 192, note 1. General Cinema Corporation, Theatre Database Information: Mall of America 14, n.d.; Besse, *Show Houses Twin Cities Style*, 144.

p. 192, note 2. *Star Tribune*, August 14, 1992.

p. 199, note 1. *Star Tribune*, February 9, 1995.

p. 205, note 1. *Star Tribune*, February 15, 1998.

p. 212, note 1. *Star Tribune*, November 2, 2002.

p. 212, note 2. Crown Theatres, e-mail to Dave Kenney, December 28, 2006.

Selected Bibliography

Berman, Hyman, and Linda Mack Schloff. *Jews in Minnesota*. St. Paul: Minnesota Historical Society Press, 2002.

Besse, Kirk J. *Show Houses Twin Cities Style*. Minneapolis: Victoria Publications, 1997.

Crawford, Merritt. "The March of the Years." *Moving Picture World*, March 26, 1927.

Downing, Michael. *Spring Forward: The Annual Madness of Daylight Saving Time*. Washington, DC: Shoemaker & Hoard, 2005.

Elzey, John Myles. "Professional Legitimate Theatre in St. Paul, Minnesota, 1890–1918." Ph.D. diss., University of Minnesota, 1972.

Fairbanks, Evelyn. *The Days of Rondo*. St. Paul: Minnesota Historical Society Press, 1990.

Galbraith, Stuart. *Motor City Marquees: A Comprehensive, Illustrated Reference to Motion Picture Theaters in the Detroit Area, 1906–1992*. Jefferson, NC: McFarland & Co., 1994.

Gomery, Douglas. *Shared Pleasures: A History of Movie Presentation in the United States*. Madison: University of Wisconsin Press, 1992.

Gray, James. "Metropolitan Books Finest Attractions of Recent Years—Casey Players Return." *St. Paul Magazine*, Fall 1929.

Grossman, Audley Mitchell. "The Professional Legitimate Theater in Minneapolis from 1890 to 1901." Ph.D. diss., University of Minnesota, 1957.

Hark, Ina Rae. *Exhibition: The Film Reader*. New York: Routledge, 2002.

Harris, Mark. "The Little Movie That Could." *Entertainment Weekly*, February 12, 1993.

Headley, Robert K. *Motion Picture Exhibition in Washington, D.C.: An Illustrated History of Parlors, Palaces and Multiplexes in the Metropolitan Area, 1894–1997*. Jefferson, NC: McFarland & Co., 1999.

Hill, Lawrence James. "A History of Variety-Vaudeville in Minneapolis, Minnesota, from Its Beginning to 1900." Ph.D. diss., University of Minnesota, 1979.

Jowett, Garth. *Film: The Democratic Art.* Boston: Little, Brown, 1976.

Kane, Lucile M., and John A. Dougherty. "Movie Debut: Films in the Twin Cities, 1894–1909." *Minnesota History* 54 (Winter 1995): 342–58.

Kenney, Dave. *Minnesota Goes to War: The Home Front during World War II.* St. Paul: Minnesota Historical Society Press, 2005.

———. *Twin Cities Album: A Visual History.* St. Paul: Minnesota Historical Society Press, 2005.

Landazuri, Margarita. "Strange Cargo." www.tcm.com.

"Limit on Movie Censorship." *Business Week,* May 31, 1952.

May, Lary. *The Big Tomorrow: Hollywood and the Politics of the American Way.* Chicago: University of Chicago Press, 2000.

McQuade, James S. "The Belasco of Motion Picture Presentations." *Moving Picture World,* December 9, 1911.

Melnick, Ross. "Rethinking Rothafel: Roxy's Forgotten Legacy." *The Moving Image* 3 (Fall 2003): 62–95.

Melnick, Ross, and Andreas Fuchs. *Cinema Treasures: A New Look at Classic Movie Theaters.* St. Paul: MBI Publishing, 2004.

Millett, Larry. *Lost Twin Cities.* St. Paul: Minnesota Historical Society Press, 1992.

Newman, Paul S. "Careers in Contrast: The Managerial Practices of L. N. Scott and Theo Hays and Their Influence on Twin Cities Entertainment, 1890–1929." Ph.D. diss., University of Minnesota, 1991.

———. "Theodore L. Hays: Theatrical Good Neighbor at the Turn of the Century." *Minnesota History* 53 (Summer 1993): 238–46.

Niderost, Eric. "'The Birth of a Nation': When Hollywood Glorified the KKK." www.historynet.com.

Orbach, Barak Y. "Antitrust and Pricing in the Motion Picture Industry." University of Michigan Law School, John M. Olin Center for Law & Economics Working Paper Series, May 2004.

Potter, Dean S. "Hiawatha: A Poem, a Legend, and Minnesota's First Movie." *Sun Country,* July-August 1986.

"Quality and Service: An Answer to the Movie Slump?" *Business Week,* September 15, 1951.

Rothapfel, Samuel. "Putting Your House in Proper Order." *Moving Picture World,* July 3, 1920.

Scherer, Herbert. *Marquee on Main Street: Jack Liebenberg's Movie Theaters, 1928–1941.* Minneapolis: University Gallery, University of Minnesota, 1982.

———. "Tickets to Fantasy: The Little Theater around the Corner." *Hennepin County History* 46 (Fall 1987): 11–15.

Schrenk, Lisa. "Birth of the Movies." *Architecture Minnesota,* November-December 1984.

Valentine, Maggie. *The Show Starts on the Sidewalk: An Architectural History of the Movie Theatre, Starring S. Charles Lee.* New Haven, CT: Yale University Press, 1994.

Walker, Gregory A. *Main Street Amusements: Movies and Commercial Entertainment in a Southern City, 1896–1930.* Washington, DC: Smithsonian Institution Press, 1995.

Wheeler, Leigh Ann. *Against Obscenity: Reform and the Politics of Womanhood in America, 1873–1935.* Baltimore, MD: Johns Hopkins University Press, 2004.

"When Stars 'Fell' on Minnesota." *Minnesota History* 44 (Fall 1974): 108–12.

Widen, Larry, and Judi Anderson. *Silver Screens: A Pictorial History of Milwaukee's Movie Theaters.* Madison: Wisconsin Historical Society Press, 2007.

Index

Photo Credits

Pages 2, 5, 6, 7, 8, 9, 11, 12, 14, 17, 18, 21, 24, 28, 30, 33, 35, 37, 40, 43, 45, 47, 49, 50, 52, 54, 56, 59, 60, 62, 66, 68, 71, 72, 73, 78, 79, 85, 86, 88, 95, 98, 100, 103, 105, 114, 117 (top), 124, 128, 131—Minnesota Historical Society collections

Pages 107, 111, 132, 137, 138, 142, 143, 156, 159, 161, 162, 166, 169, 170, 183—Minnesota Historical Society, Star Tribune photo collection

Pages 74, 75, 77, 81, 93, 96, 112, 117 (bottom), 122, 127—courtesy of the Northwest Architectural Archives, University of Minnesota Libraries

Pages 147, 149, 154, 165, 172, 176—Minnesota Historical Society, Pioneer Press photo collection

Pages 179, 186, 207—courtesy of George Heinrich

Pages 203, 211 (bottom), 212—photographed by Bill Jolitz

Pages 80, 104—courtesy of Village Communications

Pages 141, 146—provided by the Minneapolis Public Library

Pages 178, 194—Brian Peterson © 2007 STAR TRIBUNE/Minneapolis–St. Paul

Pages 191, 214—Joe Oden, Pioneer Press

Page 39—courtesy of the Jewish Historical Society of the Upper Midwest

Page 121—courtesy of the Riverview Theater

Page 130—courtesy of the Bloomington Historical Society and the Norling family

Page 153—courtesy of Jack Smith

Page 175—Mark Morson, Pioneer Press

Page 181—provided by Miller Hanson Partners Architects

Page 185—furnished by Dave Hilsgen

Page 187—Jean Pieri, the Pioneer Press

Page 192—courtesy of Michael S. Skradski

Page 199—courtesy of Landmark Theatres

Page 205—furnished by Muller Family Theatres

Page 208—courtesy of Heights Theatre Building, Inc.

Page 211 (top)—Jeff Wheeler © 2007 STAR TRIBUNE/Minneapolis–St. Paul

Page 215—Brandi Jade Thomas, Pioneer Press

Twin Cities Picture Show was designed and set in type at Cathy Spengler Design, Minneapolis. The typefaces are Miller, Frutiger, Bodega Sans, and Lux Royale. Printed by Thomson-Shore, Incorporated, Dexter, Michigan.